Literary-Critical Approaches to the Bible

A Bibliographical Supplement

Mark Minor

LOCUST HILL PRESS
West Cornwall, CT
1996

Library of Congress Cataloging-in-Publication Data

Minor, Mark.
    Literary-critical approaches to the Bible : a bibliographical
supplement / Mark Minor.
      310 p.   cm.
    Includes index.
    ISBN 0-933951-69-8 (lib. bdg.)
    1. Bible--Criticism, interpretation, etc.--Bibliography. 2. Bible
and literature--Bibliography. I. Title.
Z7770.M66 1996 Suppl.
016.2206'6--dc20   96-16495
                                                     CIP

Printed on acid-free, 250-year-life paper
Manufactured in the United States of America

To Joyce

Contents

Acknowledgments

A scholar will find himself in debt for a variety of different kinds of help from different persons in the course of writing a book such as this one. For hospitality while engaged in research, I owe thanks once again to my mother-in-law, Marvel Carncross, and to Drs. Dwight and Linda Vogel. In addition, I am grateful for the welome of Mr. Norman Beach, Steward of Wadham College, Oxford University, who provided my wife and me with accommodations and meals, and who in addition eased my entry into the Bodleian Library.

The library staff in Oxford were enormously helpful, as were those at the University of Wisconsin-Madison; at Lexington, North American Baptist and Southern Baptist Theological Seminaries; and the Joseph Regenstein Library at the University of Chicago. The indispensable element, however, was the Interlibrary Loan program at Morehead State University. Greg Mitchell and his staff funnelled an enormous number of books to me which I would never have had the time to search out myself, due to my heavy administrative responsibilities. This book would not exist without his assistance.

Likewise it is difficult for me to imagine having finished without the expert help of my two "data entry specialists," Connie Burns and Wanda Wilson. Both of them worked diligently at it during the summer of 1995, and in addition, Wanda was able to stay with the project through the fall semester, juggling the task around a full-time class load and family responsibilities. Her thoroughness and attention to detail (honed, no doubt, in many a chemistry lab), have proven vital to finishing the project on time.

The dedication page records the greatest debt of all. It would have been neither possible nor worthwhile to have undertaken this project without the loving support of my wife.

Preface

This volume was undertaken to update the original one, which was published in 1992 but with an effective terminus of mid-1991. At the same time, I also had become aware as soon as I finished the earlier book that I had missed some items which ought to have been included. Therefore, the purpose of this supplement has become twofold. Readers will find a majority of the items to be new publications since 1991; the remainder are older books and articles which I was able to locate and examine this time. Principles for inclusion are the same as in the first volume.

A breakdown by the three overall categories of items annotated in the two books reveals the following comparisons: in the original volume, 8.6% of the items dealt with the Bible as a whole, 57.2% with the Hebrew Bible, and 34.2% with the New Testament. In the supplement it is 6.5%, 47.5% and 46% respectively. Even allowing for older titles which are now included, and for the undoubted fact that once again I will have missed some items, it is obvious that there has been a shift of interest toward the New Testament among those practicing literary methods on the Bible. Whether this change is due to a greater number of New Testament critics taking up literary criticism compared to earlier years, or to fewer critics of the Hebrew Bible doing so, or some combination of these or other factors, I am not sure.

Be that as it may, the appearance of over eleven hundred items here, most of which post-date 1991, testifies dramatically to the steadily increasing interest in literary criticism of the Bible.

Abbreviations

Periodicals and Annuals Frequently Cited:

ABR   *Australian Biblical Review*
AJSL   *American Journal of Semitic Languages & Literatures*
ANRW *Aufstieg und Neidergang der Römischen Welt*
ATR   *Anglican Theological Review*
AUSS *Andrews University Seminary Studies*
BI   *Biblical Interpretation*
B Sac *Biblioteca Sacra*
BTB   *Biblical Theology Bulletin*
BTr   *The Biblical Translator*
CBQ   *Catholic Biblical Quarterly*
CL   *Christianity and Literature*
CTJ   *Calvin Theological Journal*
EL   *Essays in Literature*
ETh   *Eglise et Théologie*
ETL   *Ephemerides Theologicae Lovaniensis*
EvQ   *Evangelical Quarterly*
GTJ   *Grace Theological Journal*
HAR   *Hebrew Annual Review*
HBT   *Horizons in Biblical Theology*
HTR   *Harvard Theological Review*
HUCA *Hebrew Union College Annual*
JAAR *Journal of the American Academy of Religion*
JAOS *Journal of the American Oriental Society*
JBL   *Journal of Biblical Literature*
JBQ   *Jewish Bible Quarterly: Dor-le-Dor*
JETS   *Journal of the Evangelical Theological Society*
JJS   *Journal of Jewish Studies*
JNES *Journal of Near Eastern Studies*
JNSL *Journal of Northwest Semitic Languages*
JR   *Journal of Religion*

JSNT	*Journal for the Study of the New Testament*
JSOT	*Journal for the Study of the Old Testament*
JSS	*Journal of Semitic Studies*
JTT	*Journal of Translation and Textlinguistics*
LB	*Linguistica Biblica*
LT	*Literature and Theology*
Nov T	*Novum Testamentum*
NTS	*New Testament Studies*
OS	*Oudtestamentiesche Studien*
OTE	*Old Testament Essays*
PEGL	*Proceedings of the Eastern Great Lakes and Midwest Biblical Societies*
PIBA	*Proceedings of the Irish Biblical Academy*
PRS	*Perspectives in Religious Studies*
PWCJS	*Proceedings of the World Congress of Jewish Studies*
QJS	*Quarterly Journal of Speech*
RE	*Review and Expositor*
RQ	*Restoration Quarterly*
SBLSP	*Society of Biblical Literature Seminar Papers*
SEA	*Svensk Exegetisk Årsbok*
SJOT	*Scandinavian Journal of the Old Testament*
SR	*Studies in Religion/Sciences Religieuses*
ST	*Studia Theologica*
SWJT	*Southwestern Journal of Theology*
TB	*Tyndale Bulletin*
TJ	*Trinity Journal*
USQR	*Union Seminary Quarterly Review*
VE	*Vox Evangelica*
VT	*Vetus Testamentum*
WTJ	*Westminster Theological Journal*
WW	*Word and World*
ZAW	*Zeitschrift für die Alttestamentliche Wissenschaft*

Other Abbreviations:

HB	Hebrew Bible
KJV	King James Version
Minor I	Minor, Mark, *Literary Critical Approaches to the Bible* (Locust Hill Press, 1992)
NT	New Testament
OT	Old Testament

P	Press
Rpt	Reprinted
Tr	Translated by
U	University

Literary-Critical Approaches to the Bible

to the Bible

A Bibliographical Supplement

THE BIBLE
(Hebrew Bible and New Testament Together)

Authored Books

1. Adam, A.K.M. *What Is Postmodern Biblical Criticism?* Minneapolis (Fortress P), 1995.

   Examples and explanations of the related critical assumptions called "postmodernism," including deconstruction, ideological criticism, postmodern feminism, and "transgressive" postmodernism. How beginners might practice postmodern criticism of the Bible.

*   Culler, Arthur J. *Creative Religious Literature. A New Literary Study of the Bible.*

   See #65.

2. Edgerton, W. Dow. *The Passion of Interpretation.* Louisville (Westminster/John Knox P), 1992.

   We need to re-examine the foundations of interpretation, to think "within the dynamics of narrative." The "passionate act of interpretation" as applied to *Genesis* 22, *Luke* 24, plus other ancient and modern narratives.

3. Fabiny, Tibor. *The Lion and the Lamb. Figuralism and Fulfillment in the Bible, Art and Literature.* New York (St. Martin's P), 1992.

   An attempt "to establish a theory of typology on the basis of reader-response criticism." Definitions from the NT era into the modern criticism of Northrop Frye, Bultmann, and Brevard Childs. Sections on typology in the OT and in the NT. The Bible is "a progress of types into antitypes within a scheme of the seven phases of revelation.... The Apocalypse become[s] an anti-type, ... [and] lifts the Bible up into a new sense of reality...."

4.   Norton, David. *A History of the Bible as Literature. Volume One: From Antiquity to 1700*. Cambridge (Cambridge UP), 1993.

How people have thought about the Bible and its translations—especially about its literary aspects—from patristic times to the eighteenth century. Topics include Jerome and Hebrew poetics, non-literal readings, arguments over whether the verbal form of the text matters, slowness of the King James version to gain respect, and moves toward literary praise and appreciation of the Bible in the sixteenth century and after.

5.   Phelps, William Lyon. *Reading the Bible*. New York (Macmillan), 1919.

The literary beauty and power of the Bible; Paul as a letter-writer; short stories in the Bible. The Bible's "sublime and homely poetry."

6.   Reed, Walter L. *Dialogues of the Word: The Bible as Literature According to Bakhtin*. New York and Oxford (Oxford UP), 1993.

The "variety of dialogues formally encoded in [the Bible]", and how this literary discovery itself stands in dialogue between the centrifugal tendencies of historical analysis and the centripetal ones of theological interpretation. How Bakhtin's dialogism reveals the "recurrent forms and coherent patterns in the conversations between God and his people ..." in the HB and NT as wholes, and in *Genesis*, the gospels, *Job*, and *Revelation*. Chapter One revised from Minor I, #131; Chapter Four revised and expanded from #543.

7.   Thiselton, Anthony C. *New Horizons in Hermeneutics*. Grand Rapids (Zondervan), 1992.

Evaluation of various newer hermeneutical theories especially as applied to the Bible. Includes semiotic theories, reader response, intertextuality, speech-act theory, and deconstruction. Historical survey of the "hermeneutics of tradition" from the Patristic era through the Reformation to Schleiermacher, Gadamer, and Ricoeur. Application to Pauline texts. Liberation and feminist approaches, theories of reading.

8.   Trible, Phyllis. *Rhetorical Criticism. Context, Method, and the Book of Jonah*. Minneapolis (Fortress P), 1994.

The historical background of biblical rhetorical criticism, through its four components: classical rhetoric, literary critical theory, literary study of the Bible, and form criticism. Rhetoric as art of composition, and as art of persuasion. General guidelines for beginning an analysis. External design of *Jonah* and internal design of each of its four scenes. Guidelines for continuing, based on intentionality, subjectivity, artistry, and theology.

9.   Watson, Duane F., and Alan J. Hauser. *Rhetorical Criticism of the Bible. A Comprehensive Bibliography with Notes on History and Method.* Leiden (E.J. Brill), 1994.

Part I on the OT: sketch of rhetorical criticism since Wellhausen; its approach to the OT; bibliography by book of the OT (as distinct from the HB). Part II on the NT: a brief history of the method; contemporary practices using Greco-Roman and modern rhetoric; application to the Gospels and the letters; bibliography by topic and then by book of the NT.

10.   Wild, Laura H. *A Literary Guide to the Bible. A Study of the Types of Literature Present in the Old and New Testaments.* New York (George H. Doran), 1922.

Why studying the Bible as literature does not compromise its theological meaning. Analysis of the Bible by types of literature it contains: folklore, story, history, poetry, dramatic literature, wisdom literature, oratory, and the essay.

Edited Collections

11.   Aichele, George, and Tina Pippin, eds. *Semeia 60: Fantasy and the Bible.* 1992.

Application of literary theory of fantasy by Jack Zipes (Bible in general), Roger Schlobin (*Job*), Peter Miscall (*Exodus* 1–15), George Aichele (gospels), Tina Pippin (*Revelation*), with response to Aichele and Pippin by Joanna Dewey.

12.   Beuken, Wim, Sean Freyne, and Anton Weiler, eds. *The Bible and Its Readers.* London (SCM) and Philadelphia (Trinity P International), 1991.

Includes essays by Ben F. Meyer on literary-critical challenge to the historical method; by David Tracy on how it is both possible and necessary to integrate literary-critical approaches to the Bible into theological ones. Other essays on how the Bible was read differently by Judaism, early Christianity, the Middle Ages, the Reformation, and the Eighteenth Century.

13. Conn, Harvie M., ed. *Inerrancy and Hermeneutic: A Tradition, A Challenge, A Debate.* Grand Rapids (Baker Book House), 1988.

Essays by fourteen faculty members of Westminster Theological Seminary explaining how Calvinist Presbyterians can integrate new biblical criticism into their faith. Tremper Longman III, "Storytellers and Poets in the Bible: Can Literary Artifice Be True?" pp. 137–149.

14. Jobling, David, and Stephen D. Moore, eds. *Semeia* 54: *Poststructuralism as Exegesis.* 1991.

Poststructuralist readings of *Genesis* 11 (Derrida), David's adultery (Schwartz), *I Kings* 3–10 (Jobling), *Esther* (Bal), *Isaiah* (Miscall), *Matthew* (Burnett), women in *Mark* (Susan Graham), *Luke–Acts* (Moore), *I Corinthians* (Castelli), the betrayal by Judas (Kirk Hughes), and general application (Detweiler).

15. Krondorfer, Björn, ed. *Body and Bible. Interpreting and Experiencing Biblical Narratives.* Philadelphia (Trinity P International), 1992.

Eleven essays on various passages and books of the HB and NT which interpret the texts through recounting experiences of various forms of play, reenactment, and embodiment (dance, reading aloud, etc.). Combination of literary and anthropological methods and their therapeutic effects on the participants. *Genesis* 1–11, 19, 25–29, 34; *Exodus* 32; *Mark*; *Mark* 7.

16. Loades, Ann, and Michael McLain, eds. *Hermeneutics, the Bible, and Literary Criticism.* New York (St. Martin's P), 1992.

Ten essays, divided into three sections: three on "philosophical accounts of interpretation"; three on scriptural interpretation as practiced by Austin Farrer (especially the NT); and four on specific texts and themes: *Genesis* 32, *Psalms*, the Hebrew Bible in general, and *Genesis* 1. Six are literary-critical and are analyzed separately as #'s 36, 45, 33, 233, 472, 202.

17. Porter, Stanley E., Paul Joyce, and David E. Orton, eds. *Crossing the Boundaries. Essays in Biblical Interpretation in Honour of Michael D. Goulder.* Leiden (E.J. Brill), 1994.

Twenty-four essays on method in biblical interpretation, the HB, the NT, and extra-biblical religious topics, eight of which are literary. Analyzed separately as #'s 22, 62, 423a, 556, 575, 719, 1048, 1059.

18. Prickett, Stephen, ed. *Reading the Text. Biblical Criticism and Literary Theory.* Oxford [UK] and Cambridge [USA], (Blackwell), 1991.

Six essays by seven different scholars, tracing the interaction of biblical and literary criticism from the Middle Ages to the present: "a single connected history of that subtly intertwined relationship … each discipline owes more to the other than it is generally willing to acknowledge, and … each has been (and remains) dependent on the existence of the other for its own wellbeing."

19. Reid, Mary Esson, ed. *The Bible Read as Literature: An Anthology.* Cleveland (Howard Allen, Inc.), 1959.

Eleven essays concerning "The Scholar's Bible," covering sociopolitical, archaeological, linguistic, textual matters. Twenty further essays from Sidney, Milton, Herder, Goethe, and Whitman to Auerbach, Thomas Mann, and Robert Gordis concerning various aspects of "The General Reader's Bible." Also includes C.S. Lewis' essay on the literary impact of the KJV.

20. Ryken, Leland, and Tremper Longman III, eds. *A Complete Literary Guide to the Bible.* Grand Rapids (Zondervan), 1993.

Thirty-eight essays by twenty-eight authors: several on general topics, e.g., history of the literary approach to the Bible, biblical narrative and poetry, the OT, the NT, OT prophets, NT letters, etc; most of the rest on specific books; and several on the novelist's and poet's view of the Bible, and on the value of this approach to preaching. Overall approach is to "insure consistency in method and scope," along with "the desire to integrate literary and biblical studies more carefully than has been done to date." Individual essays analyzed separately as #'s 25, 37, 47, 53, 54, 69, 99, 130, 178, 240, 274, 300, 336, 372, 381, 437, 447, 473, 526, 553, 569, 572, 585, 593, 603, 608, 616, 645, 686, 731, 733, 825, 898, 950, 976, 1136.

Articles

21.   Barr, James. "Biblical Languages and Exegesis—How Far
       Does Structuralism Help Us?" *King's Theological Review* 7
       (1984), 48–52.

       While structuralism is undoubtedly valid as a methodology, not
       all structuralist interpretation of the Bible is necessarily worthwhile,
       and in any case it is incapable of feeding theological needs.

22.   Barton, John. "Historical Criticism and Literary Interpreta-
       tion: Is There Any Common Ground?," in #17, pp. 3–15.

       Historical critics and literary interpreters of the OT "already have
       more in common than they are prepared to acknowledge, and ...
       [t]here is considerable overlap between the questions they ask."
       Two aspects of biblical studies where "better progress could be
       made if critics of the two opposing schools collaborated more" are
       inconsistency in texts and theme.

23.   Bellis, Alice Ogden. "Objective Biblical Truth Versus the
       Value of Various Viewpoints." *HBT* 17 (1995), 25–36.

       Review of recent trends in literary biblical criticism as compared
       to traditional meaning- and author-centered methods. The desire
       for historical accuracy is more a modern than an ancient value; the
       effects the realization of this fact has on modern readers. Why the
       newer methods need to be seen as complementing the older ones
       rather than opposing them.

24.   Brown, J. Dickson. "Barton, Brooks, and Childs: A Compari-
       son of the New Criticism and Canonical Criticism." *JETS*
       36 (1993), 481–489.

       Despite arguments to the contrary, canonical criticism and the
       New Criticism are not all that similar once we examine them in de-
       tail. In fact, they "radically diverge in the presumption they make
       about their texts, the questions they ask ..., and the applications of
       authority they draw from their texts."

25.   Buechner, Frederick. "The Bible as Literature," in #20, pp.
       40–48.

       The "great drama" of the Bible, which, despite the "great miscel-
       lany of stories, characters [and] styles ... contained in this massive
       volume," and the "great divergence among the ways God is por-

trayed," somehow holds together with a single plot, and in turn holds us together as a people.

26. Campbell, Antony F., S.J. "Past History and Present Text: The Clash of Classical and Post-Critical Approaches to Biblical Text." *ABR* 59 (1991), 1–18.

"Today, in a post-critical world, ... there is room for both critical and creative readings of the biblical text.... We may signal these with antithetical balance." Such a combination will be aware both of the time and context of the composition, and the time and content of today. A pre-critical reading would not be informed or responsible."

27. Chouinard, Larry. "Changing Paradigms for Interpreting the Gospels." *RQ* 35 (1993), 71–78.

The benefits of new literary methods for analyzing scripture, and answers to those who object.

* Coleridge, Mark. "In Defence of the Other: Deconstruction and the Bible."

See #828.

28. Coleridge, Mark. "Life in the Crypt or Why Bother with Biblical Studies?" *BI* 2 (1994), 139–151.

Traditional explanations of the importance and relevance of biblical studies no longer apply in a time when the great Western cultural masterpieces have collapsed. Our ability to find an answer will depend on whether we can "discover the Bible as a new kind of meta-narrative, one that is (in Bakhtin's sense) not monologic but dialogic."

29. Ellington, John. "Wit and Humor in Bible Translation." *BTr* 42 (1991), 301–313.

"... The Bible is replete with examples of puns, irony, satire and a generally clever use of language" that must have created both amusement and serious reflection. Defines the terms, discusses "levels of linguistic play" in the Bible.

30. Eslinger, Lyle. "Inner-biblical Exegesis and Inner-biblical Allusion: The Question of Category." *VT* 42 (1992), 47–58.

"I propose, then, a self-consciously literary analysis of the textual interconnections in biblical literature. In it, we continue to use the indications of sequence that historical-critical scholarship has (improperly) relied on, but in full awareness of this reliance and without the conceit that we use a "scientific" historical framework independent of it.... For such a study, the developed theory of intertextuality provides a rich theological foundation."

31. Gerhart, Mary. "Generic Studies: Their Renewed Importance in Religious and Literary Interpretation." *JAAR* 45 (1977), 309–325.

A critical notion of "reader" is essential if the act of reading is to be meaningful. The notion of genre as a generative principle in the work of Hirsch, Gadamer, Todorov, and Ricoeur can help with this task. Thus "the notion of 'reader' makes possible a new model of the hermeneutical circle...." By means of genre the knowledgeable reader becomes the critical reader.

32. Goldingay, John. "How Far Do Readers Make Sense? Interpreting Biblical Narrative." *Themelios* 18, #2 (January 1993), 5–10.

How recent developments in narrative theory teach us that when context changes, interpretation changes. This does not, however, mean that all readings are valid, that there are not limits to what can be read out of a story. Texts "may have one intrinsic meaning ... but many significances or applications, or one sense but many references."

32a. Graham, Susan Lochrie. "On Scripture and Authorial Intent: A Narratological Proposal." *ATR* 77 (1995), 307–320.

Scripture as a special case of authorial intent, due to the rules governing its genre. It assumes the actual reader's belief. "At the very least, it is clearly possible to reinstate the critical concept of intention, and to use the insights of intertextuality and narratology in an effort to bridge the gap between biblical studies and theological interpretation."

33. Hauge, Hans. "The Sin of Reading: Austin Farrer, Helen Gardner and Frank Kermode on the Poetry of St. Mark," in #16, pp. 113–128.

While Farrer, Gardner, and Kermode agree that literary-critical methods may appropriately be applied to the Bible, they undoubtedly would not agree on how far to go, or what literary methods are relevant. On one side are Farrer and Kermode, who practice(d) a method which structuralists have been able to adapt, and on the other side is Gardner, who advocated that the meaning of a text be kept fluid and open. Gardner's position is the preferable one. Application of the work of these three critics to the gospel of Mark.

34.   Jasper, David. "Hermeneutics, Literary Theory and the Bible," in *The Study of Literature and Religion: An Introduction* (Minneapolis: Fortress P, 1989), pp. 83–96.

The bind created for hermeneutics by the powerful effects of structuralism, and how the hermeneutic strategy of Thiselton, Lundin, and Walhout in *The Responsibility of Hermeneutics* and of Bultmann and Ricoeur may provide a "means of escaping the prison-house of language"—namely replacing the literature-as-language model with a literature-as-action model. If we grant a privileged status to the Bible, it must be "hard won, not least through a critical awareness of it as literary art and language."

35.   Keegan, Terence J. "Biblical Criticism and the Challenge of Postmodernism." *BI* 3 (1995), 1–14.

Christian scholars can profitably use postmodern approaches, e.g., reader response and deconstruction, but they must be prepared to accept postmodernism's denial of objective certitude, its subjectivist implications.

36.   Klemm, David. "The Autonomous Text, The Hermeneutical Self, and Divine Rhetoric," in #16, pp. 3–26.

How two fundamental human activities, interpreting and believing, intersect. They both hold together and drive apart from one another, and understanding provides their common ground. The autonomous text as provider of possibilities, the reader as actualizer of those possibilities.

*   Longman, Tremper III. "Biblical Narrative."
      See #130.

37.   Longman, Tremper III. "Biblical Poetry," in #20, pp. 80–91.

The conventions of biblical poetry, including terseness, parallelism, imagery, and figurative language. Sample analysis of *Psalm* 114. There are four principal OT poetic types: lyric, epic, prophetic, and dramatic.

38.   Longman, Tremper III. "Storytellers and Poets in the Bible: *Can Literary Artifice Be True?*," in #13, pp. 137–149.

The Bible is both literature and history. The advantage of story over straight history or systematic theology is found in what the Russian formalists call "defamiliarization"; and of literature in general is that it speaks to the whole person: "intellect, will, and emotions." Examples from *Psalm* 114, *Job*, and *Genesis* 6–9.

39.   Longman, Tremper III. "What I Mean by Historical-Grammatical Exegesis—Why I Am Not a Literalist." *GTJ* 11 (1990), 137–155.

How the literary approach illuminates the subtlety of the Bible—much more so than traditional literalism.

40.   Macky, Peter W. "The Multiple Purposes of Biblical Speech Acts." *Princeton Seminary Bulletin*, n.s. 8 (1987), 50–61.

The "variety of speech act purposes that can plausibly be discerned as lying behind the words the biblical writers uttered," especially relational, dynamic, and exploratory examples.

41.   Medhurst, Martin J. "Rhetorical Dimensions in Biblical Criticism: Beyond Style and Genre." *QJS* 77 (1991), 214–226.

Review of the history of applications of rhetorical theory to the Bible, with some of the chief contributions since the 1970's subdivided into narration, typology, logic, linguistic rhythm, relationship to ancient and modern audiences, etc. Though the Bible does not fit easily into well-known rhetorical genres of classical antiquity, it is nevertheless valuable through its central insights into choices and effects.

42.   Noble, Paul R. "Hermeneutics and Post-Modernism: Can We Have a Radical Reader-Response Theory? Part I." *Religious Studies* 30 (1994), 419–436.

"... Fish's hermeneutics could only be imported into biblical studies if we were first to change our exegetical procedures in ways that the overwhelming majority of biblical scholars would find totally unacceptable," since his theory "is fraught with severe *internal* problems."

43.   Phillips, Gary A. "Drawing the Other: The Post-Modern and Reading the Bible Imaginatively," in David Jasper and Mark Ledbetter, eds., *In Good Company: Essays in Honor of Robert Detweiler* (Atlanta: Scholars P, 1994), pp. 403–432.

How "postmodern attention helps us to rediscover and recover the Bible critically, religiously, ethically for a new age.... Reading in a postmodern way, imaginatively, encourages biblical critics ... empowers us to imagine what else a text (the Bible) could be saying; to imagine transcendence, for example...."

44. Phillips, Gary A. "Sign/Text/Différance. The Contribution of Intertextual Theory to Biblical Criticism," in Heinrich Plett, ed., *Intertextuality* (Berlin and New York: Walter de Gruyter, 1991), pp. 78–97.

Text and reader as interpretant in an intertextual process, as illustrated in *Luke* 10. How Derrida's theories may seem to be threatening to biblical critics. "From Derrida's perspective, the disseminating quality of textuality calls for biblical critics not only to comprehend the texts that they seek to explain and interpret in terms of the discrete methodological framework that operates when they read; but also to extend that process of differentiation to the depths in order to ask what it is about the character of the critical effort itself that can be accounted for in precisely the same terms."

45. Polka, Brayton. "Interpretation and the Bible: The Dialectic of Concept and Content in Interpretative Practice." *Journal of Speculative Philosophy* 4 (1990), 66–82; rpt #16, pp. 27–45.

"... to develop a properly comprehensive concept of interpretation is to comprehend the interplay of Hegel's two claims; that the Bible cannot be interpreted like other, profane texts and that the concept of God which human beings hold expresses the content of their lives." The content of interpretation reflects how we conceive the Bible, and the content of the Bible shapes our concept of interpretation.

46. Porter, Stanley E. "Reader-Response Criticism and New Testament Study: A Response to A.C. Thiselton's *New Horizons in Hermeneutics*." *LT 8* (1994), 94–102.

Response to Thiselton's treatment of Porter's 1990 article in *Literature and Theology* 4 (Minor I, #1550). How Thiselton overlooks Porter's points about reader response there, especially his supposed dependence on Stanley Fish. Thiselton's "confusion about the fundamental nature of reading strategies." Five reasons why reader response theories and approaches have failed to take hold in biblical criticism.

47. Potok, Chaim. "The Novelist and the Bible," in #20, pp. 489–498.

How and why we can regard the Bible as sacred text and as literature, despite the suspicions and fears of Jews, Christians, and Muslims. It "does not necessarily impose humanist orientation on the contents of scripture." How archeological discoveries have increased our knowledge of the biblical world.

48.   Pyper, Hugh. "Speaking Silence: Male Readers, Women's Readings and the Biblical Texts." *LT* 8 (1994), 296–310.

"The feminist readers of the Bible can open our eyes to the fact that the male conspiracy is already betrayed in the text, betrayed both in the sense of being laid bare and of being rendered impotent. The task that the text then lays upon its male readers is to take on in faith the risk of utterance, through hearing the voice of silence."

49.   Reumann, John. "After Historical Criticism, What? Trends in Biblical Interpretation and Ecumenical, Interfaith Dialogue." *Journal of Ecumenical Studies* 29 (1992), 55–86.

The important shift from a historical to a literary frame of reference has several implications: the literary is not new, and the historical has always been literary; the historical must continue as a check on the historicism of literary criticism; the literary approach is increasingly fragmented; it is a mirror image of our age.

50.   Riley, William. "Situating Biblical Narrative: Poetics and the Transmission of Community Values." *PIBA* 9 (1985), 38–52.

"If the narrative approach [to the Bible] is to be critically grounded and avoid ... subjectivity ..., content may provide the key to the process ... *an essential content is the community dynamic of which the text is the tangible evidence.*" Supporting this are three postulates: scriptural narrative is traditional, an experiment between storyteller and audience, and it "communicates the values of the traditional community in which it functions."

51.   Robbins, Vernon K., and John H. Patton. "Rhetoric and Biblical Criticism." *QJS* 66 (1980), 327–337.

A "significant overlap" now exists between biblical studies and rhetorical scholarship. Because biblical scholars have been applying rhetoric and literary criticism to the Bible increasingly in the last decade, "a significant body of data" is now available for scholars of rhetoric to use.

52. Ryken, Leland. "Bible as Literature," in David S. Dockery et al., eds. *Foundations for Biblical Interpretation* (Nashville: Broadman and Holman Publishers, 1994), pp. 55–72.

"... as a literary anthology the Bible is a mingling of the familiar and the unfamiliar." Its "immense range of content and style" and at the same time its unifying plot; thus it "tells a single story in a way other anthologies do not." The literary approach should be our initial one; we then "move on to other considerations, especially the theological and moral."

53. Ryken, Leland. "The Bible as Literature: A Brief History," in #20, pp. 49–68.

"The idea that the Bible is literature is as old as the Bible itself," though to what degree it is "literary" became a point of debate among the church fathers. The Renaissance and Reformation "represented a remarkable flowering of literary appreciation for the Bible," while the nineteenth century's literary interest in it was "secular" because it was devoid of faith. In this century, teaching the Bible in college literature courses and the work of liberal biblical scholarship converged to create the current trends. How the method tends to work today in the light of the new pluralism in literary criticism.

54. Ryken, Leland, and Tremper Longman III. "Introduction," in #20, pp. 15–39.

Definition of the literary approach to a text, and of the identifying traits of literature—e.g., form as meaning and self-conscious artistry. How the literary and theological approaches to the Bible have differed; pitfalls of the literary approach from a biblical scholar's viewpoint; how we distinguish literary features in biblical narrative especially; the literary unity of the Bible.

55. Shea, John. "Religious-Imaginative Encounters with Scriptural Stories," in Robert Detweiler, ed., *Art/Literature/Religion: Life on the Borders* (Chico: Scholars P, 1984), pp. 173–180.

The "religious-imaginative" method allows the text to "'perform' like a sacred object," while retelling the text, "reconstructing its elements to express and communicate the experienced meaning." The "inclusive dynamics" of biblical narratives which encourages, even demands, reader participation to complete the process, though it is not precisely like either and traditional historical or literary approaches to scripture. It is rather a "poetic-religious" encounter with the text that is "playful and meditative."

56.   Stevens, Paul. "'Leviticus Thinking' and the Rhetoric of Early Modern Colonialism." *Criticism* 35 (1993), 441–446.

"... as the work of many recent literary critics bears witness, the representation of Scripture as a profoundly ironic, postmodern text often impedes the task of historicizing race and colonialism...." The work of Regina Schwartz as an example of this problem.

57.   Swanston, Hamish F.G. "Literary Categories and Biblical Imagery," in Paul Burns and John Cumming, eds., *The Bible Now: Essays on Its Meaning and Use for Christians Today* (NY: Seabury, 1981), pp. 49–60.

The author's intention "may be discerned only through and in literary forms and images that the author puts to use: an harmonious verse, an elegant narrative, an entrancing fairy tale, a quickening image.... The range of forms and images in the scriptural writings is both an acknowledgment that the divine cannot be adequately expressed unless the literary devices of many people are brought into service, and an announcement that the order insinuated by such literatures is finally discoverable in Jesus."

58.   Tomes, Roger. "Recent Developments in Biblical Studies." *Faith and Freedom* 35 (1982), 78–84.

How canonical, literary, sociological, and structural approaches to the Bible are breathing new life into biblical criticism (though they do not mean that historical criticism is dead).

59.   Weathers, Robert A. "Leland Ryken's Literary Approach to Biblical Interpretation: An Evangelical Model." *JETS* 37 (1994), 115–124.

The literary-critical work of Amos Wilder, Northrop Frye, and Leland Ryken on the Bible. The similarities and differences in their methods, and why evangelicals ought to participate in post-modern biblical criticism. Their methods applied to *Revelation*.

60.   Wilson, Robert R. "Between 'Azel' and 'Azel': Interpreting the Biblical Genealogies." *Biblical Archeologist* 42 (1979), 11–22.

The question of the accuracy of the genealogies is more complex than scholars have supposed. Historical accuracy is less important than ways in which the genealogies express the perceived reality of the authors who wrote them.

61. Wuellner, Wilhelm. "Biblical Exegesis in the Light of the History and Historicity of Rhetoric and the Nature of the Rhetoric of Religion," in #624, pp. 492–513.

"The verdict is still out on just how successful and profitable the application of rhetoric theory to the Bible has become ... today...." At least it has helped combat simplistic either/or, dogmatic biblical interpretation. "A new rhetoric and a new rhetoric criticism are ... emerging, and need to be cultivated ... to enable readers of sacred scriptures to let the reading and critical study of these texts do its work: (transforming society)...."

62. Young, Frances. "Typology," in #17, pp. 29–48.

Typology is a "'figure of speech' which configures or reads texts to bring out significant correspondences so as to invest them with meaning beyond themselves.... [It] belongs to the literary phenomenon of intertextuality...." The sacred text is no mere pretext for something else, as in allegory: rather story and symbol carry a surplus of significance.

See also #264, 620, 828.

Pedagogy and Preaching

63. Barr, David L. *New Testament Story: An Introduction.* Second Edition. Belmont, etc. (Wadsworth), 1995.

Textbook for a course on the NT emphasizing literary, social-scientific, and historical approaches. Literary analyses of *I Thessalonians*, *Romans*, plot of *Mark*, characterization in *Matthew*, literary methods in *Luke*, structure of *John*, and literary analyses of *Revelation* and the Catholic letters.

64. Bellis, Alice Ogden. *Helpmates, Harlots, and Heroes: Women's Stories in the Hebrew Bible.* Louisville (Westminster/John Knox P), 1994.

Introduction and conclusion, plus nine essays on various specific books of the HB, "designed for use in academic courses and in religious education classes...." Introduction defines "feminism" and "womanism," and explains various critical approaches to the HB, literary to scientific, as part of a feminist hermeneutic. Discussion questions after each chapter. Chapters on specific books of the HB analyzed separately as #s 172, 180, 241, 273, 295, 549, 557.

65.   Culler, Arthur J. *Creative Religious Literature. A New Literary Study of the Bible*. New York (Macmillan), 1930.

Examination of biblical literature by types, e.g., folk song; short story; fable; parable; lyric, dramatic and epic forms; biography and history; wisdom; oratory; and essay. Comparison of biblical writings with "other literature of the same type or theme." Chapter bibliographies and discussion topics and exercises.

*   Culpepper, R. Alan. "Narrative Criticism as a Tool for Proclamation: 1 Samuel 13."

See #309.

67.   Goldman, Stan. "The Problem of the Two-Testaments: Pedagogical Motives for Shifting from 'Old Testament' to 'Hebrew Bible.'" *College Literature* 20 (1993), 206–213.

In courses using a literary approach to the Bible, it is preferable to "rename" the OT as the HB for a variety of cultural, theological, literary, and historical reasons. Among these is the curiosity it creates to know more about Jewish faith and thus the tolerance which usually results; and the desirability of demonstrating to students that traditions are fluid, not fixed.

68.   Greidanus, Sidney. *The Modern Preacher and the Ancient Text: Interpreting and Preaching Biblical Literature*. Leicester (Intervarsity) and Grand Rapids (Eerdmans), 1988.

Advice on expository preaching and sermon writing, with sections on using historical, literary, and theological methods of interpretation in developing sermons. Chapters on literary characteristics of Hebrew narrative, prophetic literature gospels, and epistles.

69.   Greidanus, Sidney. "Preaching and the New Literary Studies of the Bible." *CTJ* 28 (1993), 121–130.

Five areas within the new literary approach to the Bible have had the greatest impact on homiletics: the return to the final text; detecting the textual unit and its message; historical questions; the form of the text and the form of the sermon; and the relevance of the sermon.

70. Greidanus, Sidney. "The Value of a Literary Approach for Preaching," in #20, pp. 509–519.

    The literary understanding of the Bible "has been prized by preachers from earliest times." Its advantages include a return to the final text, emphasis on a whole text, importance of style in the Bible and the sermon, and a new awareness of how stories change lines.

71. Harwell, Charles W., and Daniel McDonald. *The Bible. A Literary Survey*. Indianapolis (Bobbs-Merrill), 1975.

    Reprint of various portions of the OT and NT especially suitable for literary analysis with brief introductions to each selection. OT: *Genesis, Exodus* 1–21, *Judges* 2–5, 13–16, *Ruth*, various parts of *1* and *2 Samuel, Job* 1–14, 31, 38–42, various *Psalms, Ecclesiastes, Song of Songs, Amos, Jonah*. NT: *Mark, Matthew* 5–7, various parts of *Luke, John* 1–3, *Galatians, 2 Corinthians* 11–12, *Revelation*.

72. Lane, Robert D. *Reading the Bible. Intention, Text, Interpretation*. Lanham, NY, and London (UP of America), 1994.

    A "secular midrash and students' companion to the Bible," which is "comprised of … human stories, to be approached with curiosity, not religious awe … [like] any great literature." Chapters on "What Is the Bible?" (translations, doublet scenes, mythology, truth versus story); "Brothers, Tokens and Types" (literary devices, motifs, techniques); "History and the Bible "(*Genesis* and *Exodus*); on heroes (*Genesis*); belief and interpretations; *Job* and *Ecclesiastes*; Saul–David–Solomon narratives; various prophets; the Gospels and Pauline letters.

* Pregeant, Russell. *Engaging the New Testament. An Interdisciplinary Introduction*.

    See #625.

74. Scott, Bernard Brandon. *The Word of God in Words: Reading and Preaching*. Philadelphia (Fortress P), 1985.

    How meaning is built up in language, how the role of the reader affects meaning, how stories function—applied to understanding and preaching about the Bible.

75. Vogels, Walter. *Reading and Preaching the Bible: A New Semiotic Approach*. Wilmington (Michael Glazier), 1986.

A guide to help the laity read the Bible with confidence that they are reading in a way that is faithful to the text. How semiotics can be that method for reading. "Practical exercises" which apply the method to the "macro-texts" of *Job*, and *Genesis* 2–3, and the "micro-texts" of *Genesis* 13, and *Luke* 7 and 19. "Through their semiotic analysis the reader and the pastor have opened the text, discovered its limits, what goes on within it and noted the beautiful network of operations and relations."

See also #309, 617, 625.

THE HEBREW BIBLE

Books

76.   Alter, Robert. *The World of Biblical Literature*. [New York] (Basic Books), 1992.

Nine chapters on the need to recognize disjunctures in HBN without automatically assuming they reflect separate traditions; the sense of play in biblical literature, strategically placed specification, allusion, the role of ancient commentaries, the quest for the author, nature of HB poetry, and why reading the Bible as literature means to recover its true spiritual authority, somewhat covered by the influence of 19th-century positivism. Chs. 3 and 8 listed in Minor I, #33; 6, 7, and 9 from *Commentary* (March 1990, November 1990, August 1985).

*   Bellis, Alice Ogden. *Helpmates, Harlots, and Heroes: Women's Stories in the Hebrew Bible*.

See #64.

77.   Brenner, Athalya, and Fokkelien van Dijk-Hemmes. *On Gendering Texts. Female and Male Voices in the Hebrew Bible*. Leiden (E.J. Brill), 1993.

"Gender positions," "authority," "gendered to textuality and attributions of gender within the text," "voice," and "world view and ideological content" in various portions of the HB. Feminist method and its application to genre; female voice in *Proverbs* 1–9; text authority in biblical love lyrics—especially *Qoheleth* 3; male voice in *Ezekiel* 23 and *Jeremiah*. Briefer analyses of many books and passages.

78.   Campbell, Antony F., S.J. *The Study Companion to Old Testament Literature: An Approach to the Writings of Pre-Exilic and*

Exilic Israel. Wilmington (Glazier), 1989; rpt Collegeville (Liturgual Press), 1992.

Commentary which combines literary and historical critical approaches to the OT; separate chapters on the Pentateuch, the Deuteronomistic History, and the prophetic books as literary works, and on the thematic tensions and complexity of *Jonah* and *Job*. The OT's use of narrative and poetic devices for the purpose of communicating theological truths.

79.   Cartledge, Tony W. *Vows in the Hebrew Bible and the Ancient Near East.* Sheffield (JSOT Press), 1992.

The nature and use of vows in the ancient near east and in the HB. Literary function of vows in *Numbers* 21, *Genesis* 28, *Judges* 11, *I Samuel* 1, and *II Samuel* 15. Their literary structure is a standard four-part formula of narrative introduction, address to the deity, protasis, and apodosis, best labelled a "now account." They are also common in HBP, and have a variety of literary purposes: characterization, integral plot elements, thematic reinforcement.

80.   Crenshaw, James L. *Old Testament Story and Faith: A Literary and Theological Introduction.* Peabody, MA (Hendrickson), 1992 (c. Macmillan, 1986—original edition).

A guide to each book of the HB, emphasizing the written text rather than history, archaeology, sociology, etc. Primary aim is to "communicate an appreciation for the beauty and profundity of the sacred text," paying special attention to literary art and religious power. Includes the apocrypha.

81.   Deist, F.E., and W.S. Vorster, eds. *Words from Afar (The Literature of the Old Testament, Volume I).* Cape Town (Tafelberg Publisher), 1986.

Eight chapters by several different authors on codes of communication in OT poetic, narrative, wisdom, prophetic, apocalyptic, and legal texts. Six of the eight are literary-critical, analyzed separately as #'s 94, 125, 151, 464, 374, 604.

82.   Exum, J. Cheryl, and David J.A. Clines, eds. *The New Literary Criticism and the Hebrew Bible.* Sheffield (JSOT P) and Valley Forge (Trinity P International), 1993.

Twelve essays applying various post-structuralist forms of literary criticism (feminist, materialistic, psychoanalytic, reader-response, and deconstruction) to specific passages from *Genesis*, *Numbers*, *Isaiah*, *Jeremiah*, *II Samuel*, *II Kings*, *I Samuel*, the Former

Prophets, *Ruth*, *Amos*, *Psalms*, with an introductory essay by the editors. Individual essays analyzed separately as #'s 176, 219, 261, 271, 317, 329, 362, 390, 404, 434, 489, 562.

83.   Fewell, Danna Nolan, ed. *Reading Between Texts: Intertextuality and the Hebrew Bible*. Louisville (Westminster/John Knox P), 1992.

Fourteen essays by as many authors on how various books or passages in the HB can be illuminated using intertextuality as a method. Fewell introduces the essays; Timothy Beal urges through a reading of the work of Mieke Bal that critics "recognize the basic relations between writing and ideology, and thus between interpretation and power." Other essays analyzed as #'s 176, 382, 228, 227, 221, 327, 334, 347, 360, 361, 427, 520, 284.

84.   Garsiel, Moshe. *Biblical Names: A Literary Study of Midrashic Derivations and Puns*. Tr. Phyllis Hackett. Ramat Gan (Bar-Ilan UP), 1991 (revised and enlarged from Hebrew edition of 1987).

Various aspects of the technique, including sound and rhythm patterns, role in alliteration and punning. Sometimes deliberately ambiguous to challenge the reader. Relationship between names and their midrashic derivations. Its widespread, sophisticated use indicates that it was a recognized literary device which "played a major role in biblical poetics."

85.   Gunkel, Hermann. *The Folktale in the Old Testament*. Tr. by Michael D. Rutter with an Introduction by John W. Rogerson. Sheffield (The Almond P), 1987 (originally published 1917).

The "earnestness and sublimity of Israelite religion" rejected folktales, eradicating them whenever they said things unacceptable to Yahwism. Nevertheless, they survive in submerged form throughout the OT as, e.g., nature fables, tales of spirits, demons, and giants, tales of magic, about children and adults, etc.

86.   House, Paul R., ed. *Beyond Form Criticism. Essays in Old Testament Literary Criticism*. Winona Lake (Eisenbrauns), 1992.

Introduction assessing the rise and current state of literary criticism of the OT, and a final essay on the current status and future of the study of biblical Hebrew poetry. Bulk of the volume reprints essays listed in Minor I as #'s 112, 241, 266, 303, 327, 340, 367, 546, 559, 771, 793, 853, 900, 1132, and 1327.

87.   Jobling, David, et al., eds. *The Bible and the Politics of Exegesis:*
       Essays in Honor of Norman K. Gottwald on his Sixty-Fifth
       Birthday. Cleveland (Pilgrim), 1991.

       Part One: Socio-Literary Readings in the Hebrew Bible. Seven es-
       says on *Psalms* 9–10, *Proverbs* 1–9, *Psalms* 139, *Micah*, *Psalms*, *Genesis*
       5 and 6, and phrase "her mother's house." *Part Two*: Six essays not
       literary. *Part Three*: "The Theory and Praxis." Eight essays, one of
       which (by Jobling) is literary-critical on feminist theory; rest are
       socio-political.

88.   Pardes, Ilana. *Countertraditions in the Bible. A Feminist Ap-*
       proach. Cambridge, MA, and London (Harvard UP), 1992.

       The HB is a more heterogeneous, heteroglot text than is often ac-
       knowledged, even by feminist critics. The "tense dialogue" between
       the Bible's dominant patriarchal discourses and its "counter female
       voices." Intertextual literary analysis, together with feminist theory
       and psychoanalysis, can bring out these anti-thetical voices.
       Chapters on *Genesis* 1–2, 4–5, 25–36, *Exodus* 4, *Ruth*, *Song of Songs*,
       and *Job* analyzed separately as #'s 198, 199, 232, 252, 540, 566, 579.

89.   Rabinowitz, Isaac. *A Witness Forever. Ancient Israel's Percep-*
       tion of Literature and the Resultant Hebrew Bible. Bethesda
       (CDL P), 1993.

       Chapters on how the creators of the HB perceived words, what
       they believed about the literary process, some "anomalous" litera-
       ture, rhetorical and textual consequences of these perceptions, "the
       nature and function of *The Book of the Upright*: An ancient literary
       forerunner of the Hebrew Bible," and the HB as a literary unit.
       Many of their assumptions have results in "an array of literary ef-
       fects that quite patently defy and contradict" those of modern
       western culture.

*   Reed, Walter L. *Dialogues of the Word: The Bible as Literature*
       According to Bakhtin.

       See #6.

90.   Talmon, Shemaryahu. *Literary Studies in the Hebrew Bible:*
       Form and Content. Jerusalem (The Magnes P) and Leiden
       (E.J. Brill), 1993.

       Ten essays, all reprinted from earlier publication. Four are liter-
       ary-critical, and are listed in Minor I as #'s 154, 291, 359, and 1435.

Articles

91. Biddle, Mark E. "The Figure of Lady Jerusalem: Identification, Deification and Personification of Cities in the Ancient Near East," in K. Lawson Younger, Jr., et al., eds., *The Biblical Canon in Comparative Perspective* (Lewiston: Edwin Mellen P, 1991), pp. 173–194.

   Personification of Jerusalem through feminine imagery in the HB "rests on well-developed traditions of great antiquity and geographical scope." She is not automatically a wanton character (as in *Hosea*), and even the negative imagery need not imply identification with pagan fertility practices. Personification becomes a theological device as well.

92. Carroll, Robert P. "The Hebrew Bible as Literature—A Misprision?" *ST* 47 (1993), 77–90.

   If we ask "Is the HB literature?", we then need to ask the further question, "Compared to what?" It seems impossible to read it "straight" without reinterpretation, transformation, etc. Witness Mishna-Talmud, Philo, Qumran scrolls. Only the modern academy has attempted a straight reading, and in this has been widely condemned because it confuses "the vernacularization of the Bible ... and the re-discovery of the ancient text of the HB." The virtues and drawbacks of Alter's approach to the HB.

93. Casanowicz, Immanuel M. "Paronomasia in the Old Testament." *JBL* 12 (1893), 105–167.

   Definition and limits of paronomasia as a stylistic device; various forms found in the OT; a list of 502 examples in the OT, alphabetically arranged, and then classified by type.

94. Deist, F.E. "The Writer, His Text, and His Audience," in #81, pp. 17–38.

   Textual communication in the OT involves six factors in interrelationship: message, sender, medium, code, receiver, and content. The writer and his perspective; the text and its code; text and audience. Excurses on *Psalm* 51, *Exodus* 11–14.

94a. Garsiel, Moshe. "Puns Upon Names as a Literary Device in 1 Kings 1–2." *Biblica* 72 (1991), 379–386.

Biblical authors made subtle use of the technique of punning upon names. Examples from *Isaiah* 12, 37, 33, 35; *2 Kings* 19; *Chronicles* 26, 32, 24, 3, 29, 28; *Micah*; *Malachi*; *Hosea*.

*   Goldman, Stan. "The Problem of the Two Testaments: Pedagogical Motives for Shifting from 'Old Testament' to 'Hebrew Bible.'"

See #67.

95.   Gordis, Robert. "A Rhetorical Use of Interrogative Sentences in Biblical Hebrew." *AJSL* 49 (1932–33), 212–217.

The insertion of an implied negative in questions seeking an affirmative answer. The "heightened emotional condition" permits the omission and allows the reader to infer an automatic positive.

96.   Greenspahn, Frederick E. "A Mesopotamian Proverb and Its Biblical Reverberations." *JAOS* 114 (1994), 33–38.

Traces of an ancient Mesopotamian proverb about the limitations of human existence can be found throughout the HB, including *Deuteronomy* 30, *Qohelet* 5, *Job* 11, *Psalms* 115 and 139, and *Genesis* 11. Analysis of this last example, the Tower of Babel, where the proverb receives its most detailed treatment anywhere in the HB.

97.   Herbert, A.S. "The 'Parable' (*Masal*) in the Old Testament." *Scottish Journal of Theology* 7 (1954), 180–196.

Various forms the parable takes in the OT, including those usually labelled "prophetic figurative discourse." It is a "powerful rhetorical or literary device" used with "remarkable consistency" throughout the OT, accepted also by other ancient Near Eastern cultures. Examples from *I Samuel* 10, 24; *Ezekiel* 12, 17, 18, 21; *Psalms* 44; *Job*; *Proverbs*.

98.   Howard, David M., Jr. "Rhetorical Criticism in Old Testament Studies." *Bulletin for Biblical Research* 4 (1994), 87–104.

Review of rhetorical criticism of the OT since its self-conscious inception in 1968. Unfortunately, in OT studies, rhetorical criticism "has tended to be primarily a literary [and stylistic] concern...." Why OT scholars should practice genuine rhetorical criticism—i.e., focus on "suasive aspects of spoken discourse ... [so that] a rich, relatively unexplored field of study presents itself to Old Testament scholars...."

99. Longman, Tremper III. "The Literature of the Old Testament," in #20, pp. 95–107.

> Barriers to a proper literary appreciation of the OT. It is literature because its subject matter is "'human experience, not abstract ideas. Literature *incarnates* its meanings as concretely as possible.'" The OT not only informs the intellect, it also "arouses emotions, appeals to the will, and stimulates the imagination.... [It is] self conscious ... about its form of expression." Basic genres, themes, and plot of the OT.

100. MacDonald, Peter J. "Discourse Analysis and Biblical Interpretation," in Walter R. Bodine, ed., *Linguistics and Biblical Hebrew* (Winona Lake: Eisenbrauns, 1992), pp. 153–175.

> We must expand our sense of the content of the HB to include the linguistic framework, "human mental capabilities and strategies, and the modes of speaker-hearer interaction." Using this expanded sense, "we may some day understand ... certain aspects of the world behind a biblical text" which would even enable us "to catch glimpses of the attitudes and beliefs of ... [those] who produced and used the biblical texts during their development."

101. Mathews, Kenneth A. "Literary Criticism of the Old Testament," in David S. Dockery, et al., eds., *Foundations for Biblical Interpretation* (Nashville: Broadman and Holman Publishers, 1994), pp. 205–231.

> Newer literary methods *versus* "the traditional evangelistical and historical-critical approaches." Why a literary approach is even wanted. Various types, including archetypal, composition, "new," structuralism, discourse analysis, reader-response, deconstruction, canon criticism. Application to *Genesis* 6–9 "to illustrate the positive effects of literary theory on biblical exegesis...."

102. Muilenburg, James. "The Linguistic and Rhetorical Usages of the Particle in the Old Testament." *HUCA* 32 (1961), 135–160.

> The importance of this word for grasping Hebrew rhetorical expression. It has developed "into a vast variety of nuances and meanings, yet always preserving ... its original emphatic connotations." The importance of assessing the relationship between this particle "and Israel's understanding of time as it is reflected in terminology, syntax, literary forms and structure, and the movement of words."

103.   Parunak, H. Van Dyke. "Oral Typesetting: some Uses of Biblical Structure." *Biblica* 62 (1981), 153–168.

   "Two simple structural forms, the chiasm and the alternation, can be used to divide, unify, and emphasize biblical texts." The former will be a self-contained unit. The latter, e.g., an introductory panel, will function either as a table of contents or as a display of "how each element ... interacts with the various themes treated by each of the panels as a whole."

104.   Randall, C. Corydon. "An Approach to Biblical Satire," in Jack C. Knight and Lawrence A. Sinclair, eds., *The Psalms and Other Studies on the Old Testament* (Nashotah, WI: Nashotah House Seminary, 1990), pp. 132–144.

   The three primary types of satire are invective, sarcasm, and irony. All three are found in quantity in the HB. Examples are cited and briefly analyzed from *Isaiah* 10, 8, 1, 36, 37, 28, and 56, *Jeremiah* 14, 9, 13, 23, *Micah* 2, 3, *Psalm* 94, *Amos* 5, *Nehemiah* 3, *Habakkuk* 2, *Judges* 5, 6, 16, 11, *2 Kings* 2, 10, *1 Samuel* 17, 8, 18, *Exodus* 15, *Hosea* 8, 6, *Deuteronomy* 30, *Job* 12, 15, 40, *1 Kings* 18, 22, *Malachi* 1, *Ezekiel* 22.

105.   Richardson, H. Neil. "Some Literary Parallels Between Ugaritic and The Old Testament." *The Journal of Bible and Religion* 20 (1952), 172–175.

   Parallels of individual vocabulary words and "modes of expression." Examples of the latter from *Genesis, Psalms, Isaiah, Zechariah*. The author has collected 175 examples in these two categories.

106.   Saydon, P.P. "Assonance in Hebrew as a Means of Expressing Emphasis." *Biblica* 36 (1955), 36–50, 287–304.

   The relation between assonance and emphasis in passages from throughout the HB. These examples prove that HB writers knew and used the device (though not all assonance exists to create emphasis). How to distinguish emphatic use from aesthetic use.

107.   Tigay, Jeffrey H. "On Evaluating Claims of Literary Borrowing," in Mark E. Cohen et al., eds., *The Tablet and The Scroll: Near Eastern Studies in Honor of William W. Hallo* (Bethesda: CDL P, 1993), pp. 250–255.

   The dangers of "parallelomania": assuming that a borrowing has occurred without substantial evidence. Criteria for identifying ancient Near Eastern–biblical parallels. Examples from *Ecclesiastes* and *Gilgamesh*. An "empirical approach" to the problem. However, differences do not necessarily *disprove* a parallel, either.

108.   Trible, Phyllis. "Bringing Miriam Out of the Shadows," in #242, pp. 166–186.

"Buried within Scripture are bits and pieces of a story awaiting discovery. Unearthing the fragments and assembling them, we have crafted a mosaic for Miriam ... from overlays of patriarchy.... Lo, the fragments that the builders have rejected have become tesserae in a mosaic of salvation. Let all women and men who have eyes to behold this mosaic join Miriam in singing an updated version of her song of deliverance.... Patriarchy and its horsemen God has hurled into the sea."

109.   van Wolde, Ellen. "A Text-Semantic Study of the Hebrew Bible, Illustrated with Noah and Job." *JBL* 113 (1994), 19–35.

We need to combine literary study of textual syntagms in the HB with a linguistic study of the Hebrew language system. The important role of the reader in this process of "making visible the potentiality of meanings in ... the Hebrew Bible...." How the power and beauty of the stories of Noah and Job emerge much more completely in such a study than they may in a theoretical discussion.

See also #67.

Hebrew Biblical Narrative

Books

110.   Bar-Efrat, Shimon. *Narrative Art in the Bible*. Sheffield (Almond P), 1989.

Guide to the biblical narrative as a literary work of art. Narrator and modes of narration; shaping of characters; plot structure; time and space; style. Various narratives in *Genesis* and *I and II Samuel*, long chapter on *II Samuel* 13.

111.   Brenner, Athalya. *The Israelite Woman. Social Role and Literary Type in Biblical Narrative.* Sheffield (JSOT P), 1985.

Part One: women in professions and institutions in the HB (whether matriarch, temptress, queen, wise woman, author, prophet, etc.) and the attempt to define "women's position in the socio-political sphere...." Part Two: development of stereotypes and paradigms used repeatedly to describe women in HBN, tracing literary types corresponding to professions and institutions of Part One. Possibility of female authorship in *Song of Songs.* Literary paradigms of female types of the hero's mother (*Exodus* 2, *Matthew* 1, *Luke* 1–2), the temptress (*Genesis* 19, 38, 39, *Proverbs* 1–9, *Judges* 14–16, *Ruth*) foreign women (many of the same passages, plus *Judges* 13–16), and the ancestress (*Genesis* 2–3).

112.   Brichto, Herbert Chanan. *Toward a Grammar of Biblical Poetics: Tales of the Prophets.* NY and Oxford (OUP), 1992.

Biblical texts are "primarily creative, imaginative, and fictive, for all that their essential purpose is didactic ... and ... are presented as narratives of an essentially historical nature or as ideology in the form of narrative or precept." "Poetical grammar" means "that there is a set of rules that will when uncovered, show that the Hebrew Scriptures ... constitute a unitary design and a single 'authorial voice'...."

113.   Culley, Robert C. *Themes and Variations: A Study of Action in Biblical Narrative.* Atlanta (Scholars), 1992.

[Revised versions of *Semeia* (1980), *Genesis* 25–33, and Minor I, #706.] Study of repeated yet variable patterns of action in HBN: punishment, rescue, achievement, reward, announcement, and prohibition sequences. *Joshua* 2, 6, 7, 8; *Judges* 3, 4, 6–8, 10–12, 13–16; *I Samuel* 13, 15, 25; *I Kings* 13, 20, 21; *II Kings* 5–7; *Genesis* 2–3, 18–19, 6–9, 37–50; *Numbers* 13–14; *Exodus* 1–14.

114.   Darr, Katheryn Pfisterer. *Far More Precious Than Jewels. Perspectives on Biblical Women.* Louisville (Westminster/John Knox P), 1991.

Explanation of historical-critical, social scientific, literary-critical, rabbinical, and feminist approaches and perspectives on interpretation. The HB and succeeding chapters applying some or all of these methods to *Ruth*; Sarah, Hagar, and *Esther.*

115. Eskhult, Mats. *Studies in Verbal Aspect and Narrative Technique in Biblical Hebrew Prose*. Uppsala (Dist. by Almquist and Wiksell Int'l, Stockholm), 1990.

How the concept of verbal aspect in HB prose is linked to sentence structure, and thereby to the utterances and narratives of which they form an integrated part. As a result of the contrast between "state" and "motion" in Biblical Hebrew, "aspectual contrasts are liable to be used by a narrator in order to facilitate the apprehension of the structure of a story on the part of his audience." Examples from *I Kings 17–II Kings 10, II Samuel 13–20, Judges 6–8*.

116. Exum, J. Cheryl. *Tragedy and Biblical Narrative: Arrows of the Almighty*. Cambridge UP, 1992.

In HB narratives, e.g., *Judges 11–12, 13–16, I Samuel* and *II Samuel* (David, Saul, Michal, Jonathan, Abner, and Ishbosheth) "we encounter a vision of reality that can properly be called tragic." Concerned with theory rather than genre, defined as "Tragedy ... poses questions about the elusive and necessary reliability of guilt, suffering, and evil that it can only resolve aesthetically, not thematically." Revised versions of items listed in Minor I as #s 559, 748, 749.

117. Glatt, David. *Chronological Displacement in Biblical and Related Literatures*. Atlanta (Scholars P), 1993.

Cases of chronological displacement in Mesopotamian, biblical, and post-biblical writing all show "similarities ... with regard to ... arrangement ... motivations, and the methods through which the displaced materials were sent in their present literary locations."

118. Gunn, David M., and Danna Nolan Fewell. *Narrative in the Hebrew Bible*. Oxford (Oxford UP), 1993.

Relationship between literary and other forms of criticism of the HB over the last two millenia, as illustrated through *Genesis* 4. Importance of characters; how to read for the plot; the "lure of language" (including repetition, ambiguity, and metaphor) in HBN; readers and responsibility. Detailed analysis of *Genesis* 38, 11–12, 2–3, *Judges* 10–12, *Jonah, Daniel* 3.

119. Kessler, Martin, ed. and trans. *Voices from Amsterdam: A Modern Tradition of Reading Biblical Narrative*. Atlanta (Scholars P), 1994.

Eleven essays on HB narrative in general and on specific narratives published [in Dutch] between 1925 and the present. Most are literary, and all reflect the "Amsterdam" school of synchronic analysis. Analyzed separately as #s 134, 272, 185, 216, 245, 320, 440, 182, 217.

120.   McCarthy, Carmel, R.S.M., and William Riley. *The Old Testament Short Story. Explorations into Narrative Spirituality.* Wilmington (Michael Glazier), 1986.

Literary criticism, and the specifically narrative criticism, as a "valuable tool in the attempt to discover ... truth" in Hebrew biblical narrative. Basic narrative techniques including unity, tension and its resolution, realism, characterization, audience awareness, the role of fear. Chapters on *Ruth*, *Esther*, and *Jonah* listed separately as #s 444, 565, 592.

121.   Ostriker, Alicia S. *Feminist Revision and the Bible.* Cambridge, MA, and Oxford (Blackwell), 1993.

The possibilities of a feminist reading of the Bible, both by critics and poets. The hitherto unnoticed narrative pattern in the HB of the "buried woman"—the female character who appears early on as a major figure, but who disappears by the end: e.g., *Genesis* 22, *Numbers* 12, *Genesis* 25, others in *Judges, I Samuel* 1–2, *I Kings* 1–2.

122.   Watts, James W. *Psalm and Story; Inset Hymns in Hebrew Narrative.* Sheffield (JSOT P), 1992.

"... in the Hebrew Bible, the use of psalms in narrative contexts is a literary device used to achieve compositional (narrative) goals"—thus contradicting claims that psalms are used "merely to achieve non-narrative purposes, such as aesthetic pleasure, midrashic interpretation, or to simply find an appropriate place for them." They achieve these goals by their position, and by their thematic contents.

Articles

123.   Boyarin, Daniel. "Placing Reading; Ancient Israel and Medieval Europe," in Jonathan Boyarin, *The Ethnography of Reading* (Berkeley, Los Angeles, Oxford: U California P, 1993), pp. 10–37.

While reading the HB as fictional art "may be the only way appropriate or available for many of us to read it," we should not therefore assume that our literary categories and terms would have meant anything to the ancient authors. Yet, the very distinction between fiction and historiography which we depend on might have been meaningless in ancient Israel as well. This is true because in HB culture "reading" occurred in public, ritualistic, and controlled space, whereas in ours its space is private, ludic, and eroticized.

124.   Brenner, Athalya. "Who's Afraid of Feminist Criticism? Who's Afraid of Biblical Humour? The Case of the Obtuse Foreign Ruler in the Hebrew Bible." *JSOT* 63 (1994), 38–55.

Scornful, humorous allusions to the sexual impotence and bodily misfunctions of obtuse foreign rulers in various HB narratives. The satire centers on their mental and physical ineptitude around smarter women. "... [H]umour is an important weapon for the politically powerless. Females are inferior social agents, and their resourcefulness amplifies male (foreign) shortcomings."

125.   Deist, F.G. "Narrative Texts," in #81, pp. 72–107.

OT narrators as mediums of storytelling. The variety of fictional narrators and techniques, e.g., stereotyped forms, repetition, varying types of narration, ironic interplay of points of view, principles of character development, culturally-related functions of narratives.

126.   Friedman, Richard Elliott. "The Hiding of the Face: An Essay on the Literary Unity of Biblical Narrative," in Jacob Neusner, et al., eds., *Judaic Perspectives on Ancient Israel* (Philadelphia: Fortress P, 1987), pp. 207–222.

The archaeological and the literary are the two basic approaches to the Bible, from which all others derive. The literary method must include "all the tools of elucidating a text, namely, historical, linguistic, epigraphic, text-critical, source-critical ... and so on." Verse-by-verse analysis has tended to obscure the text's unity. Unifying components of HB plot include monotheism, national character of the materials, the writers' historical sense, and the covenant. The HB is truly *a* book.

127.   Gibson, J.C.L. "The Anatomy of Hebrew Narrative Poetry," in A. Graeme Auld, ed., *Understanding Poets and Prophets:*

Essays in Honour of George Wishart Anderson (Sheffield: JSOT P, 1993), pp. 141–148.

Even narrative poetry in the HB must be distinguished from other narratives in prose by its parallelism. We must respect the aspectual nature of the Hebrew verb when translating it. "Poetry, narrative or otherwise, shares the same aspectual verbal system with prose but, because of parallelism, disposes it quite differently."

128.   Gordon, Robert P. "Simplicity of the Highest Cunning: Narrative Art in the Old Testament." *Scottish Bulletin of Evangelical Theology* 6 (1988), 69–80.

Since the OT is mostly narration, it is "accessible to inquiry by the methods and approaches appropriate to the study of narrative prose." The role of structure, inclusio, narrative analogy, wordplay in understanding HBN.

129.   Long, Burke O. "The 'New' Biblical Poetics of Alter and Sternberg." *JSOT* 51 (1991), 71–84.

"Analysis of some recent work by Robert Alter and Meir Sternberg suggests that these two acknowledged leaders of ... the study of narrative poetics, are attempting to limit what counts as legitimate literary study of the Bible. Moreover, not claiming to be ideological readers, their writing nonetheless implies various elements of ideology. Thus, in the guise of an objectivist stance, they shield ... readers from what should be faced more forthrightly, the complicated and contestive pluralism of modern literary study."

130.   Longman, Tremper III. "Biblical Narrative," in #20, pp. 69–79.

The dynamics of narratives are mainly plot, characters, setting and point of view. How these work in the HB and NT. Characteristics of narrative style in the Bible, including repetition, omission, dialogue, and irony. Biblical narratives are both similar to, and different from, modern narratives.

131.   Marks, Herbert. "Biblical Naming and Poetic Etymology." *JBL* 114 (1995), 21–42.

The over eighty explicit etymologies contained in HB narratives have generally been regarded as insignificant, and their authors' motives misunderstood. These authors "seem ... to exploit the myth of true meaning as a generic convention, subject to the most aggressive revision." The typical etymology "is arbitrary rather than inevitable, willful rather than essential...." Focus on those "exemplary" types: "the name tradition in which an initial or explicit gloss is ironically doubled." Examples from *Genesis* and *Exodus*.

132. Milne, Pamela J. "Folktales and Fairy Tales: An Evaluation of Two Proppian Analyses of Biblical Narratives." *JSOT* 34 (1986), 35–60.

Propp's theory of classifying folk literature "and his specific heroic fairy-tale genre model" could prove useful in attempting to classify biblical texts according to genre. In the process, we must be cautious in attempting to force texts upon models and models upon texts. Jack Sasson and Joseph Blenkinsopp have not always succeeded in avoiding this pitfall in their application of Propp to *Genesis* and *Ruth*.

133. Oosthuizen, M.J. "Narrative Analysis of the Old Testament—Some Challenges and Prospects." *JNSL* 18 (1992), 145–161.

Narratology can make several contributions to OT theology: by clarifying ideological perspectives in OT narratives; by cohering with historical and theological perspectives; and by allowing adaptation of ancient biblical texts to modern readers through emphasis on storytelling.

134. Palache, Juda L. "The Nature of Old Testament Narrative," in #119, pp. 3–22 (originally published in Dutch in 1925).

Recent years have seen an undesirable extreme of historical criticism, pushing the larger view of OT narrative into the background. Narrative as the "preferred means for framing thoughts or to persuade," in the OT. "The story is not told because it happened, but becomes real by the telling.... [T]here is little concern to remove incongruities and inconsistencies.... [B]iblical writers ... likely composed materials themselves."

135. Ratner, Robert J. "Morphological Variation in Biblical Hebrew Rhetoric." *Maarav* 8 (1992), 143–159.

How authors of biblical narratives introduced variety into repetition through paired synonymous variants. Since this device occurs in all genres and periods of composition, textual critics need to beware of emending passages so as to eliminate these variants.

135a.   Riley, William. "Situating Biblical Narrative: Poetics and the Transmission of Community Values." *PIBA* 9 (1985), 38–52.

We need to ground the narrative approach to the Bible in its critical contexts—an essential one being the "community dynamic of which the text is the tangible evidence." This is because biblical narrative is traditional, an "experiment between ... storyteller and audience," and it "communicates the values of the traditional community in which it functions." The three essential tasks of the critic are to identify the truth being communicated, appreciate the aesthetics, and heed the community's function in formulating and transmitting the narrative in question.

136.   Shargent, Karla G. "Living on the Edge: The Liminality of Daughters in Genesis to II Samuel," in #296, pp. 26–42.

"Contrary to the gender assumptions of the public/private dichotomy, which would confine daughters to the private sphere, the narrative daughters of the Hebrew Bible are remarkably mobile.... As concerns belonging, though, ... daughters are unable to claim any space as inherently their own. They thus exist spatially in a liminal zone, a place that is securely rooted neither here nor there." Examples from *I Samuel* 19, *Genesis, Exodus* 2, *Numbers* 27, 36, *II Samuel, Judges* 11, 20.

137.   Sternberg, Meir. "Biblical Poetics and Sexual Politics: From Reading to Counterreading." *JBL* 111 (1992), 463–488.

Defense of the "master principle" of foolproof composition as "an alternative to a variety of dichotomies [in] ... modern literary theory" as originally set out in his book, and as attacked in Fewell and Gunn (Minor I, #588). Fewell and Gunn create "serious distortions" in my position by failing to perceive my distinction between ambiguity and ambivalence.

138.   Talmon, Shemaryahu. "The 'Topped Triad': A Biblical Literary Convention and the 'Ascending Numerical' Pattern." *Maarav* 8 (1992), 181–198.

A technique recognized as early as Lowth in the 18th century. However, it has always been grouped with the "staircase pattern." We need to see this 3/4 or 3/3+1 as an independent pattern. It occurs primarily in prose, only occasionally in poetry, and can best be characterized as a "motif bearing a message" rather than as a stylistic pattern. The motif purports to underscore the singularity of the item designated the "four."

139.   Ward, Graham. "Biblical Narrative and the Theology of Metonymy." *Modern Theology* 7 (1991), 335–349.

The "pre-suppositions for moving from word-sign to message in a theological text.... [T]he semiotics of narratives, ... and a modern reading convention that interprets Biblical narratives in terms of metaphor.... [W]here this convention goes awry, and ... how it might be corrected by reading Biblical narratives in terms of both metaphor and metonymy."

140.   Zakovitch, Yair. "Through the Looking Glass: Reflections/Inversions of Genesis Stories in the Bible." *BI* 1 (1993), 139–152.

One of the many intertextual strategies of biblical narrators is the covert use of allusions to other narratives known to author and audience—specifically where the narrator shaped a character as the antithesis of another character in another narrative. Examples discussed are *Genesis* 29 as reflection of *Genesis* 27; *Genesis* 44 as reflection of *Genesis* 31; *Genesis* 22 as reflection of *Genesis* 12; *Numbers* 10 as reflection of *Genesis* 12; *Ruth* 2 and *Genesis* 12; *Jonah and Genesis* 18–19; *II Samuel* 13 and *Genesis* 39.

Hebrew Biblical Poetry

Books

141.   apRoberts, Ruth. *The Biblical Web*. Ann Arbor (U Michigan P), 1994.

Revised and shortened version of Minor I, #394, published here as Chapter 2; expanded version of an essay in Minor I, #179, on teaching the Bible as literature published here as Chapter 3.

142.   Berlin, Adele. *Biblical Poetry Through Medieval Jewish Eyes*. Bloomington and Indianapolis (Indiana UP), 1991.

"Medieval and Renaissance views of biblical poetry and rhetoric in the context of the history of the study of biblical poetry and the context of the history of the study of medieval views of poetic language and the place of the Bible in it." Excerpts from seventeen

Jewish critics from three of the main centers of medieval Jewish culture: Spain, Provence, and Italy.

143.   Dion, Paul E. *Hebrew Poetics: A Student's Guide*. Mississauga, Ontario (Benben), 1988.

A guide restricted to the mechanics of biblical poetry, a "modest segment of the methodology required for a complete study of [poetic] books [in the HB]." Topics include Sigla, syntactic constraints, definitions, syllable count, grammatical bonding, semantic parallelism, and other devices, e.g., poetic diction, ornamentation, and figuration.

144.   Gillingham, S.E. *The Poems and Psalms of the Hebrew Bible*. Oxford (Oxford UP), 1994.

Part I: "Identifying Hebrew Poetry": poetry vs. prose in the HB, meter and rhythm, parallelism; Part II: "Poetry Outside the Psalter": poetry in law and wisdom, and popular poetry; Part III: "The Poetry of the Psalms": the psalmists as poets, poetic devices and forms in the Psalms, the psalter as a collection, its interpretation in Jewish and Christian traditions, its unity and diversity.

145.   Gordon, Alex R. *The Poets of the Old Testament*. London (Hodder and Stoughton), n.d. [1912].

General characteristics of HBP; folk-poetry; the Psalter. Themes and poetic qualities of *Job, Proverbs,* Wisdom literature, *Song of Songs, Qohelet.*

*   Lugt, Pieter Van Der. *Rhetorical Criticism and the Poetry of the Book of Job*.

See #535.

146.   Oesterley, W.O.E. *Ancient Hebrew Poems. Metrically Translated with Introductions and Notes*. New York (Macmillan), 1938.

English translation of thirty-two poems from many books of the HB with introductions to each one concerning theme, style, relationship to ancient Near Eastern writing, form, date, and authorship.

147.   Peterson, David L., and Kent Harold Richards. *Interpreting Hebrew Poetry*. Minneapolis (Fortress P), 1992.

Problems of definition and of distinguishing poetry from prose in the HB; evaluation of parallelism and meter as criteria from Lowth to the present; usefulness and limitations of theories of meter. Recent literary-critical discussions of Hebrew poetics and features of Hebrew poetic style including chiasm, inclusio, word-play, and assonance. Analysis of *Deuteronomy* 32, *Isaiah* 5, *Psalm* 1.

148. Watson, Wilfred G.E. *Traditional Techniques in Classical Hebrew Verse*. Sheffield (Sheffield Academic P), 1994.

Forty-five essays, all reprinted from earlier publications. Essays grouped into chapters on conventions of style; half-line (internal) gender-matched, and other types of parallelism; word pairs; chiasmus; figurative language; preludes to speech; patterns and rhetorical devices. Each chapter considers both Hebrew biblical and Ugaritic poetry.

Articles

149. Altham, R. "The Inverse Construct Chain and Jeremiah 10:13, 51:16." *JNSL* 15 (1989), 7–13.

The grammar of Hebrew and Ugaritic poetry is different from prose. Examples of inverted construct chains throughout the HB, especially *Jeremiah* 10 and 51 which harmonize with their context syntactically and offer chiastically structured syllabic patterns.

150. Berlin, Adele. "Azariah dé Rossi on Biblical Poetry." *Prooftexts* 12 (1992), 175–183.

The life and work on HBP of this 16th-century Italian critic, who sought to harmonize previous findings with new perspectives.

151. Burden, J.J. "What Is Poetry," in #81, pp. 39–71.

Poetic conventions, the difficulty of defining poetry precisely, the elements common to poetry and prose. The OT poet is not primarily narrator or orator, but a speaker from a "highly personal perspective." OT poetry is similar to modern poetry in its extensive use of rhetoric and stylistics, while different from modern poetry in use of parallelism. Principal forms of OT poetry.

152. Cloete, W.T.W. "The Colometry of Hebrew Verse." *JNSL* 15 (1989), 15–29.

Concepts and terminology of colometry, uncertainty of colon boundaries, importance of correct colometry—illustrated by passages from *Jeremiah*.

153.   Cloete, W.T.W. "The Concept of Metre in Old Testament Studies." *Journal for Semitics* 1 (1989), 39–53.

Though most OT scholars leave their concept of meter undefined, they should define it, given the large quantity of verse in the HB, its foreignness, and the nature of Hebrew versification system. What an appropriate definition would look like, and why many current ones fall short.

154.   Cloete, W.T.W. "Some Recent Research on Old Testament Verse: Progress, Problems, and Possibilities." *JNSL* 17 (1992), 189–204.

Survey of the "significant advances" in the study of Hebrew verse, including those that offer a comprehensive theory.

155.   Craigie, P.C. "Ugarit and the Bible: Progress and Regress in 50 Years of Literary Study," in Gordon D. Young, ed., *Ugarit in Retrospect* (Winona Lake: Eisenbrauns, 1981), pp. 99–111.

Survey of comparative Hebrew-Ugaritic studies shows it involved both progress and error: e.g., conjectural readings becoming accepted texts. Problem areas which tend to be ignored in most studies include parallel word-pairs, chronological and geographical relationships, lack of comparable genres, fragmentary Ugaritic texts, and the palimpsestic nature of Hebrew texts. Progress has been made, however, in areas of poetic form, motif, imagery, meter.

156.   Floyd, Michael H. "Falling Flat on Our Ars Poetica or Some Problems in Recent Studies of Biblical Poetry," in Jack C. Knight and Lawrence A. Sinclair, eds., *The Psalms and Other Studies on the Old Testament* (Nashotah, WI: Nashotah House Seminary, 1990), pp. 118–131.

Comparison of the strengths and weaknesses of the Robert Alter *vs.* James Kugel debate over the nature and existence of Hebrew biblical poetry. Both fail to recognize the importance of genre and setting, as well as the interplay of convention and originality in this poetry. Such criticism must be more technically adept, and at the same time able to move beyond the technical level.

*   Gibson, J.C.L. "The Anatomy of Hebrew Narrative Poetry."
        See #127.

157.   Giese, Ronald L., Jr. "Strophic Hebrew Verse as Free Verse."
        JSOT 61 (1994), 29–38.

        While Hebrew verse may or may not be metrical, "it may also
        have rhythm on the level of the strophe." Although much verse in
        the HB is non-strophic, where strophes can be discerned they may
        have rhythm at that level. It is thus neither metrical nor free verse,
        but something in between. Illustrated with *Exodus* 15.

158.   Giese, R.L. "Strophic Hebrew Verse as Free Verse." *JNSL* 17
        (1991), 1–15.

        "Hebrew verse may or may not have meter, but if [it] ... con-
        tains strophes it will contain rhythm on the level of the strophe."
        We should neither apply modern Western genres and terminology
        to HBP, nor ignore the "hyparchetypes" in both which span time
        and place. One of these could be free verse.

159.   Gitay, Yehoshua. "W.F. Albright and the Question of Early
        Hebrew Poetry," in M. Patrick Graham, et al., eds., *History
        and Interpretation: Essays in Honour of John H. Hayes* (Shef-
        field: JSOT P, 1993), pp. 192–202.

        Albright's stylistic-chronological analysis of HBP compared
        with current directions in the literary analysis of that poetry, cen-
        ters on how one describes the function of the use of prose and po-
        etry in one literary unit. Albright's assumption that "isolated po-
        etic sections within the pentateuchal narrative are the remnant of
        an earlier poetic stratum ignores the rhetorical dimension of the
        biblical narrative as a dynamic literary discourse." Thus, e.g., a
        rhetorical function of verse within prose narrative is to conclude or
        summarize specific messages.

160.   Gruber, Mayer I. "The Meaning of Biblical Parallelism: A
        Biblical Perspective." *Prooftexts* 13 (1993), 289–293.

        The debate between Robert Gordis and James Kugel over the
        basic nature of parallelism. Some gospel evidence suggests that
        this debate goes back at least 2,000 years—a possibility which
        should be investigated.

*   Hunter, J.H. "The Irony of Meaning: Intertextuality in Hebrew Poetical Texts."

    See #502.

161.   Nel, P.J. "Parallelism and Recurrence in Biblical Hebrew Poetry: A Theoretical Proposal." *JNSL* 18 (1992), 135–143.

The basic principle of all poetic texts is recurrence. Various modes of recurrence can be distinguished. The "special parameter" of OT poetry is parallelism, though identifying more and more "types of parallelism" is fruitless without an overall theory, such as is proposed here, which deals with terse formulaic couplets, congruence and distribution of semantic signs in the couplets, and the "special semantic relationship" of couplet and triplet.

162.   Pardee, Dennis. "Ugaritic and Hebrew Metrics," in Gordon D. Young, ed., *Ugarit in Retrospect* (Winona Lake: Eisenbrauns, 1981), pp. 113–130.

Problems in many studies derive from arbitrary and vague metric systems. Review of these often unsuccessful attempts, of how meter is used in describing the structures of ancient Near Eastern poetry, and of two recent theories of Ugaritic and Hebrew meter. These theories depend on syllable count or word meter. None of the four theories of how meter occurs in Ugaritic is really convincing, and the lack of traditional vocalizations for Ugaritic prevents easy comparison with biblical Hebrew poetry.

163.   Payne, Geoffrey. "Parallelism in Biblical Hebrew Verse: Some Secular Thoughts." *SJOT* 8 (1994), 126–140.

Our understanding of biblical Hebrew verse, and specifically of parallelism, "can be enriched by the wider context of literary and linguistic thought." If parallelism aims to achieve equivalence, it cannot be limited to synonymy. The "seconding effect" is neither redundancy nor ornamentation," but many and varied, both entertaining and edifying.

164.   Segert, Stanislav. "Assonance and Rhyme in Hebrew Poetry." *Maarav* 8 (1992), 171–179.

Consideration of those sound features most frequent in later biblical poetry: alliteration, assonance, and rhyme, especially the latter two. Examples from *Genesis* 4, *Isaiah* 33, *Judges* 16, *Numbers* 21. Homoeoteleutic assonance and their frequency in proportion to parallelism in *Psalms* 34, 25, 145, 119, 111, 112; *Proverbs* 31, *Lamentations* 4, *Qohelet* 3, and *Nehemiah* 9.

165.   Watson, Wilfred G.E. "Problems and Solutions in Hebrew Verse: A Survey of Recent Work." *VT* 43 (1993), 372–384.

Account of the "substantial progress ... made in the study of verse traditions in Hebrew, Akkadian, and Ugaritic" since the publication of Watson's book (Minor I, #389) in 1986. There is a "welcome trend for studying poetic texts ... in terms of larger structures" in HBP. New publications dealing with theory, aesthetics, linguistics, half-line parallelism, metathetic, antithesis, parody, as well as a number of already recognized devices.

166.   West, Mona. "Looking for the Poem: Reflections on the Current and Future Status of the Study of Biblical Hebrew Poetry," in Paul R. House, ed., *Beyond Form Criticism. Essays in Old Testament Literary Criticism*. Winona Lake (Eisenbrauns, 1992), pp. 423–431.

"Literary criticism has not liberated Hebrew poetry in the same way that it has freed biblical narrative." That is, artistic form has been liberated, but not content or the role of the reader in making meaning. Review of recent work in the field.

167.   Zevit, Ziony. "Cognitive Theory and the Memorability of Biblical Poetry." *Maarav* 8 (1992), 199–212.

The growing body of knowledge from cognitive psychology and psycholinguistics "enables us to affirm that some of the observations by practitioners of the [modern] literary approach could have been part of what Israelites found aesthetically pleasing in their poems." This may enable historians partially to reclaim the aesthetic approach to biblical poetry. Examples: *Psalms* 111, 13, and several others very briefly. In particular, these disciplines reaffirm importance of word-pairs, semantic parallelism, and texture.

168.   Zevit, Ziony. "Roman Jakobson, Psycholinguistics, and Biblical Poetry." *JBL* 109 (1990), 385–401.

Our sophisticated understanding of literature enables us to construct multi-leveled, sophisticated interpretations of HBP. "The difference, however, between us and the Israelites lies essentially in [the fact that] ... they heard it; we read it. The contribution of psycholinguistics and cognitive psychology ... lies in their ability to help us distinguish objectively between ... what is perceptible to us and ... what was apparent to them."

See also #127, 502, 535.

LAW

*   Baroody, Wilson G., and William F. Gentrup. "Exodus, Leviticus, Numbers, and Deuteronomy."

See #240.

169.   Blenkinsopp, Joseph. *The Pentateuch: An Introduction to the First Five Books of the Bible.* NY, London, etc. (Doubleday), 1992.

Not a commentary on *Genesis-Deuteronomy* so much as a discussion of important issues arising out of its study. Blends synchronic and diachronic methods to treat such questions as structure, chronology, historiographical patterns, alternate theories of formation of the Pentateuch, important themes, and the role of ritual law.

170.   Radday, Yehuda T. "Chiasm in Tora." *LB* 19 (Sept. 1972), 12–23.

Poetic parts of scripture are parallel in construction, while narrative parts are chiastically constructed. The chiastic structure of *Genesis* and its major parts in detail, and briefly that of the rest of the Pentateuch, with *Leviticus* the center of a chiasm of the five books. This leads us to conclude that the Pentateuch is an "aesthetically constructed work of one and the same author."

171.   Sailhamer, John H. *The Pentateuch as Narrative. A Biblical Theological Commentary.* Grand Rapids (Zondervan), 1992.

The narrative strategy of the Pentateuch may be traced by taking seriously the literary and historical claim that the Pentateuch "was originally composed as a single book." Even breaking it down into the traditional five books obscures its careful literary structure. A sensitivity to the author's literary skill and techniques "goes a long way" toward elucidating the author's purpose. The OT text as a system of signs and its literary form, and how these relate to the reader. The Pentateuch's basic narrative strategy is to contrast Abraham's life of faith prior to the law, and Moses' lack of (or weakening of) faith *under* the law.

See also #78, 240.

GENESIS

172.　Bellis, Alice Ogden. "The Women of Genesis," in #64, pp. 67–98.

"In spite of their lack of power, the women of Genesis are portrayed as active, strong women ... who find ways to achieve their goals. With the exception of Potiphar's wife, these goals are characterized as honorable. Nevertheless ... the lack of feminine authority and structural power made many of the women resort to trickery. It also resulted in too many of them becoming victims." Sarah (chapters 12–21); Hagar (16 and 21); the daughters of Lot (19); Rebekah (24–27); Rachel and Leah (29–35); Dinah (34); Tamar (38); Potiphar's Wife (39).

173.　Fox, E. "Stalking the Younger Brother: Some Models for Understanding a Biblical Motif." *JSOT* 60 (1993), 45–68.

The motif of the younger brother triumphant is famous and striking, especially in *Genesis* and *Samuel-Kings*. Most common recent interpretations are comparative, psychological and historical, socio-economic, Davidic, and structural-ideological. Necessity of a composite reading.

*　Marks, Herbert. "Biblical Naming and Poetic Etymology."

　　See #131.

174.　McEvenue, Sean. "Reading Genesis with Faith and Reason." *WW* 14 (1994), 136–143.

Literary methods can supplement historical readings of the Bible, especially since historical criticism of books like *Genesis* is less sure of its conclusions than heretofore. How meaning emerges from a literary reading of *Genesis* 12:5–13:7, 26, and 20, especially of the literary structure of these four chapters, all variations of the patriarch's wife.

174a.   Mikre-Selassie, G.A. "Figures of Speech in Genesis: Some
        Suggestions for Natural Translation." *BTr* 46 (1995), 219–
        225.

        How to recognize, determine location and meaning, and convey
        the meaning of figures of speech accurately in the language of the
        translation. Thirty-four examples of metaphors, similes,
        metonymy, synecdoche, idioms, and euphemisms from through-
        out *Genesis*.

175.   Nicol, George G. "Story Patterning in Genesis," in Robert P.
        Carroll, ed., *Text as Pretext: Essays in Honour of Robert
        Davidson* (Sheffield: JSOT P, 1992), pp. 215–233.

        We may find literary coherence in *Genesis* not through plot, but
        through other patterning features of the narrative. Examples
        would include the deployment of "promise theme" materials
        throughout: the phenomenon of doublet stories; chains of themes
        or motifs (despite different surface narration); sequencing of
        events, etc. This patterning gives *Genesis* a sense of direction, a co-
        hesion which makes the book an impressive literary achievement.

176.   Rashkow, Ilona N. *The Phallacy of Genesis. A Feminist-Psycho-
        analytic Approach*. Louisville (Westminster/John Knox P),
        1993.

        Readings of various parts of *Genesis*: chapters 12, 20, 1–3, 19, 17–
        18, 34. Combination of literary and psycho-analytic methods cen-
        tered on reader-response because all readings depend on one's
        own life situation. Topics include intertextuality and transference,
        dreams, daughters and fathers, and biblical deconstruction of fe-
        male sexuality. Two chapters appear in different form in #'s 82, 83.

177.   Rashkow, Ilona N. "Daughters and Fathers in Genesis …
        Or, What Is Wrong with this Picture?," in #242, pp. 22–36.

        The conspicuous absence of daughters in *Genesis* is something
        more than a general disregard of women. "My conclusion is that
        beneath the surface of father-son narration lies a suppressed
        daughter-father relationship." One clue is the fact that in *Genesis*,
        "familial and sexual integrity across Genesis seems to be observed
        more in the breach than in the maintenance."

*   Reed, Walter L. *Dialogues of the Word: The Bible as Literature
        According to Bakhtin*.
        See #6.

178. Sailhamer, John H. "Genesis," in #20, pp. 108–120.

> *Genesis* as heroic narrative and as epic. Its "fundamental concern" is to depict a believable narrative world. Two key aspects of this world are divine causality and divine retribution; three of its important narrative techniques are recursion, contemporization, and foreshadowing. Examples comparing *Genesis* 1 to 7 and 8; 2–3 to 9:20–27; 12:10–15 to 46:28–47:27; 12:17–13:4 to *Exodus* 12:31–35. The Joseph narrative.

See also #71, 72, 105, 110, 132, 135.

Genesis 1–11

179. Anderson, Bernhard W. "From Analysis to Synthesis: The Interpretation of Genesis 1–11." *JBL* 97 (1978), 23–39, rpt. #187, pp. 416–435.

> The flood story "discloses an overall design, a dramatic movement in which each episodic unit has essential function." The overall chiastic structure of the episode. We should begin with the overall structure and functional unity, not the evidence of separate sources. If we are to understand the story theologically, we must "consider how this story functions in its present context in the book of Genesis...."

180. Bellis, Alice Ogden. "The Story of Eve," in #64, pp. 45–66.

> Review of various recent feminist literary readings of *Genesis* 1–3 shows that in their view, the story is androcentric but not necessarily sexist. The "fall from grace" interpretation is probably not the original meaning of the story, but "it is an interpretation that works very well.... It also makes Genesis 3:16b easy for feminists to handle. Men's domination of women can be explained as a result of sin, rather than God's intention for humanity."

181. Bird, Phyllis A. "Sexual Differentiation and Divine Image in the Genesis Creation Texts," in Kari Elisabeth Borresen, ed., *Image of God and Gender Models in Judeo-Christian Tradition* (Oslo: Solum Forlag, 1991), pp. 11–34.

> "Genesis 1 invites, and demands, renewed reflection on the meaning of sexual differentiation as a constitutive mark of humanity and the meaning of God-likeness (image) as the defining at-

tribute of humankind." While the author's thinking is not feminist but patriarchal, his intention—as "expressed primarily by the structure of the argument," is to show that male domination is the consequence of sin, not the design of creation. An "abbreviated and entended form" of *HTR* 74 (1981), 129–159.

182.   Breukelman, F.H. "The Story of the Sons of God Who Took the Daughters of Humans as Wives," in #119, pp. 83–94.

How *Genesis* 6:1–4 functions as a "fragment" to "express the way in which the Torah criticizes popular myth." There is "much to be said for the attempt ... to interpret a text from its context, in which the narrators—who knew what they were doing—placed it and treated the subject in context."

183.   Brown, William P. "Divine Act and the Art of Persuasion in Genesis 1," in M. Patrick Graham et al., eds., *History and Interpretation: Essays in Honour of John H. Hayes* (Sheffield: JSOT P, 1993), pp. 19–32.

The dynamics of God's rhetorically nuanced speech at the creation shows the divine act not as an inbreaking but an unfolding. It is more cooperation than compulsion. The rhetorical artistry of God's speech parallels and exhibits his creative force.

184.   Carr, David. "The Politics of Textual Subversion: A Diachronic Perspective on the Garden of Eden Story." *JBL* 112 (1993), 577–595.

Genesis 2–3 "although composite, is an elegantly constructed whole." Understanding its tradition-historical dimension "can even inform consideration of more purely synchronic investigations of the text's final form." It is "irresolvably multivalent" concerning gender relations, and thus neither purely patriarchal nor purely liberating.

184a. Culley, Robert C. "Action Sequences in Genesis 2–3." *Semeia* 18 (1980), 25–33; response by Arno Hutchinson, Jr., pp. 35–39.

"... to see if a narrative like Genesis 2–3 can be described in terms of action sequences." Four main action sequences may be established: *Genesis* 2:16–17, 3:1–6, 9–13, 16–19, 3:1–5 and 14–15 (wrong/wrong punished), and *Genesis* 3:22–24 and 2:18–25 (difficulty/difficulty removed).

185. Deurloo, K.A. "The Scope of a Small Literary Unit in the Old Testament. Introduction to the Interpretation of Genesis 4," in #119, pp. 37–51.

Small literary units "must be understood in their function within the cycle [of *Genesis* as a whole]." Keyword connections create series through narrative shaping and thematic relationships. "The context in which a small unit occurs must therefore be drawn into exegesis and may even be the key to understanding the story."

186. Gordon, Cyrus H. "'This Time' (Genesis 2:23)," in Michael Fishbane and Emanuel Tov, eds., *'Sha'arei Talmon': Studies in the Bible, Qumran, and the Ancient Near East Presented to Shemaryahu Talmon* (Winona Lake: Eisenbrauns, 1992), pp. 47–51.

In *Genesis* 1 and 2 we see embedded in the second creation an assumption of a first unsuccessful fashioning of man and woman. This combination of two or more parallel narratives, widespread in the Bible, can be termed "Buildup and Climax." It also occurs in *Jonah*, for example, and in *Haggai*. Recent discoveries of Baal and Anath cycles in Ugarit cast *Genesis* 2 in a new light, since they, too, exhibit asymmetric Janus parallelism.

187. Hess, Richard S., and David Toshio Tsumura, eds. *I Studied Inscriptions from Before the Flood: Ancient Near Eastern, Literary, and Linguistic Approaches to Genesis 1–11.* Winona Lake (Eisenbrauns), 1994.

Twenty-eight essays on comparative, literary, and linguistic approaches to the primeval history. Fifteen are at least in part literary-critical; of these, six were listed and analyzed in Minor I as numbers 373, 518, 527, 535a, 549, and 550. Seven of the remaining nine are analyzed separately as #'s 193, 196, 190, 195, 179, 208, 188.

188. Hess, Richard S. "The Genealogies of Genesis 1–11 and Comparative Literature." *Biblica* 70 (1989), 241–254, rpt. #187, pp. 58–72.

Distinctions between the genealogies and ancient Near Eastern king lists and other types of ancient literature suggest that Israel may have early on developed a unique view of history and of racial equality. Formal study of the genealogies, too, has limitations because it fails to examine the narrative context of *Genesis* 1–11. We must study the onomastic environment of the time, the purpose of the narrative elements, and comparison "of the relation between the names, genealogical forms, and the narratives."

189.   Hess, Richard S. "Genesis 1–2 in Its Literary Context." *TB* 41 (1990), 143–153.

Similarities in the creation and genealogical doublets of form content, and function suggest that the writer was trying "to weave together an account of the creation of the world and of humanity using as a major technique doublets of repetitive patterns which serve to focus on a particular theme of the narratives and to provide the major means of moving the events forward into the history of a world known to the early readers of the text. Such a technique suggests a distinct literary form to the first eleven chapters of *Genesis*."

190.   Jacobsen, Thorkild. "The Eridu Genesis." *JBL* 100 (1981), 513–529; rpt. #187, pp. 129–142.

This narrative from c. 1600 BC prefigures *Genesis* creation-flood narrative in structure, but even more so is similar in style: both are interested in chronology and in numbers (very untypical of myth and folklore). While there is a "degree of dependence" of *Genesis* on Eridu, the former has decisively transformed the latter, "radically altering their original meaning and import."

191.   Kempf, Stephen. "Genesis 3: 14–19: Climax of the Discourse?" *JTT* 6 (1993), 354–377.

"Special grammatical signals" mark these verses as the grammatical climax of the discourse: where narrative tension is highest and its release begins. Verses 17–19 provide the resolution to the problem of the narrative, with greatest prominence being given to the judgment scene, and the death penalty providing resolution.

192.   Kennedy, James M. "Peasants in Revolt: Political Allegory in Genesis 2–3." *JSOT* 47 (1990), 3–14.

The creation account is a political allegory describing the struggle between royal interests and the peasant class. "The narrative of the couple's revolt against Yahweh is a literary expression of the social threat of peasant unrest and rebellion." The couching of this rebellion in a cosmogony is intended to demonstrate that peasant unrest is endemic.

193.   Kikawada, Isaac M. "The Double Creation of Mankind in *Enki and Ninmah, Atrahasis I* 1–351, and *Genesis* 1–2." *Iraq* 45 (1983), 43–45; rpt. #187, pp. 169–174.

"... there was in the Ancient Near East a literary convention of telling the story of the origin of mankind in a doublet." Many similarities exist between these stories and *Genesis* 1–2, the former providing more than a millennium of literary tradition for the biblical narrative.

194.   McKenzie, John J. "The Literary Characteristics of Genesis 2–3." *Theological Studies* 15 (1954), 541–572.

History of the debate over whether and to what extent *Genesis* 2–3 is history or myth or folklore—i.e., the correct genre of the story. The attempt to find the genre by comparing it to ancient Near Eastern creation stories. The centrality of its unity in any discussion of its literary chapter. Likely sources. The paradise narrative is a unified story with a climactic structure. The importance of the woman character.

195.   Millard, A.R. "A New Babylonian 'Genesis' Story." *TB* 18 (1967), 3–18; rpt. #187, pp. 114–128.

Comparison of the Babylonian "Atrahasis epic" with the creation and flood narratives of *Genesis* shows some intriguing similarities, though no direct evidence of influence of the former on the latter.

196.   Miller, Patrick D., Jr. "Eridu, Dunnu, and Babel: A Study in Comparative Mythology." *HAR* 9 (1985), 227–251; rpt. #187, pp. 143–168.

Comparison of two different Mesopotamian myths—the Sumerian flood story and the "Harab Myth" with *Genesis* 1–11 shows both "consonance" and "assonance." The latter used theogonic and cosmogonic elements and structures from the former. However, significant differences include the attitudes toward the foundation of cities, kingship, and what kind of people are to be blessed by God.

197.   Oden, Robert A., Jr. "Divine Aspirations in Atrahesis and in Genesis 1–11." *ZAW* 93 (1981), 197–216.

In the area of the "human crime which led to the flood" and its aftermath, "Genesis and the Atrahesis Epic speak in remarkably similar tones." Both are intensely concerned with reaffirming and carefully defining the distinction between divine and human.

198.   Pardes, Ilana. "Beyond Genesis 3: The Politics of Maternal Naming," in #88, pp. 39–59.

Analysis of *Genesis* 4–11—and especially chapters 4–5—"is essential to an understanding of both the Priestly and Yahwistic treatments of femininity in Genesis 1–3." The "naming" passages and the genealogies are the key to seeing how the dominant patriarchy is "continuously challenged by antithetical trends." We need to respect the otherness of the ancient texts.

199.   Pardes, Ilana. "Creation According to Eve," in #88, pp. 13–38.

Survey of various feminist approaches to *Genesis* 1–2 from Elizabeth Cady Stanton to Esther Fuchs and Mieke Bal shows that "there is no single monolithic feminist approach to Scripture." (Harold Bloom's *Book of J* only ends up "endorsing and venerating male rule.") They do all share, however, ideological critique of patriarchy. Thus if we "explore the historical context in which biblical texts were first formed and circulated," we will grasp their past and present influence on the creation of sexual differentiation.

200.   Perry, T.A. "A Poetics of Absence: The Structure and Meaning of Genesis 1.2." *JSOT* 58 (1993), 3–11.

The second creation narrative introduces a chiasm in both 1:2 and 2:4, and the anticipated chiasm of the latter "leads our attention to the underlying meaning." "Absence" here becomes a "presence," a descriptive device where "the reader is led to imagine removal or loss of familiar shapes," and thus to an "imaginative confrontation with his or her own existence." This reading may be supported by examining *Qohelet* 1:4–7—arguments on the futility of the created universe.

201.   Rashkow, Ilona N. *Upon the Dark Places. Anti-Semitism and Sexism in English Renaissance Biblical Translation.* Sheffield (Almond P), 1990.

How the English Renaissance biblical translators' theology, especially their attitudes toward women and Jews, affected their task. They transformed characterization of Adam and Eve (*Genesis* 1–3), Dinah (*Genesis* 34), and Ruth in the light of their NT theology—either adding levels of meaning to the original Hebrew, or revisioning them in stereotypical ways as submissive, oversimplifying morally complex plots, destroying depth of characterization.

202. Salmon, Rachel, and Gerda Elata-Alster. "Retracing a Writerly Text: In the Footsteps of a Midrashic Sequence on the Creation of the Male and the Female," in #16, pp. 177–197.

The uniqueness of Midrash is that it refuses to relinquish either term of an opposition; thus it also refuses to play language off against meaning. Its advantage is that it keeps conflicting readings alive without "forefronting" its own activity at the expense of the text in question. How the Midrash has read the creation story of Adam and Eve.

203. Scult, Allen, Michael Calvin McGee, and J. Kenneth Kuntz. "Genesis and Power: An Analysis of the Biblical Story of Creation." *QJS* 72 (1986), 113–131.

"... together the texts of Genesis 1–3 contain a full-bodied, balanced, and persuasive expression of a complete vision of power." It is a dialect of authorship and authority. This vision is "inherently persuasive" because it became an archetype "circumscribe[ing] all possible power relationships in Judeo-Christian cultures."

204. Seters, John Van. "The Primeval Histories of Greece and Israel Compared." *ZAW* 100 (1988), 1–22.

The comparison "reveals a very significant similarity both in form and context." These similarities demonstrate that separation of *Genesis* 1–11 from the rest of the book is no longer warranted, since too many themes carry over from 1–11 to 12 and beyond. Thus the Greek antiquarian tradition is more fruitful for understanding *Genesis'* form than is the Mesopotamian.

205. Stefanovic, Zdravko. "The Great Reversal: Thematic Links between Genesis 2 and 3." *AUSS* 32 (1994), 47–56.

Structural study of *Genesis* 2–3 reveals chiasm, strongly suggesting the unity of the story. "The theme of the story ... is the Great Reversal brought about by the entrance of sin...." This chiastic structure or reversed parallelism "presents the literary beauty of Genesis" through a story about God as source of perfection and man's sin as source of disorder.

206. Stordalen, Terje. "Man, Soil, Garden: Basic Plot in Genesis 2–3 Reconsidered." *JSOT* 53 (1992), 3–26.

"... Genesis 2.5 is to be read as a narrative 'program' for the basic plot of the subsequent story (Genesis 2–3).... [T]he narrative nu-

cleus in Genesis 2–3 is the account of how (wild and cultivated)
vegetation appeared in the land.... Analyzing the story that
YHWH himself only 'accidentally' and even 'unwillingly' supported that plot. His concern was with the garden, not with the
land."

207. Ward, Graham. "A Postmodern Version of Paradise." *JSOT*
      65 (1995), 3–12.

      The relationship among desire, sexuality, and representation in
      J's account of Eden, and the necessity for difference (particularly
      sexual difference). "Read through the filters of postmodernity, the
      story of paradise is an aetiological account of the origins of sexual-
      ity, desire, and representation. It is also the account of the origin of
      a patriarchal culture which has silenced the woman."

208. Wenham, Gordon J. "Sanctuary Symbolism in the Garden of
      Eden Story." *PWCJS* 9 (1986), 19–25; rpt. #187, pp. 399–
      404.

      Difficulties in the Eden story "may be explained if we see it not
      as a naive myth but as a highly symbolic narrative." The author
      views the garden as "an archetypal sanctuary, that is a place
      where God dwells and where man should worship him. Many of
      the features of the garden may also be found in later sanctuaries....
      These parallels suggest that the garden itself is understood as a
      sort of sanctuary."

209. van Wolde, Ellen. "A Reader-Oriented Exegesis Illustrated
      by a Study of the Serpent in Genesis 2–3," in C. Brekel-
      mans and J. Lust, eds., *Pentateuchal and Deuteronomistic
      Studies* ... (Leuven: Leuven UP and Uitgeverij Peeters,
      1990), pp. 11–21.

      Neither diachronic nor synchronic methods are adequate to the
      biblical text. Rather, a semiotic approach, which interrelates text
      and reader, is best. One aspect, semantic analysis, is used here,
      and contrasted with more traditional enegesis of the meaning of
      the serpent. How the semantic codes in these chapters alert the
      reader to the serpent's duplicity and unsuitedness to truth.

210. van Wolde, Ellen. "A Text-Semantic Study of the Hebrew
      Bible, Illustrated with Noah and Job." *JBL* 113 (1994), 19–
      35.

      We need to combine literary study of textual syntagms in the
      HB with a linguistic study of the Hebrew language system. The

important role of the reader in this process of "making visible the potentiality of meanings in ... the Hebrew Bible...." How the power and beauty of the stories of Noah and Job emerge much more completely in such a study than they may in a theoretical discussion.

211. van Wolde, Ellen. "The Story of Cain and Abel: A Narrative Study." *JSOT* 52 (1991), 25–41.

A narrative analysis of *Genesis* 4:1–16 shows its coherence, and its close connection with *Genesis* 2–3. It is a "concise short story marked by an elliptic use of language.... [T]he actions of (not) looking are the main ones.... YHWH is the only one called worthless one. Even the narrator is not paying much attention to him. Both YHWH's actions and the narrative ellipses intend to persuade the readers to follow YHWH's preference for the weak brother."

212. van Wolde, Ellen. *Words Become Worlds. Semantic Studies of Genesis 1–11.* Leiden (E.J. Brill), 1994.

Seven essays of semantic analysis of sections of *Genesis* 1–11, and four of theoretical background on semiotic interpretation. Eight of the essays rpt. from C. Brekelmans and J. Lust, eds., *Pentateuchal and Deuteronomistic Studies* (Leuven: Leuven UP and Uitgeverij Peeters, 1990); *JSOT* 52; one listed in Minor I, #552 and four articles originally published in Dutch; two others originally delivered as papers, and one written for this volume.

See also #15, 16, 38, 75, 87, 96, 101, 111, 113, 164, 176, 178, 265, 361.

Genesis 12–24

213. Abela, Anthony. *The Themes of the Abraham Narrative: Thematic Coherence Within the Abraham Literary Unit of Genesis II, 27–25, 18.* Malta (Studia Editions), 1989.

That the Abraham narrative was conceived as a unity can be demonstrated partly by exploring its three overarching themes: those of "blessing," "son," and "land." How each theme develops during these chapters, and how each episode contributes to this thematic development.

214.   Bandstra, Barry L. "Word Order and Emphasis in Biblical Hebrew Narrative: Syntactic Observations on Genesis 22 from a Discourse Perspective," in Walter R. Bodine, ed., *Linguistics and Biblical Hebrew* (Winona Lake: Eisenbrauns, 1992), pp. 109–123.

Principles of word order in biblical Hebrew applied to *Genesis* 22. How emphasis can be given new linguistic definition as "topicalization": taking normally nonsalient information and placing it in a position of informational prominence. "Word order is thus ... one of the most significant syntactic factors ... responsible for maintaining continuity as well as indicating thematic breaks between paragraphs."

*   Darr, Katheryn Pfisterer. *Far More Precious Than Jewels. Perspectives on Biblical Women.*

See #114.

215.   Davis, Ellen F. "Self-Consciousness and Conversation: Reading Genesis 22." *Bulletin for Biblical Research* 1 (1991), 27–40.

The activity of reading through three interpretations of *Genesis* 22: The historical, text-centered, and midrashic approaches to the story. "Conversation among those who stand in different hermeneutical traditions ... may, by arousing admiration, even envy of the riches of another tradition, make us more diligent in mining our own."

216.   Deurloo, Karel A. "Because You Have Hearkened to My Voice (Genesis 22)," in #119, pp. 113–130.

Literary critics often fail to account sufficiently for the interconnections of the story of the sacrifice of Isaac (*Genesis* 22) within the larger cycle of chapters 12–26. Motifs and forms of expression create part of the tie-in, especially variations on laughter and hearkening to a voice, and the motif of the substitute sacrifice.

217.   Deurloo, Karel. "The Way of Abraham: Routes and Localities as Narrative Data in Genesis 11:27–25:11," in #119, pp. 95–112.

Rhetorical-literary analysis of the Abraham cycle shows its "diversity of style and word usage." We must focus on this, and not on undeterminable historical matter. "The diversity of Genesis points to a process lasting generations. Narrators, accordingly, had to reckon with ancient traditional data such as the locations of Abraham at Mamre and Isaac at Beersheba."

218. Doukhan, Jacques. "The Center of the Aqedah: A Study of the Literary Structure of Genesis 22:1–19." *AUSS* 31 (1993), 17–28.

The apex of *Genesis* 22 is verses 7–8 in a chiastic structure. Thus the "central idea of the story concerns the tragic dialogue between Abraham and Isaac." It serves as the primary motif from which other motifs are derived. "... [T]he structure of the text suggests that the accent here is primarily on the human questions and silences at the center."

219. Exum, J. Cheryl. "Who's Afraid of 'the endangered Ancestress'?," in #82, pp. 91–113.

Contrasting these three type-scenes with a reversal (*Genesis* 16) demonstrates that it is not Sarah's (or Rebekah's) honor which is at stake so much as the husband's property rights (his right to his wife's sensuality). Psychoanalytic criticism helps us see that this three-fold repetition "encodes unthinkable and unacknowledged sexual fantasies," thus apparently illustrating the repetition compulsion—a symptom of the narrator's "intra-psychic conflict." "By managing fear and desire within an ordered discourse, the narrative functions as a textual working-out of unconscious fantasies, a semiotic cure for the neurosis."

220. Fields, Weston W. "The Motif 'Night as Danger' Associated with Three Biblical Destruction Narratives," in Michael Fishbane and Emanuel Tov, eds., *'Sha'arei Talmon'. Studies in the Bible, Qumran, and The Ancient Near East Presented to Shemaryahu Talmon* (Winona Lake: Eisenbrauns, 1992), pp. 17–32.

Genesis 19, *Judges* 19–21, and *Joshua* 2, all represent what in Alter's terminology might be termed a type plot: the destruction of a city or people. They share the motif of "night as danger," where the locations involved (Sodom, the cane near Zoar, and Gibeah) are scenes of crime, especially of sexual crimes. The mere mention of night in ancient Hebrew narrative "imported ... a mood of menacing and ill-omened portent," as here in these narratives.

221. Hawk, L. Daniel. "Strange Houseguests: Rahab, Lot, and The Dynamics of Deliverance," in #83, pp. 89–97.

The "striking concurrence in vocabulary" between the stories of Lot (*Genesis* 19) and Rahab (*Joshua* 2) leads us to see that the former "overlays" the latter, placing it against a "dark and threatening backdrop," thus eliciting the mood of wickedness in the latter. Likewise, the transformation of Lot's story in Rahab's raises a challenge to exclusivistic notions of salvation.

222.   Hays, J. Daniel. "Quotation Formulas in the Abraham Narratives." *JTT* 5 (1992), 348–363.

"Dialogue is a critical part of the Abraham narratives and the Quotation Formulas play an important role within the dialogue." Variation in these formulas is neither random nor arbitrary; they function "as consistent indicators of the intensity and speaker-domination dynamics that run throughout the dialogues."

223.   Irvin, Dorothy. *Mytharion. The Comparison of Tales from the Old Testament and The Ancient Near East.* Neukirchen-Vluyn (Neukirchener Verlag) and Kevelaer (Butzon and Bercker), 1978.

Careful methods are needed "for studying ancient near Eastern narrative as narrative, or for comparing ancient near Eastern with that of the Old Testament." Method based on work of Gunkel, improving the motif system in order to understand better the theology of the passage. Analysis of six stories in Genesis about a messenger from God: 16, 18, 19, 21, 22, and 28, and compared to similar stories from Sumer, Akkad, the Hittites, Ugarit, and Egypt.

224.   Kunin, Seth Daniel. "The Death of Isaac: Structuralist Analysis of Genesis 22." *JSOT* 64 (1994), 57–81.

The underlying structure of the sacrifice of Isaac in terms of two questions: what is its structural significance? and What is the structural role of the two young men? Comparison with *Genesis* 37 shows it to be an inverted version of the same myth. "The element of an actual sacrifice is significant," and the two young men "fill the structural role of brother."

225.   Lyke, Larry L. "Where Does 'the Boy' Belong? Compositional Strategy in *Genesis* 21:14." *CBQ* 56 (1994), 637–648.

The parallel stories in *Genesis* 21 and 22 as part of the author's compositional strategy of inviting comparison of Abraham's two sons. The larger narrative structure of these chapters raises the question, Who will be Abraham's heir?, as well as a variety of other questions concerning ramifications of these parallels, the attitude of God, characterization of Abraham and his favoring of Ishmael over Isaac.

226.   McKinlay, Judith E. "Dead Spots or Living Texts? A Matter of Biblical Reading." *Pacifica* 5 (1992), 1–16.

The parallel stories of the "wife/sister ploy" examined through the differing perspectives of various historical and literary methods shows that no one approach can possibly exhaust meaning. "Choosing which questions to ask of these texts is a methodological exercise which heightens the challenge of difference.... Our awareness of this challenge and our choice of questions will allow texts to challenge us in our own contexts."

227.   Penchansky, David. "Staying the Night: Inter-Textuality in Genesis and Judges," in #83, pp. 77–88.

Three stories of hospitality, and of women "powerless to direct their own lives" in *Genesis* 19, 24, and *Judges* 19. How the variations in these stories "indicate the tension or ideological struggle that occurs at the junctures of the juxtaposition." How different definitions of what constitutes the text (literary, social, or interpretive) affect our reading, including how they may "undercut [our] ... confidence in [our] ... ability to read a text."

228.   Rashkow, Ilona N. "Intertextuality, Transference, and The Reader in/of Genesis 12 and 20," in #83, pp. 57–73.

Intertextuality in these "wife-sister" stories affects not only plot and characters, but the reader also. "... [C]onventional, literal-minded expectations about meaning are defeated. The most scandalous thing about Abraham's ignominious actions is that we are forced to participate; the reader's innocence cannot remain intact since there is no such thing as an innocent reader of this text."

229.   Teugels, Lieve. "'A Strong Woman, Who Can Find?' A Study of Characterization in Genesis 24, with Some Perspectives on the General Presentation of Isaac and Rebekah in the Genesis Narratives." *JSOT* 63 (1994), 89–104.

Characterization of Isaac in the pentateuchal narratives is meager. Narrative analysis of *Genesis* 24, however, "shows that Rebekah ... is presented as a strong woman." This contrast "fits their particular task.... Isaac is the passive bearer of the blessing, while

Rebekah is the active, divinely-led helper, that assists him in keeping and passing the blessing on to the right successor."

See also #15, 75, 111, 113, 121, 174, 176, 178, 836.

Genesis 25–36

*   Bellis, Alice Ogden. "The Women of Genesis."
        See #172.

230.   Donaldson, Laura E. "Don Juan in Shechem: Rape, Romance, and Reading in Genesis 34." *EL* 20 (1993), 16–22.

The rape of Dinah has frequently been misread even by feminist critics, who wish it to mean certain things, regardless of whether it does—specifically the way the text encourages us to connect rape to romance. Thus we can see "how a social semiotic understanding of textuality reveals biblical narrative as a concurrently and contradictory process ... as a structuration of multiple, often competing codes."

231.   Jeansome, Sharon Pace. "Genesis 25:23—The Use of Poetry in the Rebekah Narratives," in Jack C. Knight and Lawrence A. Sinclair, eds., *The Psalms and Other Studies on the Old Testament* (Nashotah, WI: Nashotah House Seminary, 1990), pp. 145–152.

The importance of this verse for understanding Rebekah's role in obtaining the blessing for Jacob and protecting him from Esau. Her portrayal indicates that "the narrator recognized the importance of the second matriarch.... Thus, upon encountering Rebekah's maneuvers with Isaac, one can sympathize with her and recognize the necessity of her actions. By utilizing poetry to relay God's message, the narrator found an appropriate way to illustrate the importance of this single verse."

232.   Pardes, Ilana. "Rachel's Dream: The Female Subplot," in #88, pp. 60–78.

The interrelations between the dreams of Rachel and Jacob and the complexity of their "patriarchal specular dynamics": how dissymmetry is established and yet antithetically called into question.

Why Rachel's dream is not doomed to total frustration, despite her premature death.

* Rashkow, Ilona N. *Upon the Dark Places. Anti-Semitism and Sexism in English Renaissance Biblical Translation.*

    See #201.

233. Rogerson, John. "Wrestling with the Angel: A Study in Historical and Literary Interpretation," in #16, pp. 131–144.

    A review of interpretations of Jacob and Jabbok (*Genesis* 32) since the 19th century. The movement away from the search for a referent outside the text implies that there is no fundamental difference between biblical and literary approaches to interpretation. This in turn means that the biblical critics must turn to the literary critics for help. We stand "not above the text but beneath it and in submission to it...."

234. Sherwood, Stephen K. *"Had God Not Been on My Side," An Examination of the Narrative Techniques of the Story of Jacob and Laban. Genesis 29, 1–32,2.* Frankfurt on Main (Peter Lang), 1990.

    Close reading of Genesis 29–31, analyzing the unity of its fine episodes. Narrative analysis of basic plot structure, presence of tension, point of view, characterization, narrator's means of creating reader knowledge and interest. Stylistic analysis of each episode, its micro and macro structures, semantic fields, imagery and symbolism. The structure is loosely chiastic-thematic, the plot change one of knowledge, the characterization of Jacob ambiguous. There are many thematic links to earlier stories in *Genesis*.

See also #15, 16, 79, 121, 174, 176, 201, 219, 223, 566.

Genesis 37–50

* Bellis, Alice Ogden. "The Women of Genesis."
    See #172.

235.   Donaldson, Laura E. "Cyborgs, Ciphers, and Sexuality: Re-
        Theorizing Literary and Biblical Character." *Semeia* 63
        (1993), 81–96.

        We need to reconceptualize character as "the production of po-
        sition within a conflicted narrative field." The story of Joseph and
        Potiphar's wife as illustrative of how this might work, allowing us
        to read the latter character "as a woman who uses her sexuality to
        prevent a male homo-social redistribution of the household rather
        than to sexually harass Joseph."

*   Kunin, Seth Daniel. "The Death of Isaac: Structuralist Anal-
        ysis of Genesis 22."

        See #224.

236.   Matthews, Victor H. "The Anthropology of Clothing in the
        Joseph Narrative." *JSOT* 65 (1995), 25–36.

        Clothing as an important structural element in the Joseph narra-
        tive. The two investiture ceremonies form an inclusio in the story,
        and clothing references in the transitory material continue to serve
        as signals of changes in status and favor in the plot.

237.   O'Callaghan, Martin. "The Structure and Meaning of Gene-
        sis 38—Judah and Tamar." *PIBA* 5 (1981), 72–88.

        The structure of this chapter analyzed in five stages: theme,
        deep structure, narrative, structure, subsidiary themes and plot
        structure, and formal structure. The fundamental theme of
        life/death; Judah and Tamar as actants; the consistent use of chi-
        asm to give the story rhythm, the use of irony as key literary de-
        vice to build plot and involve the reader.

238.   Shoulson, Jeffrey S. "Daniel's Pesher: A Proto-Midrashic
        Reading of Genesis 40–41." *EL* 20 (1993), 111–128.

        The many general and particular similarities between *Genesis*
        37–50 and the chronicle in *Daniel* 1–6. Thus the latter shows a
        proto-midrashic quality, and "demonstrates particular kinship
        with Deutero-Isaiah along linguistic, thematic, and theological
        lines." There are also significant differences between these two
        narratives, partly to be accounted for by the very different histori-
        cal and political circumstances of their composition.

See also #111, 113, 118, 178, 224, 261, 361, 384, 427, 454.

EXODUS

239. Bach, Alice. "With a Song in Her Heart: Listening to Scholars Listening for Miriam," in #242, pp. 243–245.

Review of several other articles on Miriam in terms of how "If [the redactor] holds the power to narrate, he also has the power to block other narratives from forming or emerging. He can erase the memory of versions that have predated his own." It requires some skill, then, to re-vision suppressed texts about Miriam. How critics in this volume have done so, and how a sample of Graetz's suggested midrash might work.

240. Baroody, Wilson G., and William F. Gentrup. "Exodus, Leviticus, Numbers, and Deuteronomy," in #20, pp. 121–136.

The life of Moses as narrative frame for all four of these books, which contain "a marvelous collection of narrative and law ..." fused into a unity, "a fusion expressing indirectly the biblical axiom that principles and actions are inseparable." Chiasmic structure of these books as a whole, and within *Deuteronomy*. Stylistic arrangement allows; literary devices and themes.

241. Bellis, Alice Ogden. "The Women of Exodus and Numbers," in #64, pp. 99–111.

The five women who save Moses from an early death (*Exodus* 1:8–2:10); the women in Moses' adult live, e.g., Miriam (*Exodus* 15 and *Numbers* 11–12); the daughters of Zelophehad (*Numbers* 27 and 36). Some interpretations celebrate the daughters' initiative, others the story's androcentric basis, though these are not contradictory, since the daughters' motivations are not clear. On a different note, the women in Moses' life are uniformly "feisty," even defiant, and certainly not victims.

242. Brenner, Athalya, ed. *A Feminist Companion to Exodus to Deuteronomy.* Sheffield (Sheffield Academic P), 1994.

Sixteen essays on one or more of these books, of which most of those in Part One: ("Daughters") and Part Three ("Miriam: On Being A Sister") are feminist/literary, and are analyzed separately as #177, 255, 247, 266, 108, 246, 239, 262.

243.   Carroll, R.P. "Strange Fire: Abstract of Presence Absent in
        the Text Meditations on Exodus 3." *JSOT* 61 (1994), 39–58.

Meditation on *Exodus* 3 for George Steiner's 65th birthday. Intertextual reading of the text and some of its interpreters "to explore the problematics of presence in the story ... and ... the opacity
of the divine name as an evasion of presence in the narrative." The
influence of Steiner and Derrida helps us see "that the 'I' of the
text cannot be seen by the eye of the reader. In that absence all
presence in the Bible is deferred to a future unrealized in time."

244.   Cartun, Ari Mark. "'Who Knows Ten?' The Structural and
        Symbolic Use of Numbers in the Ten Plagues: Exodus
        7:14–13:16." *USQR* 45 (1991), 65–119.

"The story of the ten plagues in Exodus is filled with numerical
patterns that tie the plagues together and with cryptic, repetitive,
sprinkling of some key words. Though the meanings of the plague
groupings ... may be baffling, the overall effect amplifies lessons
and morals elsewhere explicit in the story of the Exodus."

245.   Daalen, Aleida G. Van. "The Place Where YHWH Showed
        Himself to Moses: A Study of the Composition of Exodus
        3," in #119, pp. 133–144.

Analysis of *Exodus* 3 "as an illustration of narrative technique:
how information is introduced, varied, worked out, and mutually
related." We need to read the story on two levels: questions which
confront Moses, and questions which confront the reader.

246.   Dijk-Hemmes, Fokkelien van. "Some Recent Views of the
        Presentation of the Song of Miriam," in #242, pp. 200–206.

How previous critics, including feminist ones, have failed to see
that Miriam's song does not echo Moses' but originates it. Miriam
and the women "are the ones who call Moses and the men/people
to sing songs of praise to God. They take the lead."

247.   Exum, J. Cheryl. "Second Thoughts about Secondary Char-
        acters: Women in Exodus 1.8–2.10," in #242, pp. 75–87.

A reconsideration of Exum's article in *Semeia* 28 (Minor I, #641)
in light of developments in feminist literary criticism over the last
decade. "The case of Miriam in *Numbers* 12 offers but one example
of the way women's experience ... is expressed but has been displaced and distorted.... [A]ttempting to account for the distortion

or absence or suppression of female presence after the opening stories in Exodus 1 and 2 in terms of biblical gender politics, rather that treating it as if it were unmotivated, is, I think, a step in the right direction.

*   Giese, R.L. "Strophic Hebrew Verse as Free Verse."

        See #158.

248.   Hendrix, Ralph E. "A Literary-Structural Overview of Exodus 25–40." *AUSS* 30 (1992), 123–138.

        Exodus 25–40 "has at least three maxi-structural axes: literary, topical, and terminological ..., [with] at least one subsidiary, mini-structural axis: grammatical. Its structural integrity ... has given strong argument for approaching the biblical text in its canonical form."

249.   Holbert, John C. "A New Literary Reading of *Exodus* 32, The Story of the Golden Calf." *Quarterly Review* 10, #3 (Fall 1990), 46–68.

        Close reading of this story of a challenge to Moses' leadership in terms of its structure, style, narrative accomplishments, plot, and characterization.

250.   Jackson, Bernard S. "Practical Wisdom and Literary Artifice in the Covenant Code," in B.S. Jackson and S.M. Passamaneck, eds., *The Jerusalem 1990 Conference Volume* (Atlanta: Scholars P, 1992), 65–92.

        How wisdom functions "as an alternative dispute-resolution technique" in 2 *Samuel* 20 and 14, and examples of practical wisdom in the "Covenant Code" of *Exodus* 21–23. Structural relations in the latter, as well as literary allusions, structural divisions, and chiastic patterns based on theme.

251.   Krašovec, Jože. "Unifying Themes in Exodus 7,8–11,10," in C. Brekelmans and J. Lust, eds., *Pentateuchal and Deuteronomistic Studies* (Leuven: Leuven UP and Uitgeverij Peeters, 1990), pp. 47–66.

        How the content and literary devices in this narrative help clarify its theological meaning. Thematic unity of *Exodus* 3–14 based on God's repeated demands and Pharaoh's repeated failure to submit, as well as on the idea of the exodus itself. The theological significance of this pattern is that Pharaoh knows he is wrong and yet proceeds in his course.

*   Marks, Herbert. "Biblical Naming and Poetic Etymology."
          See #131.

*   Miscall, Peter D. "Moses and David: Myth and Monarchy."
          See #317.

252.   Pardes, Ilana. "Zipporah and the Struggle for Deliverance,"
          in #88, pp. 79–97.

          The enigmatic role of Zipporah in the "Bridegroom of Blood"
          story of *Exodus* 4:24–26 in fact exposes a weak point in monothe-
          ism and patriarchy. Her tricking of a male deity "becomes an anti-
          thetical element that unsettles its textual surroundings both in its
          antipatriarchal bent and in its anticovenautal ... spirit."

253.   Patrick, Dale. "The Rhetoric of Revelation." *HBT* 16 (1994),
          20–40.

          "The exchanges between YHWH and Moses at the burning bush
          fit J.L. Austin's description of performative utterance. They create
          a 'reality', [an] ... *ethos*." Further, important use in *Exodus* is made
          of a narrative strategy for incorporating the knowledge of the
          reader into the drama through a "new type of suspense which
          cannot be resolved by knowledge of the outcome." Ways in which
          the canonical status of scripture "seem[s] to deconstruct the per-
          formative force of accounts like the exodus."

254.   Seters, John Van. *The Life of Moses. The Yahwist as Historian in
          Exodus-Numbers*. Louisville (Westminster/John Knox P),
          1994.

          The J source "is a comprehensive, unified, literary work, extend-
          ing from the primeval history in Genesis to the death of Moses ...
          meant to be an introduction to the national history of Dtr H." Thus
          we need not posit multiple redactors for this material. J's presen-
          tation of Moses is "radically new." Its profound influence on later
          books of the HB.

255.   Siebert-Hommes, Jopie. "But If She Be a Daughter ... She
          May Live! 'Daughters' and 'Sons' in Exodus 1–2," in #242,
          pp. 62–74.

          Remarkably, daughters in *Exodus* 1–2 occupy a special place
          alongside sons, an active role as subjects. The continuation of his-
          tory depends on the daughters—i.e., the twelve women who en-
          able Moses to survive.

256. Sprinkle, Joe M. *'The Book of the Covenant.' A Literary Approach.* Sheffield (JSOT P), 1994.

Seeks to determine "whether a synchronic 'literary approach' to biblical law might not be superior to the heavily source-oriented methodologies that ... have dominated the study of biblical law." Relationship of *Exodus* 20–23 with the surrounding narrative makes it appear "purposefully positioned" there. Organizing principles of the laws themselves, their interrelationship, point of view, and connection to other legal formulations outside of *Exodus*.

257. van der Westuizen, J.P. "Literary Devices in Exodus 15:1–18 and Deuteronomy 32:1–43 as a Criterion for Determining Their Literary Standards," in W.C. van Wyk, ed., *Studies in the Pentateuch* (Johannesburg: Weeshuispers, n.d. [1977?]), pp. 57–73.

Investigation and clarification "of certain literary devices used in the song of Miriam ... and the Song of Moses and the extent to which these may be applied as a criterion in determining the literary standards of these hymns of praise." Three types: devices for sound (rhyme, assonance/alliteration, onomatopoeia); devices for sense (simile, metaphor, hendiadys, etc); devices for form (chiasm, parallelism, etc.). The relative frequency of each in the two passages.

See also #11, 15, 71, 72, 104, 112, 113, 124, 135, 157, 178, 270, 458.

LEVITICUS

* Baroody, Wilson G., and William F. Gentrup. "Exodus, Leviticus, Numbers, and Deuteronomy."

See #240.

* Brenner, Athalya, ed. *A Feminist Companion to Exodus to Deuteronomy.*

See #242.

258. Carmichael, Calum M. "Laws of Leviticus 19." *HTR* 87 (1994), 239–256.

To understand legal material in the Pentateuch, we must first realize that it is embedded in narrative. Then, we must see that writers of both narrative histories and of laws "exercise their historical imagination in creating their material." Finally, biblical (and all ancient) law existed before any institutionalized legal system came into being. Narratives, therefore, is a logical embodiment of such law.

259. Rendsburg, Gary A. "The Inclusio in Leviticus XI." *VT* 43 (1993), 418–421.

This technique is usually associated with Hebrew poetry, but is in fact widespread in the Pentateuch, even in the legal portions. It is a rhetorical device. Its appearance in *Leviticus* 11.

260. Whitekettle, Richard. "Leviticus 15:18 Reconsidered: Spatial Structure and the Body." *JSOT* 49 (1991), 31–45.

"The chiastic structure of *Leviticus* 15 is significant for the interpretation of its content. The reproductive system, as perceived through the filter of these laws, is in a homologous relationship with the tabernacle. Both the tabernacle and the setting of sexual intercourse are at one end of a continuum, which has as its other end the characteristics wilderness/non-life/waste."

See also #240.

NUMBERS

261. Bach, Alice. "Good to the Last Drop: Viewing the Sotah (Numbers 5.11–31) as the Glass Half Empty and Wondering How to View It Half Full," in #82, pp. 26–54.

In *Numbers* 5:11–31, the "central concern is the control of women's sexuality." How traditional readings "have preserved patriarchal values while containing woman as the object of male anxieties," and how a Derridean reading can expose this anxiety by refusing to accept that texts have firm borders which cannot be transcended. *Genesis* 39, *Proverbs* 5 and 7, and *Deuteronomy* 22 form relevant "con-texts" which enable this new reading to take place and challenge the male point of view as universal or normative.

* Baroody, Wilson G., and William F. Gentrup. "Exodus, Leviticus, Numbers, and Deuteronomy."

  See #240.

* Bellis, Alice Ogden. "The Women of Exodus and Numbers." See #241.

* Brenner, Athalya, ed. *A Feminist Companion to Exodus to Deuteronomy.*

  See #242.

262. Graetz, Naomi. "Did Miriam Talk Too Much?," in #242, pp. 231–242.

  Various questions which may be raised about this chapter, especially with regard to Miriam's status and her relationship to patriarchal authority. Readings which emphasize Aaron's pain at the expense of Miriam's "assault our sense of the meaning of the text by smoothing over the injustice inherent in the original story.... We must start imaginatively to re-engage with our sacred texts by writing midrash."

263. Horn, Bernard. "Spies, Sacrifices, and Fringes." *EL* 20 (1993), 31–53.

  The distinction between the God of the narrative and that of the legal passages must be dealt with in any discussion of the unity of *Numbers*. All three central characters in the book—God, Moses, and the people—"undergo a transformation appropriate to the movement from slavery to freedom." Even God must learn and change, and therefore must be treated by readers of *Numbers* as a character.

264. Sakenfeld, Katharine Doob. "New Approaches to Understanding and Study of the Bible" [with responses by Melvin K.H. Peters and J. Ramsay Michaels], in Howard Clark Kee, ed., *The Bible in the Twenty-First Century* (Philadelphia: Trinity P International, 1993), pp. 125–158.

  Applications to *Numbers* 12 of literary and structural and of feminist and African-American perspectives, in part to demonstrate how these new approaches alter the questions we ask about a biblical text. How these new questions might affect both academic and congregation-centered bible study. Peters: Sakenfeld's analysis is too narrowly Protestant, and suffers also from failing to distinguish between methods (literary and structural) and audiences (feminist and African-American). Michaels: ditto for objection 2, and also notes how literary methods are not all that new.

265.   Savran, G. "Beastly Speech: Intertextuality, Balaam's Ass and the Garden of Eden." *JSOT* 64 (1994), 33–55.

"The anomalous feature of animal speech in *Genesis* 3 and in *Numbers* 22 is only the most obvious point in common between the two texts. The serpent and the she-ass play complementary roles in relation to the human actors in the stories, and a comparison of their functions reveals further similarities. Both the garden story and the Balaam narrative focus on the themes of blessing and curse, vision and understanding, and obedience/disobedience to God. The intertextual relationship between the stories uncovered in this analysis sheds light on larger patterns of inner-biblical interpretation within the Pentateuch."

*   Seters, John Van. *The Life of Moses. The Yahwist as Historian in Exodus-Numbers.*

See #254.

266.   Sterring, Anke. "The Will of the Daughters," in #242, pp. 88–99.

Various ramifications of the the usual inheritance arrangements for the daughters of Zelophehad. The story "can be read as an inspiring narrative for women. It demonstrates that seemingly rigid social structures can be modified. Even a commandment established by God [is] ... altered through speaking the right word at the time. The story also exhibits the backlash of women's achievement, the reaction of patriarchy when it suspects its existence is threatened."

See also #79, 113, 121, 124, 135, 164, 240, 247, 416.

DEUTERONOMY

*   Baroody, Wilson G., and William F. Gentrup. "Exodus, Leviticus, Numbers, and Deuteronomy."

See #240.

*   Brenner, Athalya, ed. *A Feminist Companion to Exodus to Deuteronomy.*

See #242.

267.   Christensen, Duane L. *A Song of Power and the Power of Song. Essays on the Book of Deuteronomy.* Winona Lake (Eisenbrauns), 1993.

Twenty-five essays using various approaches and methods to analyze parts or the whole of *Deuteronomy.* Three essays in Part 5: "New Directions in Recent Research," by Robert Polzin, Casper J. Labuschagne, and Duane L. Christensen, employ some form of literary-critical methodology.

268.   Kaufman, Stephen A. "The Structure of Deuteronomic Law." *Maarav* 1/2 (1978–79), 105–158.

The Deuteronomic Law (12–25) is "a unified masterpiece of jurisprudential literature created by a single author ... who combined ancient civil and cultic regulations with intentional civil reforms ... with wisdom teachings, with speculations on the propriety of patriarchal institutions, and with a program of politico-religious centralization into a highly patterned whole—an expanded decalogue."

269.   Lenchak, Timothy A. *"Choose Life!" A Rhetorical-Critical Investigation of Deuteronomy 28, 69–30, 20.* Rome (Editrice Pontificio Istituto Biblico), 1993.

Rhetorical analysis of Moses' Third Discourse, emphasizing argumentation/persuasion rather than stylistics or strictly literary analysis. Fundamentals of ancient and modern rhetoric. Audience and rhetorical situation of this discourse. Enthymemes and arguments of association explicit or implicit in this material. Literary structure and style in *Deuteronomy* 28–30. It is primarily deliberative, but shows features of epideictic rhetoric as well.

270.   O'Connell, Robert H. "Deuteronomy IX 7–X7, 10–11: Panelled Structure, Double Rehearsal and the Rhetoric of Covenant Rebuke." *VT* 62 (1992), 492–509.

"... the means by which the panelled presentation of YHWH's double giving of the commandments was designed to serve a rhetoric of covenant rebuke...." Also the "rhetorical design of its double rehearsal of YHWH's giving of the ten commandments, its double allusion to Exodus xxxii and its function in the context of Deuteronomy iv–xi."

270a. Polzin, Robert. "Dialogic Imagination in the Book of Deuteronomy." *Studies in Twentieth-Century Literature* 9 (1984–85), 135–143.

Deuteronomy, "as a supremely artful and artistic work of prose, struggles powerfully 'against various kinds and degrees of authority' ... [and] paradoxically destroys the monologic tendencies of the authoritative word even as it appears on the surface simply to be transmitting it." The "central struggle" in Deuteronomy, between the word of God and the word of Moses, is won by the latter.

*   van der Westuizen, J.P. "Literary Devices in Exodus 15:1–18 and Deuteronomy 32:1–43 as a Criterion for Determining Their Literary Standards."

See #257.

See also #96, 104, 147, 240, 261.

PROPHETS

Former Prophets

271.   Pyper, Hugh S. "Surviving Writing: The Anxiety of Historiography in the Former Prophets," in #82, pp. 227–249.

The oft-noted absence of references to writing in the Former Prophets is in reality a "repression of writing ... tied to a wider anxiety, what we might call an anxiety of utterance." Writing is consistently linked there with violence and death, which is a paradox, since only through an utterance can we avoid death while the utterance is death. The anxiety of genealogy, since offspring are also a form of utterance, and since surviving the demise of the Davidic kingdom creates anxiety in the very art of writing about it. How Freudian theory illuminates these situations.

JOSHUA

272. Beek, M.A. "Joshua the Savior," in #119, pp. 145–153.

> *Joshua* was given the function not only of bridging the gap be-tween Torah and the Former Prophets, but of preparing hearers for the history of salvation introduced in *Judges*. Literary analysis helps us understand that *Judges* "originated in a period during which the scriptures were rearranged according to new princi-ples.... It was Joshua, the ideal savior, who assembled *all* the peo-ple in *one* country around *one* Torah."

273. Bellis, Alice Ogden. "The Women of Joshua and Judges," in #64, pp. 112–139.

> Rahab (*Joshua* 2) and women of *Judges*, e.g., Deborah and Jael (*Judges* 4–5), Manoah's wife and Delilah (*Judges* 13–16), Jephthah's daughter (*Judges* 11) and the unnamed woman of chapter 19 "present us with stark contrasts," yet they are all in their way heroic (at least according to some interpreters) and in any case not victims (except for the last two named). It is a "cause for concern" that these last "are among the most atrocious stories of victimiza-tion ... anywhere."

*   Fields, Weston W. "The Motif 'Night as Danger' Associated with Three Biblical Destruction Narratives."
> See #220.

274. Gros Louis, Kenneth R.R., and Willard van Antwerpen, Jr. "Joshua and Judges," in #20, pp. 137–150.

> The literary approach and the questions about human life which it asks. Why these two books are more like Homer than, say, the *Anglo-Saxon Chronicles*. "Pattern-creating events" in *Joshua* and *Judges*; progression of history in the former; linking stories; the "surprises" of *Judges*. "Paradox" and history in the books.

275. Hawk, L. Daniel. *Every Promise Fulfilled: Contesting Plots in Joshua*. Louisville (Westminster/John Knox P), 1991.

> Literary analysis of *Joshua* shows that its incongruities are cir-cumstances of its plot, and that "the configuring of the story gives rise to its tensions...." Thus this analysis explores the patterns in the story and "the agendas which underlie them." Its rhetoric shows a story that illustrates "the tension between the structuring

operations of dogma, Israel's need to be faithful to Yahweh and the circumstances of experience—the tendency of the land to dilute this faithfulness."

276.   Robinson, Robert B. "None but Thine: Joshua 6 and the Ethics of Reading." *EL* 20 (1993), 84–99.

The complex morality and theology of *Joshua* 6 speaks to modern readers who have experienced the Holocaust, but at the same time creates a dilemma for us, since both ethically engaged interpretations and textually sensitive ones may be inadequate in one way or another. We must recognize that, because we approach ancient texts *via* other texts, their moral force "is exerted precisely in the continuous act of one story interpreting another...."

277.   Rowlett, Lori. "Inclusion, Exclusion and Marginality in the Book of Joshua." *JSOT* 55 (1992), 15–23.

Analysis of "the literary dynamics of the conquest story in the book of Joshua," based on Foucault's theory of power. *Joshua* "uses the rhetoric of warfare and nationalism as an encouragement and a threat to its own population to submit voluntarily to a ... government struggling to organize itself.... In order to justify violent action, the dynamics of the literature of warfare usually consist of a division between self and other...."

See also #113, 221, 266.

JUDGES

278.   Beem, Beverly. "The Minor Judges: A Literary Reading of Some Very Short Stories," in K. Lawson Younger, Jr., et al., eds., *The Biblical Canon in Comparative Perspective* (Lewiston: Edwin Mellen P, 1991), pp. 147–172.

How these stories work together "and how they relate to the larger stories surrounding them and contribute to the Book of *Judges* as a whole. They are not isolated units placed at random, but are strategically arranged to connect with the heroic narratives. They add comment and a linear movement, helping move us toward the Samson story and then toward kingship."

*   Bellis, Alice Ogden. "The Women of Joshua and Judges."

           See #273.

279.   Brenner, Athalya, ed. *A Feminist Companion to Judges*. Sheffield (Sheffield Academic P), 1993.

           Fifteen essays by twelve critics on all or parts of Judges, using literary/feminist criticism. Four essays on the female characters in the whole book, and on whether it is "a woman's satire on men who play God." Two essays each on chapters 4–5, 11, 13–16; three essays on chapters 19–21; introduction and afterword by the editor. Brenner essay on *Judges* 4–5 rpt. from Minor I, #733; Exum essay on *Judges* 11 rpt. from Minor I, #748.

280.   Brettler, Marc. "Never the Twain Shall Meet? The Ehud Story as History and Literature." *HUCA* 62 (1991), 285–304.

           The Ehud story as center of the argument over whether biblical historical texts should be analyzed as literature. Evaluations of the discussions by Alter and Halpern. "... [T]he Ehud pericope should be understood as political satire, a literary genre that is best understood within a historical context. Therefore, a literary approach which also considers ancient historical settings is most appropriate for understanding this unit."

*   Fields, Weston W. "The Motif 'Night as Danger' Associated with Three Biblical Destruction Narratives."

           See #220.

281.   Fokkelman, Jan P. "Structural Remarks on Judges 9 and 19," in Michael Fishbane and Emanuel Tov, eds., *'Sha'arei Talmon': Studies in the Bible, Qumran, and the Ancient Near East Presented to Shemaryahu Talmon* (Winona Lake: Eisenbrauns, 1992), pp. 33–45.

           Actantial analysis of *Judges* 9 shows Abimelech as both subject and object of his quest for power. The correct structure of *Judges* 19 shows it to consist of nine elements or segments. This in turn helps us see its relation to the larger *inclusio* of *Judges* 17–21. The correspondences make these nine segments into a chiasm rather than a linear sequence.

282. Garsiel, Moshe. "Homiletic Name Derivations as a Literary Device in the Gideon Narrative: Judges vi–viii." *VT* 43 (1993), 302–317.

The author creates a number of puns, of correspondences between names and the plot. It is possible, then, that the names were made up to fit the plot; more likely, the author has handled his material so as to "suggest links between the names of characters and the events of the plot," i.e, as an organizing device, a literary technique of allusions which form part of the structure of the plot and suggest certain theological conclusions as well.

283. Greene, Mark. "Enigma Variations: Aspects of the Samson Story (Judges 13–16)." *VE* 21 (1991), 53–79.

General literary analysis of the Samson story as a suspense story, tension being created through structure, repetition, ambiguity, puns, delayed climax, etc. Themes include "seeing," right *vs.* wrong, obedience. Samson as type of Israel.

*   Gros Louis, Kenneth R.R., and Willard van Antwerpen, Jr. "Joshua and Judges."

See #274.

284. Gunn, David M. "Samson of Sorrows: An Isaianic Gloss on Judges 13–16," in #83, pp. 225–253.

A counter-reading which questions the critical consensus on Samson as a comic figure lacking the tragic dignity and sense of purpose of a Saul. Samson is a "dealer in death," who is "defeated in his search for an ordinary life of his own by God allied with the evil in the hearts of other people.... Both trust in and acceptance of this god become moot for Samson.

285. Hudson, Don Michael. "Living in a Land of Epithets: Anonymity in Judges 19–21." *JSOT* 62 (1994), 49–66.

Employment of "disintegrating characterization" to reflect dehumanization of Israelite society of the author's time, and of the concept of anonymity as a "major literary technique" to display both ethical anarchy and annihilation of familial, tribal, and national identity and wholeness.

286. Jonker, L.C. "Samson in Double Vision: Judges 13–16 from Historical-Critical and Narrative Perspectives." *JNSL* 18 (1992), 49–65.

The probable history of composition of various parts of the cycle. How the addition of Chapter 16 clarifies themes, adds nuance to characterization, and creates overall narrative unity with units that "complement and articulate one another on a literary level." How Samson himself can be interpreted within this literary whole.

287. Kim, Jichan. *The Structure of the Samson Cycle.* Kampen (Kok Pharos Publishing House), 1993.

Survey of previous research on *Judges* 13–16 by source, form, tradition, and rhetorical critics, and why each of these methods has ultimately failed to do justice to the Samson cycle. How a new method—linguistic-structural criticism based on the nature of Northwest Semitic documents—can succeed in illuminating authorship, unity, fictive nature of the narrative, and relationship to the deuteronomistic historian, among other issues. Detailed verse-by-verse analysis of the narrative.

288. Niditch, Susan. "Samson as Culture Hero, Trickster, and Bandit: The Empowerment of the Weak." *CBQ* 52 (1990), 608–624.

Close reading of the content and structure of *Judges* 13–16 reveals "Israelite versions of traditional and crossculturally evidenced narrative *topoi*. The overriding theme and concern of these *topoi* ... is the marginal's confrontation with oppressive authority ... the victory of the weak over seemingly implacable forces."

*   Penchansky, David. "Staying the Night: Intertextuality in Genesis and Judges."

See #227.

289. Robbins, Vernon K. "The Ritual of Reading and Reading a Text as Ritual: Observations on Mieke Bal's *Death and Dissymmetry*," in David Jasper and Mark Ledbetter, eds., *In Good Company: Essays in Honor of Robert Detweiler* (Atlanta: Scholars P, 1994), pp. 385–401.

Three ways in which socio-rhetorical criticism "could be used in the context of Bal's analysis and interpretation": as a guide to independent analysis of the same passage in *Judges*; as a guide to a "programmatic display of Bal's interpretation of the texture" of these passages; and as a guide to an analysis of her book "as a twentieth century text designed to make a cultural and ideological statement about biblical interpretation itself."

290.   Satterthwaite, P.E. "Narrative Artistry in the Composition of Judges XX 29ff." *VT* 42 (1992), 80–89.

The narrator of *Judges* 20 has not only written a unified story; he has been extremely effective in exploiting "necessities imposed upon him by the nature of his narrative ... striking juxtapositions of word and event ..."; creation of telling effects, suspense, and vivid depiction of relentless pursuit.

291.   Satterthwaite, Philip, "'No King in Israel': Narrative Criticism and Judges 17–21." *TB* 44 (1993), 75–88.

Narrative techniques of Alter and Sternberg applied to *Judges* 17–21 produces a coherent interpretation based on repetition, narrative analogy, and use on narration and dialogue. As a result, we see that the narrator "takes a negative view of premonarchic Israel."

292.   Tanner, Paul J. "The Gideon Narrative as the Focal Point of Judges." *B Sac* 149 (1992), 146–161.

The narrator of *Judges* wishes to convince the reader by the time the Samson story is reached that another judge is not the answer for Israel. Through elaborate chiastic patterning, the author constructs not only a narrative whose focal point will be the Gideon story of Chapters 6–8, but also a similar pattern for the Gideon story itself: both of which will dramatize this theme.

293.   Williams, Jay G. "The Structure of Judges 2.6–16.31." *JSOT* 49 (1991), 77–85.

Judges is not the product of "clumsy editors" who arranged independent blocks of material, but is "carefully constructed according to the cycle of the solar year. Each of the twelve judges can be identified with a different tribe and each tribe with a month.... The cycle is carefully balanced on to geographic locations and maternal origin of the respective tribes. The role of women ... seems to mirror the role of the earth in the agricultural cycle."

294.   Younger, K. Lawson, Jr. "Heads! Tails! Or the Whole Coin?! Contextual Method and Intertextual Analysis: Judges 4 and 5," in K. Lawson Younger, Jr., et al., eds., *The Biblical Canon in Comparative Perspective* (Lewiston: Edwin Mellen P, 1991), pp. 109–146.

Analysis of promising ancient Near Eastern texts where, as in *Judges* 4–5, parallel accounts of a battle exist side by side. Thus we have "demonstrated that neither account must be dependent on the other, but rather that both probably derive from a common source ... and possess a complementary relationship."

See also #71, 79, 104, 111, 113, 115, 116, 118, 121, 124, 135, 164.

SAMUEL

295. Bellis, Alice Ogden. "The Women of 1 and 2 Samuel," in #64, pp. 140–159.

While Samuel contains no stories as horrible as *Joshua* and *Judges*, rape and murder continue in the former to be the lot of many women. Analyses of Hannah the woman, Rizpah, Michal, Abigail, Bathsheba, Tamar, and the wise women of Tekoa and Abel.

296. Brenner, Athalya. *A Feminist Companion to Samuel and Kings.* Sheffield (Sheffield Academic P), 1994.

Sixteen essays on specific chapters or books of Samuel and Kings of which ten are literary critical; one is a reprint of Minor I, #813. The other nine are analyzed as #136, 337, 303, 315, 316, 302, 342, 354, 359.

297. Deeley, Mary Katherine. "The Rhetoric of Memory in the Stories of Saul and David: A Prospective Study." *SBLSP* (1988), 285–292.

How memory as it is given to characters in the stories of Saul and David functions as a persuasive device by providing allusions to specific events, and thus "a coherent symbol-system ... a world-view." This rhetoric of memory enables the author to be persuasive: "Whether one is for or against, Saul's story disrupts Israel's history and its characters fail to take that history into account."

298. Edelman, Diana. "The Deuteronomist's Story of King Saul: Narrative Art or Editorial Product?," in C. Brekelmans and J. Lust, eds., *Pentateuchal and Deuteronomistic Studies* (Leuven: Leuven UP and Uitgeverij Peeters, 1990), pp. 207–220.

How literary analysis can work as a basis for source analysis of a biblical text. The main structural patterns, themes, and *Leitwörter* of these chapters, and how they can be used to evaluate current theories about the date and *Sitz in Leben* of the sources of these 25 chapters. Five main structuring devices, three overlapping patterns, one theme and one *Leitwört* can be discerned, all used to facilitate plot deviation—e.g., the three-part kingship ritual, the regnal account pattern, and the two-part division of Saul's career, and the theme of Johnathan's personal covenant with David. All these make major pre-biblical narratives unlikely as sources.

299. Edelman, Diana Vikander. *King Saul in the Historiography of Judah*. Sheffield (JSOT P), 1991.

The patterns which mark *I Samuel 8–II Samuel* 1 as "an intentional subunit within a larger account of Israel's relationship to its god Yahweh through time"—this larger account being the "Deuteronomistic History." These patterns include themes, *Leitwörter*, structuring and stylistic devices. Analysis of the actual, intended, and ideal readers of this narrative. Attempt to read the narrative chapter by chapter as though encountering it for the first time, with knowledge of historical background but only of those narratives which precede *I Samuel* 8 in the canon.

*   Linafelt, Tod. "Taking Women in Samuel: Readers/Responses/Responsibility."

See #327.

300. Long, V. Philips. "First and Second Samuel," in #20, pp. 165–181.

Three basic literary traits of the Samuel narratives are the scenic character of the narrative, its succinctness, and its subtlety. Overview of patterns, pivotal events, and plot; keywords, use of irony, and characterization. Sample analysis of the narrative of Saul's rise (*I Samuel* 9–13).

301. Reinhartz, Adele. "Anonymity and Character in the Books of Samuel." *Semeia* 63 (1993), 117–141.

The effect of anonymity of character on a mimetic reading of the narrative is largely positive on both characterization and plot development. Survey of anonymous characters in *I* and *II Samuel* and detailed study of three women: the medium of Endor (*I Samuel* 28); wise woman of Tekoa (*II Samuel* 14); and wise woman of Abel (*II Samuel* 20).

302. Valler, Shulamit. "King David and 'His' Women: Biblical Stories and Talmudic Discussions," in #296, pp. 129–142.

Comparison of biblical narratives about the women in King David's story with rabbinic interpretations of those narratives shows that concepts of masculinity and femininity "are quite different" in the two. Discussions of Michal, Abigail, Bathsheba, and Abishag in both sources shows that in the rabbinic interpretations David's character develops quite differently from the biblical accounts, as do those of the women. To show David as ideal man they "sometimes change the women's narrative roles" into, e.g., subdued instead of independent wives, "sexual and scheming" women instead of victims.

See also #71, 72, 110, 615.

1 Samuel

303. Amit, Yairah. "'Am I Not More Devoted to You Than Ten Sons?' (1 Samuel 1,8): Male and Female Interpretations," in #296, pp. 68–76.

How a woman's point of view "may shed fresh light" on a biblical narrative: in this case, that of Hannah's "delicacy and virtue ... the noble and silent way in which she expresses her protest."

304. Amit, Yairah. "'The Glory of Israel Does Not Deceive or Change His Mind': On the Reliability of Narrators and Speakers in Biblical Narrative." *Prooftexts* 12 (1992), 201–212.

"Only the narrator and God appear as reliable in biblical narrative. The other characters, including prophets, must be examined individually." No unreliable narrators are used in the HB. "The reliability of the narrator is ... a judgmental criterion for assessing other aspects of reliability throughout the story."

305. Blenkinsopp, Joseph. "Jonathan's Sacrilege. 1 Samuel 14, 1–46: A Study in Literary History." *CBQ* 26 (1964), 423–449.

Literary and stylistic study of the episode of Jonathan's breaking of the fast. The simple, functional and yet rhythmic, almost poetic dialogue, swift action, stylistic patterns, lack of description, motifs in the plot. Literary differences among the likely sources.

306. Brueggemann, Walter. "Narrative Coherence and Theological Intentionality in I Samuel 18." *CBQ* 55 (1993), 225–243.

The narrative of *I Samuel* is an "artistic rendering of human interaction" which constitutes a "powerful theological statement." Its function and placement are designed to introduce key themes and issues of the narrative to follow. Though an "odd collection of literary fragments," the chapter nevertheless demonstrates "internal coherence and intentionality."

307. Clines, David J.A., and Tamara C. Eskenazi, eds. *Telling Queen Michal's Story: An Experiment in Comparative Interpretation*. Sheffield (JSOT P), 1991.

Twenty-eight essays, of which seven are previously unpublished and six are literary-critical: Richard G. Bowman on *2 Samuel* 1–8; D.J.A. Clines on sequential plot; Tamara Eskenazi on Hebrew sources; P.D. Miscall on Michal and her sisters; Robert Polzin on "multivoiced look" at the narratives.

308. Craig, Kenneth M., Jr. "Rhetorical Aspects of Questions Answered with Silence in 1 Samuel 14:37 and 28:6." *CBQ* 56 (1994), 221–239.

These two chapters "are organized around a single literary thread.... The multiple effects of the picture of a king unable to get answers combine to support the theme of decline, and the near duplication of images signals a distinct rhetorical strategy.... Subtle, important shifts in language [play] ... an important role in characterization ...," which is achieved through analogy.

309. Culpepper, R. Alan. "Narrative Criticism as a Tool for Proclamation: 1 Samuel 13." *RE* 84 (1987), 33–40.

How narrative criticism approaches a biblical text. Narrative critical analysis of the first crisis in Saul's kingship. Preaching such a narrative involves "retelling the biblical story so that hearers are drawn into [its] narrative world." It also entails focusing on the conflicts and struggles within the story, "showing how the text speaks to hearers involved in similar struggles." How the complexity of Saul's character carries a message for readers.

310. Deist, F.E. "'By the way, Hophni and Phinehas Were There: An Investigation into the Literary and Ideological Func-

tions of Hophni, Phinehas and Shiloh in 1 Samuel 1–4."
JNSL 18 (1992), 33–40.

The narrated encounters between Samuel's parents and the father of Hopni and Phinehas, and the constant contrasts drawn by the narrator between Samuel and these seemingly unimportant characters as prominent features of the narrative.

311. Deist, Ferdinand. "Coincidence as a Motif of Divine Intervention in I Samuel 9." *OTE* 6 (1993), 7–18.

Yahweh tends to fade as a visible actor in human affairs in later parts of the HB. The probable literary reason for this phenomenon is that reflective and philosophical parts of a story allow Yahweh to direct affairs from a distance without losing control. Overt and covert divine intervention, and coincidence in *I Samuel* 9 as illustration of this principle.

312. Garsiel, Moshe. *The First Book of Samuel. A Literary Study of Comparative Structures, Analogies, and Parallels.* Ramat-Gan (Revivim Publishing House), 1985.

Various themes and motifs in *1 Samuel* as related to the author's presumed intentions in using "linkage systems" and techniques in his narratives about Samuel, Saul, and David. Some of these comparative structures appear close together in the text, while others do not—some even provide the keys to understanding the book's concern with comparing, past and present.

313. Gitay, Yehoshua. "Reflection on the Poetics of the Samuel Narrative: The Question of the Ark Narrative." *CBQ* 54 (1992), 221–230.

"The story of the ark in I Samuel 4:1b–7:1 is an integral part of the entire plot.... The story ... is told in a particularly literary manner which might have been chosen intentionally." Since the abandonment of the ark was a national trauma, "the reciting of the story in a legendary form is the appropriate stylistic means of enabling the narrator to cope with the situation." The colorful descriptive and satiric presentation heightens dramatic tension.

* Jobling, David. "Ruth Finds a Home: Canon, Politics, Method."

See #562.

314. Jobling, David. "What, if Anything, Is 1 Samuel?" *SJOT* 7 (1993), 17–31.

How virtually all literary commentators distance themselves from the political dimension of the text. They legitimize and thus "deproblematize" David's kingship. How our reading can avoid becoming trapped in ideological context.

315.   Klein, Lillian R. "Hannah: Marginalized Victim and Social Redeemer," in #296, pp. 77–92.

The "emotional marginalization of Hannah" as significant component of her narrative. She is a "woman in a boundary situation," who becomes a "social redeemer" for men. "Victim and redeemer, Hannah reinforces the patriarchal image of women."

316.   Meyers, Carol. "Hannah and Her Sacrifice: Reclaiming Female Agency," in #296, pp. 93–104.

Hannah's centrality in her narrative, and her "agency in a ritual act" reveals otherwise hidden aspects of women's cultic life. Additionally, Hannah's sacrifice reveals activity with national implications. "By the very individuality of her characterization and behavior, she is represented as contributing to the corporate welfare of ancient Israel."

317.   Miscall, Peter D. "Moses and David: Myth and Monarchy," in #82, pp. 184–200.

The often-remarked ambiguity and doubling of the narratives in *I Samuel* 1–17 is designed "to present kingship and its origins in a decidedly negative light ... through the narrative pace that delays the appearance of the first two kings, Saul and David," compared to the "strong mythic quality," of the Pentateuchal story. Kingship is treated at length in *I Samuel* because it lasted 400 years, not because it is viewed positively by the narrator.

318.   Reis, Pamela Tamarkin. "Collusion at Nob: A New Reading of I Samuel 21–22." *JSOT* 61 (1994), 59–73.

Attention to the subtleties of narrative characterization in *I Samuel* 21–22 enables us to argue "that David and Ahimelech know Doeg's presence in the sanctuary at Nob and collude to mislead him." Such a reading resolves various problems present in earlier interpretations and "enhances the characterization of David, Ahimelech, Saul, and Doeg, and implicates a rationale for the massacre at Nob."

See also #79, 97, 104, 113, 116, 121, 135, 295, 301, 562, 836.

2 Samuel

319.   Bach, Alice. "Signs of the Flesh: Observations on Character-
        ization in the Bible." *Semeia* 63 (1993), 61–79.

        The need to retrieve female characters "who may have been flat-
        tened or suppressed by the weight of the story that is not [theirs]."
        Contra structuralism, we recognized that character can exist "as an
        element independent of the story in which the character was orig-
        inally discovered." The figure of Bathsheba as both object of male
        sexual fantasy and as a good mother.

*   Bar-Efrat, Shimon. *Narrative Art in the Bible.*
        See #110.

320.   Beek, M.A. "David and Absolom: A Hebrew Tragedy in
        Prose?," in #119, pp. 155–168.

        While we have no evidence of any plays being performed in
        ancient Israel, the story of David and Absolom is a tragic tale. The
        "fate of the *dramatis personal* is tragic. Crime and punishment are
        clearly linked, there are no accidental circumstances. The king
        bore his burden of guilt, repentance and suffering. The author
        wrote well, but he wrote to be heard, not to be praised."

*   Clines, David J.A., and Tamara C. Eskenazi, eds. *Telling
        Queen Michal's Story: An Experiment in Comparative Inter-
        pretation.*
        See #307.

321.   Conroy, Charles. "A Literary Study of 2 Samuel 17, 1–14,"
        in Vicente Collado and Eduardo Zurro, eds., *El Misterio de
        la Palabra* (Madrid: Ediciones Cristiandad, 1983), 177–192.

        How the author of *2 Samuel* 17 passes judgment on Ahitophel
        and Hushai through use of direct speech, repetition, pause, im-
        plicit criticism of skill in speech, and diction.

*   Cotterell, Peter, and Max Turner. *Linguistics and Biblical In-
        terpretation.*
        See #620.

322.   Craig, Kenneth M., Jr. "The Character(ization) of God in 2
        Samuel 7:1–17." *Semeia* 63 (1993), 159–176.

   Characterization is achieved here primarily through dialogue,
   with almost every phrase illuminating God's character through
   "subtle yet significant artistic measures." The role of indirect discourse, point of view, direct speech, etc., in conveying God's psychological and ideological points of view.

323.   Eslinger, Lyle. *House of God or House of David. The Rhetoric of
        2 Samuel 7.* Sheffield (Sheffield Academic P), 1994.

   The narrative rhetoric of one of the key speeches in the
   deuteronomistic narratives. The need for analyzing this chapter,
   given its seeming contradictions about the covenant. These problems concern the past, present, and future relations in the
   deuteronomistic narrative. Various forms of parallelism and chiastic structure in the chapter.

324.   Garsiel, Moshe. "The Story of David and Bathsheba: A Dif-
        ferent Approach." *CBQ* 55 (1993), 244–262.

   Historical inquiry and literary study cannot be separated. When
   combined, they show that biblical narrative is an ancient historiography ... based upon a theological, social, and political world view
   ... directed toward ... didactic messages.... Analysis of rhetorical
   and literary aspects of II Samuel 11, "in the light of the historical
   background which it reflects." The author deliberately avoids
   submerging us in mental lines of his characters because to do so
   would tempt readers to identify with one side or the other, thus
   losing sight of the moral issues involved.

*   Jackson, Bernard S. "Practical Wisdom and Literary Artifice
        in the Covenant Code."

   See #250.

325.   Kleven, Terence. "Hebrew Style in 2 Samuel 6." *JETS* 35
        (1992), 299–314.

   "... [T]he study of Hebrew style heightens our awareness of the
   subtleties of the Hebrew language that have all too often been at-
   tributed to carelessness in manuscript transmission," among other
   causes. The stylistic characteristics of *2 Samuel* are "deliberate uses
   of language" to develop a forceful narrative about a complex
   David.

326. Kleven, Terence. "Reading Hebrew Poetry: David's Lament Over Saul and Jonathan (2 Samuel 1:17–27)." *PEGL* 11 (1991), 51–65.

Reading of this passage "must attend to the full force of all its stylistic characteristics." Failure to do so has weakened recent literary studies of the lament, either by giving one stylistic aspect priority over all others, or by basing needless emendations on these partial analyses. Only all its stylistic elements together make it poetry.

327. Linafelt, Tod. "Taking Women in Samuel: Readers/Responses/Responsibility," in #83, pp. 99–113.

The theme of taking women as a sign of male power, and how its having been ignored by the dominant readings of 2 *Samuel* 12 helps us "unmask the androcentric ideological investment of contemporary biblical discourse." An "ironic counter-reading" of 2 *Samuel* 8 as an "intertext" of 2 *Samuel* 12. The narrator shows that even YHWH is "not immune to the seductions of politics."

328. McEvenue, Sean. "The Basis of Empire: A Study of the Succession Narrative," in *Interpretation and Bible. Essays on Truth in Literature* (Collegeville: Liturgical P, 1994), pp. 142–157.

"The author of this narrative chose to write about the succession ... mostly because he or she had searched for and discovered a traditional faith ... in the experience of ambiguous human interaction. The reader who seeks 'objective' historical data, or who admires literary skill will find much to praise in this text."

329. Polzin, Robert. "Curses and Kings: A Reading of 2 Samuel 15–16," in #82, pp. 201–226.

The important but brief exposition in 15:1–6 introducing Absalom, and its effective paronomasia. Signals of literary composition within 2 *Samuel* 9–20 that "highlight a central aspect of the story," including of language. Thematic emphasis of chapters 15–19 on being with the king or not. Context of 2 *Samuel* 16 in its preceding chapters, and its "complex interaction of two related themes concerning the house of David," related to curses invoked upon the ruling house.

330. Polzin, Robert. *David and the Deuteronomist: A Literary Study of the Deuteronomic History. Part Three: 2 Samuel.* Bloomington and Indianapolis (Indiana UP), 1993.

The "philosophy of language and the love of literature that are associated with Mikhail Bakhtin [as] ... the major contemporary inspiration for my retelling of an ancient classic." Extension of the author's method (found in Minor I, #679 and #806) of detailed chapter-by-chapter analysis of characterization, narrative voice structure, and ideology in *II Samuel*.

331.   Pyper, Hugh S. "The Enticement to Re-Read: Repetition as Parody in 2 Samuel." *BI* 1 (1993), 153–166.

Pairs (or even series) of stories "in which the later versions can be interpreted as comic or satirical recapitulations of the story as first read which serve to undermine its sobriety." An example is *2 Samuel* 12 and *2 Samuel* 14—the latter being a deliberate bathetic parody of the former. When we notice similar strategies in ancient Greek novels, we discover that this results in the reader throwing into question the categories of reading strategies we apply to the text.

332.   Schwartz, Regina M. "Nations and Nationalism: Adultery in the House of David." *Critical Inquiry* 19 (1992), 131–150.

The problems caused by the tendency of biblical studies and political assumptions to merge in some peoples' minds in some prominent ideologies. The Bible as the site of of struggles over identity and power—especially the conflict over David's adultery: the preoccupation of the narrative with both sexual and divine fidelity. What we might learn about present-day Israel's claim to autonomy over Palestine from this.

333.   Tilborg, Sjef Van. "Metaphorical versus Visionary Language." *Neotestamentica* 28, #3 (1994), 77–91.

The nature of metaphorical language, and its complexity. The interaction theory of metaphor applied to *2 Samuel* 12 and *Revelation* 17; the semiotics of these parables.

334.   Willey, Patricia K. "The Importunate Woman of Tekoa and How She Got Her Way," in #83, pp. 115–131.

The "mirror halves" of one sequence of events in *2 Samuel* 11–14: David violates Bathsheba and arranges the murder of Uriah; Amnon rapes his half-sister Tamar and is in turn killed by her brother Absalom. Yet despite these parallels and numerous others, the latter story "gain[s] much of its effect from its clever parody of the contours of the previous story." Readers over the centuries, then, have been "convicted and convinced by Nathan, but coerced and confused by Joab."

See also #79, 110, 115, 116, 135, 137, 250, 295, 301, 361.

KINGS

335. Bellis, Alice Ogden. "The Women of 1 and 2 Kings," in #64, pp. 164–176.

"The books of Kings contain many more strong women than the books of Samuel." Analyses of examples including Jezebel, the Queen of Sheba, Athaliah, Huldah, and the women associated with Elijah and Elisha. Other, more circumscribed women include Ahishag, Bathsheba and various wives, concubines, and harlots around Solomon. *Kings* probably misleads us into thinking that there was less female victimization during this period.

* Brenner, Athalya. *A Feminist Companion to Samuel and Kings.*

See #296.

336. Hagan, G. Michael. "First and Second Kings," in #20, pp. 182–192.

Storytelling is the writer's vehicle in Kings to recount the history of Israel from Solomon to the fall of the two kingdoms. The interplay of chronological and narrative time; character portrayal, plot, storytelling techniques. Sample analysis of *I Kings* 13.

337. Reinhartz, Adele. "Anonymous Women and the Collapse of the Monarchy: A Study in Narrative Technique," in #296, pp. 43–65.

The narrator's "penchant for comparing and contrasting his characters: anonymous female characters as "narrative antonyms of the major [male] players.'" Three categories of such characters: consorts of Solomon, women pressing a king for judgment, and women petitioning a prophet on behalf of an ill or starving son. Results of this anonymity for a literary understanding of the text.

1 Kings

338.   Brettler, Marc. "The Structure of 1 Kings 1–11." *JSOT* 49 (1991), 87–97.

> Although traditionally the Solomon material has been divided into two parts (*I Kings* 1–10 and *I Kings* 11), they are really one narrative. The structural clues are found in the use of formal markers dividing it into three sections.

339.   Bruns, Gerald L. "The Hermeneutics of Midrash," in *Hermeneutics Ancient and Modern* (New Haven and London: Yale UP, 1992), pp. 104–123.

> Revised version of essay analyzed as Minor I, #864.

340.   Burns, John Barclay. "Solomon's Egyptian Horses and Exotic Wives." *Forum* 7 (1991), 29–44.

> The relevance and importance of intertextuality for biblical study, especially in rhetoric, reader-response, and structuralist criticism. Application of its principles to these two parallel passages about Solomon, and to related treatments of horse chariots in other HB books, shows the accuracy of its Egyptian reference. These, and the texts on Solomon's foreign wives reveal "a narrative world of texts edited, reinterpreted, and transformed by various authors," who disagree among themselves about the relative wisdom and merit of Solomon's actions.

341.   Dwyer, Timothy. "Prominent Women, Widows, and Prophets: A Case for Midrashic Intertextuality." *EL* 20 (1993), 23–30.

> The interrelatedness of three texts regarding widows and prophets (*1 Kings* 17, *2 Kings* 4, and *Mark* 5) "says much about the functioning of biblical intertextuality." All these texts struggle for preeminence among themselves. This may be a more complete way of reading the Bible than those more conventional literary readings which stress unity above all else. To read the Bible as midrashically intertextual can be one way in which the frictions are allowed to stand and play together."

342.   Fontaine, Carol R. "A Response to 'The Bearing of Wisdom,'" in #296, pp. 161–167.

How we become the products of traditions of academic timidity, and how the juxtaposition of the two texts "offers once again a telling insight into the ways that patriarchal ideology cracks and breaks open under the weight of its own assumptions."

343. Frisch, Amos. "Structure and Its Significance: The Narrative of Solomon's Reign (I Kings 1–12, 24)." *JSOT* 51 (1991), 3–14.

Literary-theological considerations lead us to conclude that the scope of this narrative "consists of nine units arranged in a concentric structure, at the centre of which stands the description of the temple (6.1–9.9). This structure ... also suggests criticism of Solomon after the focal unit.... [T]he contrast between the last units and their parallels gives weight to the concept reward and punishment...." Response by Kim Ian Parker pp. 15–21, and Frisch, 22–24.

344. Garsiel, Moshe. "Puns Upon Names as a Literary Device in 1 Kings 1–2." *Biblica* 72 (1991), 379–386.

Puns upon names are especially important. "By creating a correlation between names and plot materials, the biblical author evokes an atmosphere of order and coherence which occasions a sense of predestination" in the narrative.

345. Hamilton, Jeffries M. "Caught in the Nets of Prophecy? The Death of King Ahab and The Character of God." *CBQ* 56 (1994), 649–663.

Reflection on God as a character in the Ahab story leads us to several conclusions: that the story of Ahab is a tragedy in the classical sense; that God's ability to foresee, control, and will what happens is limited; and that the mechanics of the narrative "are in large degree functions of theology done as narrative rather than as abstract argumentation."

346. Holt, Else K. "'... Urged by his Wife Jezebel'—A Literary Reading of 1 Kings 18 in Context." *SJOT* 9 (1995), 83–95.

The leitmotif of the hunt for the person who is responsible for the drought and for the more comprehensive corruption of the Yahwist faith. Using René Girard's notion of the scapegoat, at first it appears that the Baal priests are the guilty ones: However, a closer look shows the priests to be the scapegoats for Jezebel. Simultaneously, the king appears less guilty than is usually thought.

347.   Lasine, Stuart. "Reading Jereboams's Intentions: Intertextu-
        ality, Rhetoric, and History in 1 Kings 12," in #83, pp.
        133–152.

        How diachronic studies of *I Kings* 12 and Jeroboams's intentions
        usually result in a distorted picture of author and original audi-
        ence, and how a synchronic analysis contributes to a more precise
        grasp of the ancient Israelite audience and the circumstances of
        composition related to Hezekiah's cult reforms of the late 8th cen-
        tury.

348.   Lasine, Stuart. "The Ups and Downs of Monarchical Justice:
        Solomon and Jehoram in an Intertextual World." *JSOT* 59
        (1993), 27–53.

        Response to Pyper (#351): ways in which intertextuality, narra-
        tive analogy, and inverted world are used by biblical, literary, and
        social critics. How to distinguish between intertextual echoes of
        little import and those which are rhetorical devices designed to
        convey a message. Pyper's "support-subvert" dichotomy does not
        do justice to the subtle intertextuality of these two narratives.

*   McEvenue, Sean. "The Basis of Empire: A Study of the Suc-
        cession Narrative."

        See #328.

349.   Newing, Edward G. "Rhetorical Art of the Deuteronomist:
        Lampooning Solomon in First Kings." *OTE* 7 (1994), 247–
        260.

        The Deuteronomist systematically undermines the traditional,
        positive view of Solomon found in *I Kings* 3–5, using various
        rhetorical devices, e.g., contradiction, repetition and dislocation for
        this purpose. Two voices are to be heard in the narrative: tradi-
        tional and authorial.

350.   Nicol, George G. "The Death of Joab and the Accession of
        Solomon: Some Observations on the Narrative of 1 Kings
        1–2." *SJOT* 7 (1993), 134–151.

        A literary reading of the account of Joab's death suggests that
        David's charges against Joab (used also by Solomon) cannot be
        sustained. He had to die "because having supported the succes-
        sion, his loyalty was not transferable to Solomon."

351.   Pyper, Hugh S. "Judging the Wisdom of Solomon: The Two-Way Effect of Intertextuality." *JSOT* 59 (1993), 25–36.

Response to Lasine (#348): the influence of 2 *Kings* on our reading of *I Kings* 3. We "are led to see that there is more consistency to the ideology of the final form of the books of Kings than Lasine seems to allow.... [T]he text is always aware of ... [containing] the seeds of its own destruction." Thus the two chapters do not contrast so much as show the same ambiguous attitude toward the monarchy.

352.   Smelik, K.A.D. "The Literary Function of 1 Kings 17," in C. Brekelmans and J. Lust, eds., *Pentateuchal and Deuteronomistic Studies* (Leuven: Leuven UP, 1990), pp. 239–243.

The historical unlikelihood, but literary appropriateness at this point in *I Kings*, of the story of the widow of Zarephath. She acts as a "positive counterpart to Queen Jezebel," and her narrative prepares the reader for the Queen's, shows a "double-edged attitude of the Lord towards mankind," and narrows the gap between the beginning of the drought and the ordeal on Mt. Carmel.

353.   Talstra, E. *Solomon's Prayer. Synchrony and Diachrony in the Composition of I Kings 8, 14–61.* Kampen (Kok Pharos), 1993.

An attempt "to throw more light" on the relationship between synchronic and diachronic analyses of biblical texts. The language, literary function, and genesis of the prayer of Solomon in comparison with other texts in the Deuteronomistic History. Surface structure, vocabulary, and roles in the text.

354.   Tarlin, Jan. "Toward a 'Female' Reading of the Elijah Cycle: Ideology and Gender in the Interpretation of 1 Kings 17–19, 21 and 2 Kings 1–2.18," in #296, pp. 208–217.

"... [W]hen a 'male' scholar discovers that he can produce a reading, then the dualistic Western gender system collapses. At that point we can glimpse in the flawed textual mirror of the Elijah cycle forms of subjectivity that humanity has dreamt of ... but which ideological pressures on our scholarly language still deny us the words to name."

355.   Todd, Judith A. "The Pre-Deuteronomistic Elijah Cycle," in Robert B. Coote, ed., *Elijah and Elisha in Socioliterary Perspective* (Atlanta: Scholars P, 1992), pp. 1–35.

Close analysis of the language and structure of the Elijah stories shows that they "form a composition crafted almost entirely on the basis of the Elisha stories that follow." The presumed purposes of this cycle vis à vis the royal house of Omri.

356.   Trible, Phyllis. "Exegesis for Storytellers and Other Strangers." *JBL* 114 (1995), 3–19.

"... [A]uthorial-editorial intentionality and reader response have converged for interpretive compatibility" that we should love Elijah and hate Jezebel. Yet this unrelenting polarity only forces us to take both of them together: "Though we may find the convergence repugnant, we can be sure that we are heirs to it, indeed that we participate in it.... [Therefore, we should] allow storytellers and other strangers a place in the enterprise. Their presence may just upset our cherishing of polarity."

357.   Walsh, Jerome T. "Methods and Meanings: Multiple Studies of I Kings 21." *JBL* 111 (1992), 193–211.

Causes of the variety of different readings of a biblical text produced by synchronic methods, as illustrated by analysis of *I Kings* 21. Stylistic, syntagmatic, and paradigmatic analyses all show a "strongly unified reading," whereas historical-critical analysis generally does not. However, altering the text on historical-critical basis does change the stylistic and structural analyses of it. In addition, different readings result from different levels and aspects of the text which that method actualizes.

See also #104, 112, 113, 115, 121, 328, 336, 458, 939.

2 Kings

358.   Conroy, Charles. "Reflections on the Exegetical Task, Apropos of Recent Studies on 2 Kings 22–23, " in C. Brekelmans and J. Lust, eds., *Pentateuchal and Deuteronomistic Studies* (Leuven: Leuven UP, 1990), pp. 255–268.

We need a two-phased view of the exegetical task, phase one being "final form analysis," and phase two source analysis, roughly analogous with synchronic and diachronic analysis, respectively. Both phases are then taken with equal seriousness by biblical scholars. Brief application to key problems raised by 2 *Kings* 22–23.

359. Dijk-Hemmes, Fokkelien van. "The Great Woman of Shunam and the Man of God: A Dual Interpretation of 2 Kings 4.8–37," in #296, pp. 218–230.

One interpretation illuminates the "strategies with which the patriarchal order attempts to prove itself, and the position women occupy within it: they are victims." The second interpretation is also necessary: "The struggle the woman-in-the-text has to undertake in order to acquire a blessing, ... becomes visible through it." Why one reading does an injustice, while the other does not.

* Dwyer, Timothy. "Prominent Women, Widows, and Prophets: A Case for Midrashic Intertextuality."

See #341.

360. Garcia-Treto, Francisco O. "The Fall of the House: A Carnivalesque Reading of 2 Kings 9 and 10," in #83, pp. 153–171.

A Bakhtinian, carnivalized reading of 2 *Kings* 9 and 10 within the large narrative design of the Deuteronomistic history; an intertextual reading especially of the central motif of "house." The house of Ahab is viewed with repulsion and hostility, yet by "relativizing the past," it says emphatically "that the old world is dead, so that out of its grave the future may be born...."

361. Granowski, Jan Jaynes. "Jehoiachin at the King's Table: A Reading of the Ending of the Second Book of Kings," in #83, pp. 173–188.

The theological and literary facets of the closing lines of *Kings* explored "in order to make sense of the ending they provide." Its pessimism coexists with its optimism, judgment with hope. Jehoiachin's death is not, after all, "the end" of God's people, nor even of the Davidic line. It is an ending "ripe with intertextual possibility," with its motif echoes of 2 *Samuel* 9, *Genesis* 11, and 40–41.

362. Lasine, Stuart. "Manasseh as Villain and Scapegoat," in #82, pp. 163–183.

The schematic, composite-like portrait of Manasseh which invites readers to fill in the blanks by contrasting Manasseh to other rulers. The stereotypical portrait of Manasseh compared to the "nuanced and extensive descriptions" of Jereboam and Ahab. The complex rhetorical problem of for whom the text was designed: probably an audience seeking to escape a morally chaotic situation, and thus an audience in need of both a stereotype and a scapegoat.

363.   Lundbom, Jack R. "Elijah's Chariot Ride." *JJS* 24 (1973), 39–50.

"There is evidence, therefore, that legendary material was cast into deliberate structural forms as it was collected and preserved. If we plot the geographic points ... we can see that the controlling structure is a chiasmus which binds all four legends together." Identifying this structure aids in interpretation. We see that Elijah must have been abducted by the king, and Elisha remembered the disappearing chariot as Elijah going to heaven.

*   Pyper, Hugh S. "Judging the Wisdom of Solomon: The Two-Way Effect of Intertextuality."

See #351.

364.   Shields, Mary E. "Subverting a Man of God, Elevating a Woman: Role and Power Reversals in 2 Kings 4." *JSOT* 58 (1993), 59–69.

This story at first seems a straightforward miracle story designed to enhance Elisha's prestige. However, disjunctions in the story invite us to question this perspective and to see the roles and power of Elisha and the Shunammite woman as reversed. Yet the final word (and in *2 Kings* 8 as well) suggests that the patriarchal perspective, subverting the woman's status and power, returns.

*   Smelik, Klaas A.D. "King Hezekiah Advocates True Prophecy: Remarks on Isaiah xxxvi and xxxvii//II Kings xviii and xix."

See #392.

365.   Smelik, Klaas A.D. "The Portrayal of King Manasseh: A Literary Analysis of II Kings xxi and II Chronicles xxiii." *OS* 28 (1992), 129–189.

The different problems faced by the authors of *2 Kings* and *2 Chronicles*, and how each attempted to solve them, as revealed by literary analysis. They had no real historical interest in King Manasseh, but their writings here are important for literary and theological research into these books.

*   Tarlin, Jan. "Toward a 'Female' Reading of the Elijah Cycle: Ideology and Gender in the Interpretation of 1 Kings 17– 19, 21 and 2 Kings 1–2.18."

    See #354.

See also #94a, 104, 112, 113, 115, 341, 348, 351, 355, 392, 444, 458, 615.

Latter Prophets

366.   Bailey, Randall C. "Prophetic Use of Omen Motifs: A Pre- liminary Study," in K. Lawson Younger, ed., *The Biblical Canon in Comparative Perspective* (Lewiston: Edwin Mellen P, 1991), pp. 195–215.

"... particular genres of speech and actions employed by prophets had counterparts in divination," thus demonstrating "another way they attempted to insure the reception of their mes- sage." They reshaped omen motifs to fit their purposes, illus- trating the cosmopolitan nature of the ancient Near East.

367.   Bellis, Alice Ogden. "The Women of the Prophets," in #64, pp. 67–98.

"The prophetic corpus provides many difficult texts for femi- nists, especially the frequent use of women as representative of sinful Israel. However, ... [one] interpretation of Second and Third Isaiah's use of the barren woman motif provides us with an in- triguing positive reading of some imagery in the prophetic litera- ture, literature that elsewhere often denigrates women."

368.   Chisholm, Robert B. "Wordplay in the Eighth-Century Prophets." *B Sac* 144 (1987), 44–52.

Among its many uses in the prophets, its "most energetically significant uses are to indicate correspondence and contrast (or re- versal)," to emphasize theme, especially "to draw attention to the appropriate ... nature of divine justice."

369. Dobbs-Allsopp, F.W. *Weep, O Daughter of Zion: A Study of the City-Lament Genre in the Hebrew Bible.* Rome (Editrice Pontificio Istituto Biblico), 1993.

Analysis of the genre's conventions, and how they are used or subverted at different times. Different ancient near Eastern traditions contain the same genre: comparisons of Lamentations and Mesopotamian laments; use of the Israelite city-lament in the prophets and Psalms.

370. Houston, Walter. "What Did the Prophets Think They Were Doing? Speech Acts and Prophetic Discourse in the O.T." *BI* 1 (1993), 167–188.

Review of speech act theory, and of R.P. Carroll's application to prophetic books. Judgment prophecy "should be understood as having the illocutionary force of a declaration placing the hearers ... under judgment. The response narrated or expected ... is ... ambiguous as between mourning ... and prayer for mercy, and this is seen to be appropriate to an illocutionary act of that kind." *Isaiah* 55, 3, 30, *Jeremiah* 5, *Amos* 1, *Jonah*, among others.

371. Jemielity, Thomas. *Satire and the Hebrew Prophets.* Louisville (Westminster/John Knox P), 1992.

The connection between prophecy and satire. They are "near of kin because both are preponderantly criticism or judgment." How prophecy and satire share a rhetorical character to expose and humiliate; their tendency to parody; their "rhetoric of credibility"; how Hebrew prophets "Speak of themselves and their mission in roles very similar to those assumed by satirists."

372. Patterson, Richard. "Old Testament Prophecy," in #20, pp. 296–309.

Various theological and literary attempts to define "prophecy." It may perhaps be best thought of as proclamation. Typical unity and structure is through authorial perspective in prophetic books. Typical forms of prophetic speech. The importance of poetry in prophecy. Homily as the best analogy of genre.

373. Peckham, Brian. *History and Prophecy. The Development of Judean Literary Traditions.* New York (Doubleday), 1993.

How and why the writers of the books wrote, their interrelationships, and their part in "an ongoing, developing tradition." This tradition was literate from the beginning, with constant reciprocity between prophecy and history. It made use of many epic, poetic, and narrative genres.

374. le Roux, J.H. "Texts with a Prophetic Perspective," in #81, pp. 130–165.

Development of prophecy in Israel and the ancient Near East. Nature of the prophetic perspective. Various literary and textual forms used by the prophets, especially "annunciation of judgment" and "oracle of salvation."

* Vorster, W.S. "Texts with an Apocalyptic Perspective."

See #604.

See also #72, 78, 369, 604.

ISAIAH

375. Carr, David. "Reaching for Unity in Isaiah." *JSOT* 57 (1993), 61–80.

Evidence which calls into serious question various attempts in recent years to find narrostructural literary unity in Isaiah.

376. Clements, R.E. "The Unity of the Book of Isaiah," in James Luther Mays and Paul J. Achtemeier, eds., *Interpreting the Prophets* (Philadelphia: Fortress P, 1987), pp. 50–61.

"... the overall structure of the book shows signs of editorial planning and ... at some stage in its growth, attempts were made to read and interpret the book as a whole." Rather than assuming its unity results from a late, superficial stage of editing, we should recognize that the overall structure and unity are too complex for that. The thematic connections among the three major units of Isaiah are strong.

377. Darr, Katheryn Pfisterer. *Isaiah's Vision and the Family of God.* Louisville (Westminster/John Knox P), 1994.

A "reader-oriented construal ... that focuses especially upon its recurring female and child tropes and the themes to which they are integral." Isaiah's "rhetoric of rebellion" in the literary contexts of its metaphorical representation of Israel as God's rebellious children; how Isaiah exploited common stereotypes of women, his "female city imagery and his theme of "inability to bring to birth." Isaiah as a complex literary unity.

378. Darr, Katheryn Pfisterer. "Isaiah's Vision and the Rhetoric of Rebellion." *SBLSP* (1994), 847–882.

Reader-response criticism of Isaiah discerns recurring and unfolding themes unavailable to "pericopal" readings. The development of the "rhetoric of rebellion" theme, already introduced in Isaiah I "contributes significantly" to its coherence as a literary work through "rebellious child imagery as a shaper of the book's rhetorical power."

379. Darr, Katheryn Pfisterer. "Two Unifying Female Images in Book of Isaiah," in Lewis M. Hopfe, ed., *Uncovering Ancient Stones: Essays in Memory of H. Neil Richardson* (Winona Lake: Eisenbrauns, 1994), pp. 17–30.

Concern for the fate of Jerusalem, and its personification as a woman "accounts in significant measure for the plethora of female images throughout the book." Two deserve special attention: the woman in travail and the inability to bring to birth (and miraculous reversal).

380. Eidevall, Göran. "Lions and Birds as Literature. Some Notes on Isaiah 31 and Hosea 11." *SJOT* 7 (1993), 78–87.

Intertextual connections between *Isaiah* 31 and *Hosea* 11. Similarities of genre and style.

381. Gentrup, William F. "Isaiah," in #20, pp. 310–323.

Various ways in which Isaiah has been seen as having a unifying strategy." Its literary genre most closely resembles that of the sermon. Its unity, despite diverse parts, derives from a pattern of warning and promise, a progression of "intertwining of judgments and blessings." The "hinge" function of certain chapters. Themes, functions of the narrator, and poetic features.

382. Miscall, Peter D. "Isaiah: New Heavens, New Earth, New Book," in #83, pp. 41–56.

"Isaiah's allusive, transumptive style sets in motion a series reaching back into ANE myths, Genesis and Exodus—a series that Isaiah seeks to close by precluding further figuration. This is a new book and a new vision of the new heavens and the new earth which the LORD is the things of the past ... are to be forgotten. Read Isaiah and not these other books!"

383. O'Connell, Robert H. *Concentricity and Continuity. The Literary Structure of Isaiah.* Sheffield (Sheffield Academic P), 1994.

Isaiah "comprises seven asymmetrically concentric sections, each of which presents a complex frameworking pattern of repetition among its subunits, and ... the rhetoric of the book is closest to that of the prophetic covenant disputation genre." How this structure serves the interests of rhetorical development in the book. The likely single authorship of the book.

384. Paul, Shalom M. "Polysensuous Polyvalency in Poetic Parallelism," in Michael Fishbane and Emanuel Tov, eds., *'Sha'arei Talmon': Studies in the Bible, Qumran, and the Ancient Near East Presented to Shemaryahu Talmon* (Winona Lake: Eisenbrauns, 1992), pp. 147–163.

Examples of polysensuous double entendre from *Song of Songs* 2, *Genesis* 49, *Isaiah* 7, 9, 49, 19, 27, 52, 57, 60, *Jeremiah* 9, *Hosea* 2, *Amos* 1, *Nahum* 3, *Zephaniah* 3, *Lamentations* 1, and *Job* 9. Definitions of "polyvalency" and "polysensuous."

385. Rendtorff, Rolf. "The Book of Isaiah: A Complex Unity. Synchronic and Diachronic Reading." *SBLSP* (1991), 8–20.

How the two types of reading differ, yet have in recent years led to remarkable and promising common progress in understanding the Book of *Isaiah*.

* Witt, Douglas A. "The Houses Plundered, The Women Raped: The Use of Isaiah 13 in Zechariah 14:1–11."

See #461.

386. Worgul, John E. "The Quatrain in Isianic Poetry." *GTJ* 11 (1990), 187–204.

Isaiah integrates couplets into quatrains by "sophisticated interplay on the grammatical, semantic, and rhetorical levels." How Isaiah used these poetic devices to express theological meaning in ways that prose could not.

See also #105, 147, 164.

Isaiah 1–39

387. Anderson, Bernhard W. "The Slaying of the Fleeting, Twist-
      ing Serpent: Isaiah 27:1 in Context," in Lewis M. Hopfe,
      ed., *Uncovering Ancient Stones: Essays in Memory of H. Neil
      Richardson* (Winona Lake: Eisenbrauns, 1994), pp. 3–15.

      Study of this verse using history of religions, form—critical
      analysis, stylistic/rhetorical criticism, placement within structure
      of chapters 24–27, and function in the entire book of Isaiah. Liter-
      ary pattern of the "Isaiah Apocalypse."

388. Finley, Thomas J., and George Payton. "A Discourse Analy-
      sis of Isaiah 7–12." *JTT* 6 (1993), 317–335.

      Various markers of prominence within the discourse of these
      chapters help to uncover its structure. Rather than rambling, it is
      carefully structured with a unified theme. The speeches (proce-
      dural, hortatory, or predictive) are the principal factors, the story
      line the basic content, with historical events only as background.

389. Gitay, Yehoshua. *Isaiah and His Audience. The Structure and
      Meaning of Isaiah 1–12*. Assen and Maastricht (Van Gor-
      cum), 1991.

      The form and content of the prophetic utterances of chapters 1–
      12. Isaiah in these thirteen speeches "reveals himself as a profound
      thinker," arming himself with a number of rhetorical devices be-
      cause of the hostility of his audience. These complex utterances re-
      veal different styles in a "profound intellectual and literary en-
      deavor." They are arranged in the book in a thematic order.

*   Irwin, William H. "Conflicting Parallelism in Job 5,13; Isa
      30,28; Isa 32,7."

      See #533.

390. Landy, Francis. "Tracing the Voice of the Other: Isaiah 28
      and the Covenant with Death," in #82, pp. 140–162.

      Poetry as "antagonist of death" in any culture. The poet speaks
      for a radical otherness. So Isaiah "is a movement between that
      other voice and his own, inscribing the trace of the ... 'wind/
      spirit' on the other side of disaster." There are two paradigms in
      chapter 28: one "is composed of the chain: drunkenness-excre-

ment-nonsense-death.... [T]he other paradigm is that of the new age and its new language, of which the primary symbol in Isaiah is children."

391. Roberts, J.J.M. "Double Entendre in First Isaiah." *CBQ* 54 (1992), 39–48.

The presence of many double entendres in *Isaiah* 1–40 should caution us against moving too quickly to resolve exegetical ambiguities. Some of these ambiguities enhance the power of the message in which they appear.

392. Smelik, Klaas A.D. "King Hezekiah Advocates True Prophecy: Remarks on Isaiah xxxvi and xxxvii//II Kings xviii and xix." *OS* 28 (1992), 93–128.

Literary analysis of *Isaiah* 36–37 shows that they belong as an integral part of that book, rather than belonging in *2 Kings*. These chapters are "another instance of the literary technique ... [of] retrojection of contemporary problems into the past."

See also #94a, 370, 384, 416, 461.

Isaiah 40–55

393. Ceresko, Anthony R. "The Rhetorical Strategy of the Fourth Servant Song (Isaiah 52:13–53:12): Poetry and the Exodus-New Exodus." *CBQ* 56 (1994), 42–55.

The poetry, concentric structure, and subtle evocation of the theme of the exodus, and rhetorical strategy of the Fourth Servant Song. How the poem skillfully elicits the sympathy of the reader, and taps into "anti-imperialist sentiments implicit in those exodus traditions."

395. Dion, Paul E. "The Structure of Isaiah 42.10–17 as Approached through Versification and Distribution of Poetic Devices." *JSOT* 49 (1991), 113–124.

Fresh analysis of its structure, "based on a colometric arrangement of the text and a charting of its poetic and 'rhetorical' features adapted from M. O'Connor's system.... [M]ethodological priority is given to devices bonding small braces of verse. A loose envelope structure ... emerges...."

396.   Franke, Chris. *Isaiah 46, 47, and 48: A New Literary-Critical Reading*. Winona Lake (Eisenbrauns), 1994.

The importance of the poem in Isaiah 47 to a study of the entire book. The "devices, techniques, and patterns [that] ... make it a superb literary piece ... [and the] structuring elements [which] ... demonstrate that it is a unity.... Comparison of the rhetorical devices, structure, theme and content of chapters 46 and 48. How the poetry of deutero-Isaiah is related to other biblical Hebrew poetry.

397.   Johnston, Ann. "A Prophetic Vision of an Alternative Community: A Reading of Isaiah 40–55," in Lewis M. Hopfe, ed., *Uncovering Ancient Stones: Essays in Memory of H. Neil Richardson* (Winona Lake: Eisenbrauns, 1994), pp. 31–40.

The chiastic structure of second Isaiah. Its core image is contained in 44:21–45:19—Yahweh forms Israel again as the only living, creating, redeeming God. "The successive inclusios contrast and compare ... the work of this God.... This holistic way of rhetorical patterning heightens and deepens the central thought."

398.   Merrill, Eugene H. "Survey of a Century of Studies on Isaiah 40–55" and "Literary Genres in Isaiah 40–55." *B Sac* 144 (1987), 24–43 and 144–156.

Survey of 100 years of form and rhetorical criticism of deutero Isaiah, and the conclusions of contemporary scholarship. The power of literary criticism of the Bible if used properly.

399.   Motyer, Alec. "Three in One or One in Three: A Dipstick into the Isianic Literature." *Churchman* 108 (1994), 22–36.

The stylistic argument for three different authors of the book of *Isaiah* is weak. Rather we should note the incomparable and powerful command of language in *Isaiah* versus the "pedestrian" Hebrew of *Jeremiah* or the "fidgety" style of *Ezekiel*. The common themes of all parts of the book.

400.   Payne, D.F. "Characteristic Word-Play in 'Second Isaiah': A Reappraisal." *JSS* 12 (1967), 207–229.

C.C. Torrey's interpretation of Second Isaiah (published 1928) exaggerated the amount of word play present in those chapters, and has been influential on questions of unified authorship as well. In fact, Torrey's examples failed to relate this phenomenon to widespread repetition in Isaiah and throughout HBP. While occasional paronomasia occurs, it is not as frequent nor as significant as had been thought.

401. Walsh, Jerome T. "Summons to Judgement: A Close Reading of Isaiah XLI 1–20." *VT* 43 (1993), 351–371.

Examination of the poetic style and organization of *Isaiah* 41:1–20 shows "that it is indeed a cohesive unit, marked by internal symmetry and completeness." The whole poem is arranged concentrically.

See also #238, 370, 384, 604.

JEREMIAH

402. Bozak, Barbara. *Life "Anew": A Literary-Theological Study of Jeremiah 30–31*. Rome (Editrice Pontificio Istituto Biblico), 1991.

Poetic analysis of *Jeremiah* 30–31 in terms of diction, parody, syntax, and imagery. Ideas of suffering and punishment are as important as the theme of salvation. Analysis of the use of feminine imagery shows it to be a portrayal of Israel, in order to reflect realities of Babylonian society, and to function as an archetype.

403. Carroll, R.P. "Inscribing the Covenant: Writing and the Written in Jeremiah," in A. Graeme Auld, ed., *Understanding Poets and Prophets: Essays in Honour of George Wishart Anderson* (Sheffield: JSOT P, 1993), pp. 61–76.

The ambiguity of various statements about writing in *Jeremiah*— especially 8:8–9. On balance, these verses seem to "call into question any writing that claims to represent YHWH's torah." It is a "statement on behalf of the living voice ... over against the written as false."

404. Carroll, Robert P. "Intertextuality and the Book of Jeremiah: Animadversions on Text and Theory," in #82, pp. 55–78.

The persuasiveness and inevitability of intertextuality in the HB in general, and *Jeremiah* specifically. The fact that *Jeremiah* 52 is also *2 Kings* 25 draws our attention to the fact that *Jeremiah* "is a book in dialogue with the [Deuteronomistic] History and also dependent on it," since the "language, discourse analysis, topic, and other concerns of the Deuteronomistic writers are also to be found in Jeremiah." Since much of *Jeremiah* is pieced together, its own text is also intertextual. Reflections of other of the latter prophets in *Jeremiah*, as well as of Psalms.

405.   Clendenen, E. Roy. "Discourse Strategies in Jeremiah 10:1–16." *JBL* 106 (1987), 401–408.

Whether the chapter has a reasonable structure, and its relationship to the rest of the book, have long baffled commentators. The importance of thematic contrast based on strophic structure, chiasmus, and code-switching in grasping the discourse structure of the chapter.

*   Cloete, W.T.W. "The Colometry of Hebrew Verse."

See #152.

406.   Dorn, Louis. "The Unexpected as a Speech Device: Shifts of Thematic Expectancy in Jeremiah." *BTr* 37 (1986), 216–222.

J's use of figures and expression for a theme and for its reverse. The latter is undoubtedly a way of creating shock and surprise, and readers and translators should thus be alert to this technique.

407.   Gitay, Yehoshua. "Rhetorical Criticism and the Prophetic Discourse," in #629, pp. 13–24.

The "drought poem" (*Jeremiah* 14:2–15:9) analyzed through rhetorical criticism: what is the nature of the poem? its style? its structure? Rhetorically, it is one unit designed to reach an audience.

408.   Heyns, Dalene. "History and Narrative in Jeremiah 32." *OTE* 7 (1994), 261–276.

"Biblical history is presented to us in the complex form of historical narrative in which writers created meaning by imaginatively reconstructing the past according to their understanding of present situations. The historical reality recorded does therefore not correspond to history in the modern, rationalized sense of the word, but is intimately related to the narrative meaning." Application of this thesis to *Jeremiah* 32.

409.   House, Paul R. "Plot, Prophecy and Jeremiah." *JETS* 36 (1993), 297–306.

Jeremiah is an "innovative prophecy that strikes out in new literary directions. It uses characterization extensively, and welds together two seemingly irreconcilable ideas in its conclusion.... Its artistry escapes interpreters who only examine its rich historical background.... Once understood, however, its unified plot exhibits great artistry, great vision and great beauty."

410. Jackson, Jared J. "Jeremiah 46: Two Oracles on Egypt." *HBT* 15 (1993), 136–145.

This chapter contains two "oracles against the nations": vv 3–12, and 14–24. "Taunt songs, mocking, irony and satire seem to be the principal tools of the OANs. In these cases, they form a matching pair, showing the prophet's skill as both theologian and poet."

411. Lundbom, Jack R. "Jeremiah and the Break-Away from Authority Preaching." *SEA* 56 (1991), 7–28.

Rhetorical analysis of the "assertive mode" in *Jeremiah*, and the transition (visible in that book) to a more dialogic rhetoric where prophet and audience pursue the discovery of earthly truth together.

412. Lundbom, Jack R. "Rhetorical Structures in Jeremiah 1." *ZAW* 103 (1991), 193–210.

"... [I]f Jeremiah I is to be understood properly ... the macro-structures in chapter 1 must be recognized as being rhetorical in nature.... Simple but nevertheless effective techniques of Hebrew rhetoric lie embedded in the text, their function being to enhance the reception of the text before its ancient audience."

413. Miller, Patrick D., Jr. "Trouble and Woe: Interpreting the Biblical Laments." *Interpretation* 37 (1983), 32–45.

One of the most important hermeneutical clues to interpreting the Psalms is that "the language ... is open and metaphorical." How the laments in Psalms and Jeremiah resonate "between lament and human story ... [thus] opening up...examples of the human plight that may be articulated through the richly figurative but stereotypical language...."

414. Shields, Mary E. "Circumcision of the Prostitute: Gender, Sexuality, and the Call to Repentance in Jeremiah 3:1–44." *BI* 3 (1995), 61–74.

Various shifts in and from male and female imagery in 3, and their meaning. Shifts in mode of address from feminine to masculine are equally important, being used "rhetorically to pressure the audience into identifying with one or the other." How these shifts in imagery and address construct gender and sexuality in the chapter, and how these in turn construct the call to repentance.

415.   Westhuizen, J.P. van der. "A Stylistic-Exegetical Analysis of Jeremiah 46:1–12." *JBQ* 20 (1991–92), 84–95.

Exploration of poetic devices in Jeremiah 46 including histories, synonymous parallelism, rhythm, assonance, simile, hendiadys, meter, alliteration. These devices elucidate the structure of the passage, showing that verses 9, 10, and 12 help explain verses 3–6 to emphasize satire and irony, while verses 7 and 8 form a link between the sections.

416.   Zipor, Moshe A. "'Scenes from a Marriage'—According to *Jeremiah*." *JSOT* 65 (1995), 83–91.

Peculiar marriages occur not only in Hosea, but in Numbers 12, Isaiah 8, and Jeremiah 2–3. The "seemingly sporadic metaphors" of the vine and the washing of blood are actually connected. In Jeremiah "we have ... a metaphor within a metaphor: the prophet is speaking of the unfaithful with metaphors ... and appears to forget that the hated-beloved woman, with whom he is settling accounts, does not really exist and is only a metaphor."

See also #77, 104, 149, 152, 367, 370, 384, 399, 419, 458.

EZEKIEL

417.   Boadt, Lawrence, C.S.P. *Ezekiel's Oracles Against Egypt. A Literary and Philological Study of Ezekiel 29–32*. Rome (Biblical Institute P), 1980.

Form, stylistic, and structural criticism of the "Oracle Against Nations" in *Ezekiel* reveals its basic theological structure in the "Recognition Formula," its use of mythic imagery, the "frequent close literary or semantic parallels ... between Ezekiel's oracles and ... comparative material from neighboring cultures," as well as with other biblical prophets. The importance of climax structure, repetition and chiasmus in the rhetoric of these chapters.

418. Bodi, Daniel. *The Book of Ezekiel and the Poem Erra.* Göttingen (Vandenhoeck and Ruprecht); Freiburg (Universitäts-verlag), 1991.

Ezekiel's extensive use of the Babylonian "Poem of Erra," as well as other ancient near eastern literary works. His was a "creative adaptation of individual motifs, expressions or themes to a new end"—a "literary metamorphosis" of pagan materials.

419. Brisman, Leslie. "Satanic Verses of the Bible: Swallowing Ezekiel's Loathsome Word." *EL* 20 (1993), 3–15.

Passages in *Ezekiel* as examples of a need throughout the book to "occlude God's benevolence by insisting on His omnipotence and omnipresence," where God works for evil ends behind the scenes. Ezekiel seems "to broker [this kind of scene] with greatest assiduity." Ezekiel may be, e.g., in chapter 20, deliberately mis-reading Jeremiah through a kind of anxiety of influence.

420. Bruns, Gerald L. "Canon and Power in the Hebrew Bible," in *Hermeneutics Ancient and Modern* (New Haven and London: Yale UP, 1992), pp. 64–82.

Revised version of essay listed in Minor I as #970.

421. Van Dijk-Hemmes, Fokkelien. "The Metaphorization of Woman in Prophetic Speech: An Analysis of Ezekiel xxiii." *VT* 43 (1993), 162–170; rpt #77, pp. 168–176.

Metaphorical language in Ezekiel 23 requires, or at least entices, its readers (ancient and modern), to participate in construction of both a humiliating and violent speech act, but it distorts female sexual experience even more because, while it allows males an es-cape, it doesn't allow females any.

422. Newsom, Carol A. "A Maker of Metaphors: Ezekiel's Ora-cles Against Tyre," in James Luther Mays and Paul J. Achtemeier, eds., *Interpreting the Prophets* (Philadelphia: Fortress P, 1987), pp. 188–199.

How metaphor works, and its importance as an exegetical tool for the biblical critic. How Ezekiel both "creates and criticizes metaphors that purport to give insight into the relationship [between human power and divine sovereignty]."

423. Polk, Timothy. "Paradigms, Parables, and *Mesalim*: On Reading the *Masal* in Scripture." *CBQ* 45 (1983), 564–583.

The comparisons inherent in the *Masal* in *Ezekiel*, as elsewhere in the HB, "must have been thought to model a reality always capable of impinging upon a particular readership." That readership was necessarily a religious one.

THE TWELVE

423a.   Coggins, R.J. "The Minor Prophets—One Book or Twelve?," in #17, pp. 57–68.

"... the redactional process did bring about a unified Book of Twelve, something which produced a coherent whole, something which deserves attention in its own right as well as being divided into its component parts...."

424.   Nogalski, James. *Literary Precursors to the Book of the Twelve. (BZAW 217).* Berlin and New York (Walter de Gruyter), 1993.

"... a long neglected catchword phenomenon opens significant avenues of interpretation which illuminate the growth, unity, and intentions of the Book of the Twelve." In addition, "the editorial activity in these writings exhibits intertextuality with other prophetic writings," especially *Isaiah*. Concentration on *Hosea, Amos, Micah, Zephaniah, Haggai,* and *Zechariah* 1–8 because these six were likely part of a multivolume corpus predating The Twelve.

See also #77, 97, 104, 367, 399, 706.

Hosea

425.   Botha, P.J. "The Communicative Function of Comparison in Hosea." *OTE* 6 (1993), 57–71.

How meaning is expressed or augmented through analogy, simile, and metaphor in Hosea. The importance of semantic tension, connotation, association and culture in these comparisons. Some images in Hosea were speech acts used to inform, express attitude, elicit emotions, or argue, etc.

*   Eidevall, Göran. "Lions and Birds as Literature. Some Notes
         on Isaiah 31 and Hosea 11."

         See #380.

426.   England, Archie W. "Hosea, A Prophet with Style: Rhetoric
         and the Prophetic Message." *Mid-America Theological Jour-
         nal* 17 (1993), 51–61.

         Rhetorical and structural elements at the micro and macro levels
         in *Hosea* enable it to "flow flawlessly like a film." Its rhetoric and
         style "rivals that of even the Greco-Roman rhetorical classics."

427.   Krause, Deborah. "A Blessing Cursed: The Prophet's Prayer
         for Barren Womb and Dry Breasts in Hosea 9," in #83, pp.
         191–202.

         Intertextual reading of this chapter can "draw out more fully the
         literary and thematic depth of the text." Hosea's prayer is not a call
         for mercy but for judgment, and its formulation produces several
         ironic reversals. Judgment becomes a central theme, but judgment
         with instruction. Its intertextual relationship with other parts of
         Hosea, and with *Genesis* 49.

428.   Landy, Francis. "In the Wilderness of Speech: Problems of
         Metaphor in Hosea." *BI* 3 (1995), 35–59.

         Metaphor in current theory is more a process than a transfer. Its
         instability, and its tendency to seek to make sense of a fragmented
         world while risking nonsense. Metaphorical language in Hosea "is
         often fractured, baffling, and claims a status verging on madness....
         [I]t seeks mimetically both to depict social and political entropy,
         and to interpret it, thus reconstructing and repairing its world."

See also #94a, 104, 367, 380, 384, 424.

Joel

429.   Marcus, David. "Nonrecurring Doublets in the Book of
         Joel." *CBQ* 56 (1994), 56–67.

         Nonrecurring doublets differ from key words both in number of
         occurrences (only twice) and function (to underscore previously
         mentioned thoughts). The various, subtle ways in which doublets

may occur. They emphasize complementary ideas, illustrate reversals, and link sections through allusion. Further, the presence of
these doublets in all four chapters strengthens the argument for
the unity of the book.

430.   Prinsloo, Willem S. "The Unity of the Book of Joel." *ZAW*
(1992), 66–81.

The unity of *Joel* is based on the interrelationship of the various
pericopes in a step-by-step progression or ascending pattern, with
the final pericope forming the climax of the book.

Amos

431.   Ceresko, Anthony R. "Janus Parallelism in Amos's 'Oracles
the Nations' (Amos 1:3–2:16)." *JBL* 113 (1994), 485–490.

In *Amos* 1–2, we should perhaps read *"šybnw"* as the hiphil of
nsb. This accords with the imagery, and as an example of Janus
parallelism helps us better appreciate the poet's high order artistry
in his "'skillful exploitation of twin meanings.'"

432.   Dorsey, David A. "Literary Architecture and Aural Structuring Technique in Amos." *Biblica* 73 (1992), 305–330.

Despite disruptive features of *Amos*, rhetorical-structural analysis demonstrates its overall unity, the "deliberate and well-con-
ceived structural designing" of the book. Devices include "many
aurally-oriented structuring techniques devised to aid the listening
audience. In fact, even the apparent structural anomalies appear to
serve crucial functions in rhetorically oriented structural patterns."

433.   Freedman, David Noel. "Confrontations in the Book of
Amos." *Princeton Seminary Bulletin*, n.s. 11 (1990), 240–252.

Examination of the structure of *Amos* 7 "to see how the arrangement of the parts affects our understanding and interpretation of the contents." The purpose of the author is "confrontation
between divine reality and human exigency," and he has "taken
great pains to enhance his thesis by the positioning of the story ...
and specifically framing the narrative by the second pair of visions."

434. Garcia-Treto, Francisco O. "A Reader-Response Approach to Prophetic Conflict: The Case of Amos 7.10–17," in #82, pp. 114–124.

Reading *Amos* 7:10–17 from two elements: "expressions of power relations and characterizations of power, and ... the sort of performative intertextuality which ... can be called 'Signifyin(g).'" Thus we find that "Amos needs to revise Amaziah's exclusionary text in order precisely to remain in the power game, to 'clear a space' for himself ..." which in fact he succeeds in doing.

435. House, Paul. "Amos and Literary Criticism." *RE* 92 (1995), 175–187.

"Working definition" of literary criticism; survey of recent literary-critical approaches to *Amos*; brief analysis of its structure, plot, and characterization.

436. Noble, Paul R. "The Literary Structure of Amos: A Thematic Analysis." *JBL* 114 (1995), 209–226.

Previous analyses of the overall structure of *Amos* have given insufficient attention to literary criteria while formal criteria have received greater prominence than they merit. Thematic considerations, especially, can yield better results. The author "saw no need to mark formally ... [the] main divisions" of the "complex and subtle structure of Amos...." Structural parallelism and parallelism and thematic correspondence create the literary pattern of the book.

437. Ryken, Leland. "Amos," in #20, pp. 337–347.

Amos as a satire, and the tradition of informal satirical writing into which the book fits better than does any other one in the Bible. The necessity of knowing its objects of attack, as well as the satiric norm, for readers to grasp its meaning. Satiric structure and satiric imagination in the book, and the author's skill at parody.

See also #71, 104, 370, 384, 424, 458.

Obadiah

438. Bliese, Loren F. "Chiastic and Homogeneous Metrical Struc-
      tures Enhanced by Word Patterns in Obadiah." *JTT* 6
      (1993), 210–227.

      How key words are used within the overall structure of *Obadiah*
      to give it cohesion and emphasis. Repetition of keywords in
      climaxes, use of inclusio and of a looser chiasmic pattern than that
      found in Hosea. The book may be analyzed as six poems which
      present an ABC:C'B'A' thematic inversion. How this pattern fur-
      thers the theme of the book.

Jonah

439. Barré, Michael L. "Jonah 2, 9 and the Structure of Jonah's
      Prayer." *Biblica* 72 (1991), 237–248.

      A key word in *Jonah* 2:9 enables us to understand the overall
      structure of Jonah's prayer. It shows that 2:9 is connected to 2:8,
      leaving 2:10 as an independent stanza. This in turn demonstrates
      that the whole poem has seven stanzas, with the major caesura at
      7d.

440. Beek, M.A. "Saturation Points and Unfinished Lines in the
      Study of Old Testament Literature," in #119, pp. 23–35.
      (Originally published in Dutch in 1968.)

      How the "literary science" of such critics as Alonso Schökel and
      Weiss impacts biblical studies. *Jonah* 2 as example of a text which
      form criticism regards as an intrusion, but which literary criticism
      can show is integral to the story by anticipating the rescue of the
      prophet. Narrative sections lend themselves more easily to literary
      analysis than do legal sections of the Pentateuch.

441. Craig, Kenneth M., Jr. *A Poetics of Jonah. Art in the Service of
      Ideology*. Columbia (U of South Carolina P), 1993.

      All of the multi-faceted art of Jonah is a means to evaluation,
      "potential vehicles of an evaluating or ideological point of view."
      A full working poetics of Jonah will disclose the aesthetic and the
      social dimensions of the book in the service of ideology. Narrator

and characters, Jonah and the reading process, Jonah and poetry, characterization.

442. Crouch, Walter B. "To Question an End, To End a Question: Opening the Closure of the Book of Jonah." *JSOT* 62 (1994), 101–112.

Chapter 4 of *Jonah* re-opens the closure experienced by the reader at the end of chapter three. This is a literary device "used to involve the reader in the ideological conflict that propels the plot." The narrative frame is blurred in the final scene, so as to "focalize on the external world of the reader."

443. Kahn, Paul. "An Analysis of the Book of Jonah." *Judaism* 43 (1994), 87–100.

The value of a literary analysis of the structure of *Jonah* for solving its "enigma." The signal of God's ultimate tolerance of Jonah's position, and its relationship to exiled Israel.

444. McCarthy, Carmel, and William Riley. "The Book of Jonah: A Conflict Of Wills," in #120, pp. 112–139.

Jonah is a satire, now generally recognized as a work of fiction. Jonah as the more usual OT prophet: foretelling good rather than bad for Israel (2 *Kings* 14). Round and flat characterization in the story (including Yahweh as one of the former). Structure of the book, and its theme of suffering as potential for renewal.

* Trible, Phyllis. *Rhetorical Criticism. Context, Method, and the Book of Jonah.*

See #8.

445. Wilt, Timothy Lloyd. "Lexical Repetition in Jonah." *JTT* 5 (1992), 252–264.

Lexical repetition as one of the basic cohesive devices in *Jonah* on the paragraph, section, and text levels. How these repetitions indicate themes of the book.

446. Woodard, Branson L. "Death in Life: The Book of Jonah and Biblical Tragedy." *GTJ* 11 (1990), 3–16.

"Literary analysis of ... Jonah indicates a number of features found in the OT tragedies about Samson and Saul.... Relating Jonah to ancient Hebrew tragedy suggests a broader, more sophisticated expression of the Hebrew tragic vision [than previ-

ously thought].... Jonah is a tragic figure whose spiritual es-
trangement throughout the narrative intensifies his death-in-life."

447.   Woodard, Branson L. "Jonah," in #20, pp. 348–357.

Jonah is unique among the minor prophets for its highly-unified,
compact, and clearly-structured narrative. While many recent
critics label it as satire, it more nearly resembles tragedy. Its characteristics here include a reliable narrator, historical purpose, and
"factual (though imaginatively constructed) plot." It displays several phases of OT tragedy: "dilemma, choice, catastrophe, suffering ... realization of one's error, and death...."

448.   Zimmerman, Frank. "Problems and Solutions in the Book of
       Jonah." *Judaism* 40 (1991), 580–589.

The coherence of the second episode of *Jonah* "can be affirmed
... on literary and psychological grounds."

See also #71, 78, 112, 118, 186, 370.

Micah

449.   Beal, Timothy K. "The System and the Speaking Subject in
       Hebrew Bible: Reading for Divine Abjection." *BI* 2 (1994),
       171–189.

In *Micah* 1:8–9 the speaker is not the prophet, but "YHWH as the
profoundly unstable speaking subject of this objectionable dirge,"
and as such is "rendered entirely ambivalent...." this reading
draws inspiration for Kristeva's "theories of textuality and the
construction of the speaking subject in discourse" while both prob-
lematizing her reading of the divine subject and using it to evolve
a new reading of this text.

450.   Shaw, Charles S. *The Speeches of Micah: A Rhetorical-Historical
       Analysis.* Sheffield (JSOT P), 1993.

Based on the assumption that differences in *Micah* need not
preclude a unified work by one author, and that the prophets
functioned in similar ways to the orators of ancient Greece, we can
explore the rhetorical situations and themes to define six discourses in the book. Each discourse uses a variety of persuasive
methods to address "a unique matrix of events and circum-

stances." The likely historical setting of each discourse covers, all together, about 747–721 BCE.

See also #87, 94a, 104, 424.

Nahum

451. Floyd, Michael H. "The Chimerical Acrostic of Nahum 2:1–10." *JBL* 113 (1994), 421–437.

We should abandon the hypothesis of an alphabetical acrostic in *Nahum* 2:1–10, partly because the evidence for it is doubtful, "but also because the claim that the existence of an acrostic is supposed to support, namely, that Nah 1:2–10 is basically a hymn, is also not viable." If we abandon this idea, then "the interpretation of Nahum can begin to take a potentially more fruitful turn."

452. Patterson, Richard. "A Literary Look at Nahum, Habakkuk, and Zephaniah." *GTJ* 11 (1990), 17–27.

All these prophets "were skilled authors who composed their prophecies with careful design and utilized polished literary techniques to achieve their purposes...." All three display extensive use of synechdoche, metaphor, alliteration, and parallelism, among other literary devices.

453. Sweeney, Marium A. "Concerning the Structure and Generic Character of the Book of Nahum." *ZAW* 104 (1992), 364–377.

The problems with previous theories of the structure and genre of *Nahum*. The book can be shown to have "a coherent structure based on the refutation pattern of the disputation speech."

454. Tsumura, David Toshio. "Janus Parallelism in Nah 1:8." *JBL* 102 (1983), 109–111.

This unusual Hebrew poetic device was first identified in 1978 in *Song of Songs*, and in 1980 was found in *Genesis* 49:26. *Nahum* 1:8 contains a third example, showing both synthetic and synonymous parallelism in a sophisticated poetic artistry.

See also #384.

Habakkuk

*   Patterson, Richard. "A Literary Look at Nahum, Habakkuk, and Zephaniah."
       See #452.

See also #104.

Zephaniah

*   Patterson, Richard. "A Literary Look at Nahum, Habakkuk, and Zephaniah."
       See #452.

See also #384, 424.

Haggai

455.   Christensen, Duane L. "Impulse and Design in the Book of Haggai." *JETS* 35 (1992), 445–456.

       Haggai is constructed of three "cantos," each showing careful and elaborate chiastic structure. Noticing this helps reveal the main themes of the book.

456.   Clark, David J. "Discourse Structure in Haggai." *JTT* 5 (1992), 13–24.

       Many discourse features found in *Zechariah* also occur in *Haggai*. There are a number of "major discourse markers" in both books. A chart of the overall discourse structure of *Haggai* shows no overarching pattern, but does reveal "a certain degree of structural parallelism" between sections 1 and 3, and between 2 and 4.

457.   Clines, David J.A. "Haggai's Temple, Constructed, Deconstructed and Reconstructed." *SJOT* 7 (1993), 51–77.

Various meanings of the word "temple" for Haggai. At points Haggai's "construction" of the temple deconstructs itself in concepts of "honor," "uncleanness," and the oracle to Zerubbabel. A "reconstruction" of Haggai's concept of the temple should focus on the composition and reception of the book. How the book inadvertently reveals its own attempts to suppress social conflicts.

See also #186, 424.

Zechariah

458. Butterworth, Mike. *Structure and the Book of Zechariah.* Sheffield (JSOT P), 1992.

How we should develop a theory of structure for biblical books, and examples from past analyses of the supposed structure of *Psalms* 3, 15, 1, 2, 4, 30, 29, 58; *Isaiah* 60; *Kings*; *Amos* 5; *Jeremiah*; *Exodus* 6. All of these analyses are seriously flawed, as can be illustrated when we "discover" elaborate chiasm even when verses from *Isaiah* 67 are rearranged randomly. These guidelines for proper structural analysis produce what we call rhetorical criticism; its application to larger and smaller structures in *Zechariah*. We conclude that evidence for editorial structuring in chapters 1–8 is very strong, more varied and less precise in chapters 9–14.

*   Clark, David J. "Discourse Structure in Haggai."

See #456.

459. Hartle, James A. "The Literary Unity of Zechariah." *JETS* (1992), 145–157.

Unifying factors of *Zechariah* include grammatical characteristics (particularly unusual expressions), metonymy, and specialized words, but most importantly thematic development. There are four themes: covenant restoration, divine judgment, cleansing, and blessings of God.

460. Kline, Meredith G. "The Structure of the Book of Zechariah." *JETS* 34 (1991), 179–193.

The parts of *Zechariah* are "structurally interlocked ... by means of an intricate triple-hinge mechanism." This curious plan argues the unity of a single author rather than later redaction.

461.   Witt, Douglas A. "The Houses Plundered, The Women
        Raped: The Use of Isaiah 13 in Zechariah 14:1–11." *PEGL*
        11 (1991), 66–74.

        Zechariah recalls Isaiah's oracle against Babylon and applies it in
        a new context: a "negative recasting of the familiar Conflict myth,"
        in which Yahweh as Divine Warrior overcomes the forces
        threatening the faithful." Redactional, socio-historical, and liter-
        ary-critical analysis.

See also #105, 424.

Malachi

462.   Clendenen, E. Roy. "Old Testament Prophecy as Hortatory
        Text: Examples from Malachi." *JTT* 6 (1993), 336–353.

        Robert Longacre's stress on discourse typology provides new
        insights into the hortatory discourse and structure of OT prophetic
        books. Application of this theory to *Malachi* (particularly chapter 1)
        shows it to have a very clear structure and cohesion, and a
        "skillful familiarity" with the "semantic slots of hortatory dis-
        course."

463.   Snyman, S.D. "Antitheses in the Book of Malachi." *JNSL* 16
        (1990), 173–178.

        Antithesis is "a prominent and typical feature throughout the
        book of Malachi." It is marked by the use of several prominent an-
        tithetic word-pairs: love-hate, blessing-curse, and good-evil.

See also #94a, 104.

WRITINGS

464.   Loader, J.A. "Texts with a Wisdom Perspective," in #81, pp.
        108–129.

Definition of the Wisdom perspective. Textual codes in these books, including linguistic (chiastic) organizations, use of numerous figures, parallelism, differences in types of sayings, textual organizations and functions, audience and reception. Argumentation and description as the most frequent modes in Wisdom literature. Similarities and differences between Wisdom poetry and poetry in other sections of the OT.

* Peckham, Brian. *History and Prophecy. The Development of Late Judean Literary Traditions.*

See #373.

465. Shupak, Nili. *Where Can Wisdom Be Found? The Sage's Language in the Bible and in Ancient Egyptian Literature.* Fribourg (Fribourg UP) and Göttingen (Vandenhoeck and Ruprecht), 1993.

Attempt to determine "the presence or absence of contact between the vocabularies of Biblical and Egyptian wisdom literature, and to fix the semantic boundaries of selected Hebrew wisdom terms in comparison with the same genre in Egyptian literature." Biblical material covered includes *Proverbs, Qoheleth, Job,* and some of *Psalms.* Topical chapters on teaching and learning, negative and positive human types, foolishness, consequences of wisdom, parts of the body, and wisdom words.

See also #373.

PSALMS

466. Brueggemann, Walter. *Abiding Astonishment: Psalms, Modernity, and the Making of History.* Louisville (Westminster/ John Knox P), 1991.

The "Psalms of Historical Recital": 78, 105, 106, 136, and the interface in these poems between history and rhetoric. "'What' ... happened turns out to be dependent upon and determined by how the happenedness is shaped in the speech practices of the remembering community.... Both the formation and the continued use of these Psalms ... mediated Israel's remembered past to Israel's present.... Thus 'history' is in every instance a chosen mode of rhetoric."

467.   Cumming, Charles Gordon. *The Assyrian and Hebrew Hymns of Praise*. New York (Columbia UP), 1934.

To understand the Psalms adequately, we must move beyond philology to several other methods: classification of the poems on the basis of similarities; arrangement of these "according to the principle of development from the lower to the higher stages of religious experience"; and comparison of Hebrew psalms with those of other ancient Near Eastern and Asian cultures. The similarities of Assyrian and Hebrew literary cultures, and resulting similarities of their psalms, due to the influence of the former on the latter.

*   Dobbs-Allsopp, F.W. *Weep, O Daughter of Zion. A Study of the City-Lament Genre in the Hebrew Bible*.

See #369.

468.   Ferris, Paul Wayne, Jr. *The Genre of the Communal Lament in the Bible and the Ancient Near East*. Atlanta (Scholars P), 1992.

An attempt "to develop a unified comparative description of the Hebrew communal lament in light of the phenomenon of public lament in neighboring cultures as preserved in their literature." Influence the various laments may have had upon one another. Isolation of thematic elements in the laments. The Hebrew laments were not learned directly from the Babylonians during the exile; rather their "unique flexibility of form and style" shows their relationship to the common Near Eastern culture.

*   Gillingham, S.E. *The Poems and Psalms of the Hebrew Bible*.

See #144.

469.   Hauge, Martin Ravndal. *Between Sheol and Temple: Motif Structure and Function in the I-Psalms*. Sheffield (Sheffield Academic P), 1995.

The tension between the "background of traditional, even stereotypical expositions" and the "highly individual expressions" of the same concepts and motifs in several of the Psalms. The "I" figure in the text as a paradigmatic figure. Separate chapters on Psalms 5, 26, 27, 36, 42–43, 62, 73, 84, and 140.

470.   Hunter, J.H. "The Literary Composition of Theophany Passages in the Hebrew Psalms." *JNSL* 15 (1989), 97–107.

"... theophany texts not only adhered to a fixed formula, but ... in spite of this formula authors of theophany texts were creative in their use of the traditions ... and in fact, were refashioning the traditions to leave behind texts characterized by originality and individuality." Examples primarily from Psalms 50, 144, 97, 68, 18.

471. Levine, Herbert J. *Sing Unto God A New Song. A Contemporary Reading of the Psalms.* Bloomington and Indianapolis (Indiana UP), 1995.

Survey of the history of interpretation of the Psalms, including how the anthropology of ritual "can provide a nondoctrinaire starting point"; setting the Psalms "amid the realia of Temple worship"; application of several approaches to speech act theory and literary discourse theory to the Psalms; sacred time and space in the Psalms. The "central story" of these poems is the conflict between faith and experience, and they were written "in an environment open to profound theological questioning."

472. Levine, Herbert. "The Dialogic Discourse of Psalms," in #16, pp. 145–161.

Quoting another's words, "the concept so central to the discourse theory of Mikhail Bakhtin," is a crucial stylistic trait of the Psalms. Despite Bakhtin's denial of true dialogism to poetry, the Psalms may be said to exhibit what he himself calls "an internally persuasive discourse." Examples from Psalms 81, 95, 82, 10, 73 in detail, with briefer mention of many others.

473. Longman, Tremper III. "Psalms," in #20, pp. 245–255.

There is a long history of literary approach to the Psalms, as compared to other biblical books; they are rightly described as lyric poetry. How generic analysis of the book based on mood and tone. Characteristics of HBP in the Psalms and their intertextuality. Sample analysis of Psalm 131.

474. McCann, J. Clinton, ed. *The Shape and Shaping of the Psalter.* Sheffield (JSOT P), 1993.

Nine essays focusing on the Psalms as a coherent literary whole. Essays by James L. Mays, Roland L. Murphy, Walter Brueggemann, David M. Howard, Jr., and two by Gerald H. Wilson discuss this issue. Further essays by Patrick D. Miller, J. Clinton McCann, and David M. Howard, Jr., on particular sections of the Psalter are analyzed separately as #484, 485, 497.

475.   Mikre-Sellassie, G. Ammanuel. "Metonymy in the Book of
        Psalms." *BTr* 44 (1993), 418–425.

        Extreme care needed when translating to identify and under-
        stand this device, especially in *Psalms*, where so many examples of
        this and other poetic devices occur. Classifies various types, with
        examples.

476.   Miller, Patrick D., Jr. "Current Issues in Psalms Studies."
        WW 5 (1985), 132–143.

        A review of recent work, the issues it raises and addresses, con-
        cerning the function of the Psalms in ancient Israel, reinterpreta-
        tion of the Psalms in terms of intertextual connections, the Psalter
        as a collection, and literary study of the Psalter.

477.   Miller, Patrick D., Jr. *Interpreting the Psalms*. Philadelphia
        (Fortress P), 1986.

        Current issues in interpreting the Psalms, especially those which
        have led critics toward a literary approach. Clues from their his-
        tory and content. Several contemporary literary methods of ana-
        lyzing the Psalms. Interpreting the biblical laments and hymns.
        Detailed analyses of Psalms 1, 2, 14, 22, 23, 82, 90, 127, 130, 139.
        Reprints essay listed in Minor I as #1131.

*   Miller, Patrick D., Jr. "Trouble and Woe: Interpreting the
        Biblical Laments."

        See #413.

478.   Parkander, Dorothy. "'Exalted Mauna': The Psalms as Lit-
        erature." *WW* 5 (1985), 122–131.

        A general appreciation of the literary power of the Psalms, with
        consideration of their influence on English poets.

479.   Seybold, Klaus. *Introducing the Psalms*. Translated by R.
        Graeme Dunphy. Edinburgh (T and T Clark), 1990.

        History of the Psalter; origins of the Psalms; their literary form:
        sound patterns, style, line structure, arrangement, and text struc-
        ture. Purposes, classification by content and type, cosmology, re-
        lationship to oriental psalmody, and subsequent influence.

480.   Smith, Mark S. *Psalms: The Divine Journey*. NY and Mahwah
        (Paulist P), 1987.

Attempt "to recover the psalmists' language, worldview and religious experience. The psalms are "poetic masterpieces which disclose their spiritual insights through images, metaphors, poetic parallelism," etc.

481.   Viviers, Hendrik. "The Coherence of the Ma$^{\hat{a}}$lôt Psalms (PSS 120–134)." *ZAW* 106 (1994), 275–289.

"The (original) literary unity of the Ma$^{\hat{a}}$lôt collection is confirmed by a network of word repetitions, corresponding constructions, similar figures of speech, a main theme of trust in Yahweh and a (non-rigid) chiastic synthesis overall. It was probably derived from post-exilic ... scribal circles (meditation book) in a disconsolated situation."

482.   Wilson, Gerald H. "The Shape of the Book of Psalms." *Interpretation* 46 (1992), 129–142.

Organization techniques in *Psalms* call attention to "a rather complex, purposeful structure ... that gives shape to the whole Psalter." These literary techniques include competing editorial frames and central pivot point, and demonstrate "that the Psalter assumed final form at a time when sages had the upper hand in restructuring the community's perception of ... cultic traditions." Analysis of Psalm 73.

See also #16, 71, 87, 105, 145, 369, 404, 465, 486.

INDIVIDUAL PSALMS

Psalm 1

483.   Botha, P.J. "The Junction of the Two Ways: The Structure and Theology of Psalm 1." *OTE* n.s. 4 (1991), 381–396.

What syntactic, rhetorical, semantic and stichometric analyses tell us about the structure of Psalm 1 differ in certain respects. Semantic analysis should be the preferred method because "the psalm's polar structure seems to be a key factor in its interpretation."

See also #147.

Psalm 1 and 2

484. McCann, J. Clinton, Jr. "Books I–III and the Editorial of the Hebrew Psalter," in #474, pp. 93–107.

Additional evidence can be found to support Gerald Wilson's contention that the purpose of the Psalter was "to address the apparent failure of the Davidic covenant in light of the exile, the diaspora and the oppression of Israel by the nations in the postexilicera." This evidence relates to the shape of Books I, II, and III, and in particular to the Psalms (1, 2, 42–44, and 73–74) which begin each book, and thus serve as thematic links.

485. Miller, Patrick D. "The Beginning of the Psalter," in #474, pp. 83–92.

The introductory functions of Psalms 1 and 2; literary and thematic links between Psalms 1–2 and 3–10. How these psalms (and especially 1 and 2) provide a fitting introduction to Book 1, and to the Psalter as a whole. They tell us how to read the book.

See also #477.

Psalm 3

See #485.

Psalm 4

See #485.

Psalm 5

*   Hauge, Martin Ravndal. *Between Sheol and Temple: Motif Structure and Function in the I-Psalms.*

See #469.

See also #485.

Psalm 6

See #485.

Psalm 7

See #485.

Psalm 8

See #485, 536.

Psalm 9

See #87, 472, 485.

Psalm 10

See #87, 472, 485.

Psalm 13

*   Zevit, Ziony. "Cognitive Theory and the Memorability of
       Biblical Poetry."
       See #167.

Psalm 14

See #477.

Psalm 18

486.   Berry, Donald K. *The Psalms and Their Readers: Interpretive
       Strategies for Psalm 18.* Sheffield (JSOT), 1993.

Four separate analyses of Psalm 18, in order to test the hypothesis that a reader-oriented approach "can offer substantially new and productive insights on the psalm itself and Psalms study in general." These analyses show first textual, then form-critical, rhetorical, and finally speech-act theory and other reader-oriented strategies, "with particular attention to the reader/hearer." The strengths and weaknesses of each of the four methods.

See also #470.

Psalm 19

487.   Magonet, Jonathan. *A Rabbi Reads the Psalms*. London (SCM P), 1994.

A reading, informed by basic literary assumptions, of selected psalms. Chapter on "biblical poetry for beginners." Detailed analyses of Psalms 19, 22, 23, 25, 73, 90, 92, 115, 121, 124, 134, 145, and 146.

Psalm 22

488.   Davis, Ellen F. "Exploding the Limits: Form and Function in Psalm 22." *JSOT* 53 (1992), 93–105.

Rhetorical and form criticism can both be utilized for theological interpretation of Psalm 22. "… attention to the function of poetic language complements and deepens insights to which formal analysis points." The form of Psalm 22 shows an "essential integrity" with a single theme throughout.

See also #791.

Psalm 23

See #477, 791.

Psalm 24

489. Clines, David J.A. "A World Established on Water (Psalm 24): Reader-Response, Deconstruction and Bespoke Interpretation," in #82, pp. 79–90.

Psalm 24 is "riddled with religious ideas as unacceptable as its cosmology, and ... it is not even internally coherent," making it "ideologically and religiously alien today...." The two basic objectionable ideas are that holiness attaches to places, and that victory in war is glorious. Yet it also deconstructs itself in several respects, because "the qualities demanded of the worshippers are deconstructed by the qualities praised in the deity they worship." How a "goal-oriented hermeneutic" can help us deal with such text by reminding us of the fragility of texts and interpretations, as well as of our need to make sense of texts.

490. Mazor, Yair. "Psalm 24: Sense and Sensibility in Biblical Composition." *SJOT* 7 (1993), 303–316.

The seemingly ramshackle structure of this psalm in fact hides a unity of aesthetics and ideology, as revealed by literary analysis. Its "impressive systematic order," as constituted by its layers of theme, structure, rhetoric, ideology, and alliteration.

Psalm 25

491. Freedman, David Noel. "Patterns in Psalms 25 and 34," in Eugene Ulrich, et al., eds., *Priests, Prophets and Scribes: Essays on the Formation and Heritage of Second Temple Judaism in Honour of Joseph Blenkinsopp* (Sheffield: JSOT P, 1992), pp. 125–138.

Certain unusual features that these two psalms have in common suggest a "planned, rather intricate poetic structure" which can hardly be the result of chance. They were even designed to be of equal length.

See also #164.

Psalm 26

*   Hauge, Martin Ravndal. *Between Sheol and Temple: Motif Structure and Function in the I-Psalms.*
     See #469.

Psalm 27

*   Hauge, Martin Ravndal. *Between Sheol and Temple: Motif Structure and Function in the I-Psalms.*
     See #469.

Psalm 29

492. van der Westhuizen, J.P. "A Proposed Reinterpretation of Psalm 29 Based on a Stylistic-Exegetical Analysis." *Journal for Semitics* 5 (1993), 111–122.

      Psalm 29 evidences a number of Canaanite elements which bear resemblance to Ugaritic poetry. It is metrically and structurally well-balanced, showing not only parallelism and various sound devices, but various figures including hendiadys, synecdoche, metonymy, merismus, hyperbole, metaphor and antithesis.

Psalm 31

See #468.

Psalm 34

See #164.

Psalm 35

See #468.

Psalm 36

* Hauge, Martin Ravndal. *Between Sheol and Temple: Motif Structure and Function in the I-Psalms.*

See #469.

Psalm 40

See #1091.

Psalms 42, 43

* Hauge, Martin Ravndal. *Between Sheol and Temple: Motif Structure and Function in the I-Psalms.*

See #469.

See also #468.

Psalm 44

See #97, 468.

Psalm 50

See #470.

Psalm 56

See #468.

Psalm 59

See #468.

Psalm 60

See #468.

Psalm 61

493.   Bellinger, W.H., Jr. "How Shall We Read the Bible? The Case of Psalm 61." *PRS* 20 (1993), 5–17.

Literary criticism teaches us that a text has no one definitive meaning, though it may be full of meaning. This approach liberates the exegete of the Bible. The literary approach illustrates by application to the levels of meaning in Psalm 61.

Psalm 62

*   Hauge, Martin Ravndal. *Between Sheol and Temple: Motif Structure and Function in the I-Psalms.*

See #469.

Psalm 67

494.   Prinsloo, W.S. "Psalm 67: Harvest Thanksgiving Psalm, (Eschatological) Hymn, Communal Prayer, Communal Lament or ...?" *OTE* 7 (1994), 231–246.

Various debates over the verbs, structure, strophic segmentation, and poetic quality of Psalm 67 can be resolved through a "text-immanent" analysis, emphasizing morphology, syntax, style, and semantics. The psalm is revealed by this analysis as a persuasive text.

Psalm 68

See #470.

Psalm 69

See #468, 916.

Psalm 72

495. Jobling, David. "Deconstruction and the Political Analysis of Biblical Texts: A Jamesonian Reading of Psalm 72." *Semeia* 59 (1992), 95–127.

    Three readings of Psalm 72: structural analysis "shows its failure to reconcile mythic inevitability and political cause and effect"; the second reading "shows it to 'demythologize' the royal ideology in the direction of a more realistic politics and economics"; the third reading relates its contradictions to contradictions in the social formation of monarchist Israel.

496. Skehan, Patrick W. "Strophic Structure in Psalm 72 (71)." *Biblica* 40 (1959), 302–308.

    How analyzing the metric structure of Psalm 72 helps us understand its structural pattern, and how all of its seemingly discordant parts fit together.

Psalm 73

*   Hauge, Martin Ravndal. *Between Sheol and Temple: Motif Structure and Function in the I-Psalms.*

    See #469.

See also #472, 482.

Psalm 74

See #468.

Psalm 77

See #468.

Psalm 78

See #466.

Psalm 79

See #468.

Psalm 80

See #468.

Psalm 81

See #472.

Psalm 82

See #472, 477.

Psalm 83

See #468.

Psalm 84

*   Hauge, Martin Ravndal. *Between Sheol and Temple. Motif Structure and Function in the I-Psalms.*
        See #469.

Psalm 85

See #468.

Psalm 89

See #468.

Psalms 90–94

497. Howard, David M., Jr. "A Contextual Reading of Psalms 90–94," in #474, pp. 108–123.

     There are significant lexical links "between every consecutive psalm in Psalms 90–94, and between many non-adjacent psalms as well." A tripartite discussion in Book III manifests itself. Psalms 90–94, 95–100, and 101–106, with the same coherence evident in each of the three groups. Thus the structure of the book seems to be dependent on these groupings.

See also #104, 477, 468.

Psalm 95

498. Riding, Charles Bruce. "Psalm 95: 1–7c as a Large Chiasm." *ZAW* 88 (1976), 418.

     The chiasm especially evident here creates a "natural, poetic and beautiful flow and development of thought," highlighting the theme of Yahweh as savior over that of the theme of Yahweh as creator.

See also #472.

Psalm 97

See #470.

Psalm 102

See #468.

Psalm 103

499. Willis, T.M. "'So Great Is His Steadfast Love': A Rhetorical Analysis of Psalm 103." *Biblica* 72 (1991), 525–537.

     Style, thematic development, structure and themes of Psalm 103 as they relate to its message. Such analysis clarifies the fact that the focus is on the Lord and his mercy and grace. Thus its intent is not merely to provoke others to praise God, but is hortatory, even evangelistic.

Psalm 105

See #466.

Psalm 106

See #466.

Psalm 109

See #468.

Psalm 111

500.   Pardee, Dennis. "Acrostics and Parallelism: The Parallelistic Structure of Psalm 111." *Maarav* 8 (1993), 117–138.

The acrostic structure of Psalm 111 did not permit abandonment of the parallelism typical of West Semitic poetry. "It did, however, provide a framework so clear that semantic parallelism in regular, inner-colonic distribution could be practically discarded." Other types of parallelism—namely distant repetitive—then took over as a means of emphasizing principal themes.

*   Zevit, Ziony. "Cognitive Theory and the Memorability of Biblical Poetry."
         See #167.

See also #164.

Psalm 112

See #164.

Psalm 114

501.   Geller, Stephen A. "The Language of Imagery in Psalm
        114," in Tzvi Abusch, et al., eds., *Lingering Over Words:
        Studies in Ancient Near Eastern Literature in Honor of
        William L. Moran* (Atlanta: Scholars P, 1990), pp. 179–194.

    "Despite its great simplicity, Psalm 114 makes sophisticated use
    of motifs drawn from two well-attested areas of biblial imagery,
    theophany and creation, to evoke two dimensions of Israel's reli-
    gious expression, history and myth, respectively."

502.   Hunter, J.H. "The Irony of Meaning: Intertextuality in He-
        brew Poetical Texts." *Journal for Semitics* 1 (1989), 229–243.

    Different concepts of intertextuality among deconstructionist
    critics. HB poetic texts "borrow material from different traditions
    and refashion [them] ... to fit [their] purposes." Interpreters must
    take this intertextual borrowing into account when explicating
    these texts. Psalm 114 as example.

*   Longman, Tremper III. "Biblical Poetry."
        See #37.

See also #38.

Psalm 115

See #96.

Psalm 116

503.   Prinsloo, W.S. "Psalm 116: Disconnected Text or Symmetri-
        cal Whole?" *Biblica* 74 (1993), 71–82.

    Morphological, syntactic, stylistic and semantic analysis of the
    structure of Psalm 116 shows that, while it lacks the chiastic struc-
    ture claimed by many critics, it is characterized by "numerous
    verbal and thematic repetitions" which "give rise to a complex
    network of connections between the various parts of the psalm
    without being trapped in a scheme."

Psalm 119

504.   Freedman, David Noel. "The Structure of Psalm 119: Part
        II." *HAR* 14 (1994), 55–87.

        Questions of quantity and meter in this psalm. Line-by-line syl-
        lable count, and the difficulties in being precise about the count;
        frequency and distribution of second m.s. suffixed forms; line
        length. The "highly intricate" structure of the poem, and its links
        with theme. The poem is a "mechanical and technical marvel."

See also #164.

Psalm 127

505.   Estes, Daniel J. "Like Arrows in the Hand of a Warrior
        (Psalm CXXVII)." *VT* 41 (1991), 304–311.

        The arrow simile of verses 4 and 5a "provides a plausible the-
        matic key to the total psalm.... [T]he figure of the arrow links the
        two superficially disparate segments into a profound statement on
        human significance."

See also #477.

Psalm 130

See #477.

Psalm 131

See #473.

Psalm 132

506.   Houk, Cornelius B., and Ronald E. Bee. "Psalm 132, Literary
        Integrity and Syllable-Word Structures...." *JSOT* 6 (1978),
        41–48, 49–53, 54–57.

Debate about the extent to which, and whether, word length and related scansion can establish the unity of authorship of a poem, e.g., Psalm 132.

Psalm 136

See #466.

Psalm 137

See #468.

Psalm 139

See #87, 96, 477.

Psalm 140

*   Hauge, Martin Ravndal. *Between Sheol and Temple: Motif Structure and Function in the I-Psalms.*
        See #469.

Psalm 142

See #468.

Psalm 144

See #470.

Psalm 145

507.   Kimelman, Reuven. "Psalm 145: Theme, Structure, and Impact." *JBL* 113 (1994), 37–58.

The degree to which the structure and content of Psalm 145 "converge to promote the idea of the extension of divine sovereignty." Thus it is not surprising to find this psalm at the head of a series of psalms which introduce the recitation of the Shema in the morning rabbinic liturgy.

See also #164.

JOB

508.   apRoberts, Ruth. "Waiting for Gödel; Or, Hierarchy and the Book of Job," in #141, pp. 61–73.

"... in the Book of Job, the Voice out of the Whirlwind is glorious and resonant, in good measure because of the precedent lengthy, widely exploratory, discursive, exhaustive rationalizations of the comforters, notorious in their failure. The Voice is an enfranchisement."

509.   Aufrecht, Walter E., ed. *Studies in the Book of Job*. Waterloo (Wilfrid Laurier UP), 1985.

Four essays on *Job*, of which two are literary-critical: Ronald J. Williams, "Current Trends in the Study of the Book of Job" (pp. 1–27) includes sections on language, literary criticism, and irony and satire. Peter C. Craigie, "Job and Ugaritic Studies" (pp. 28–35) includes comment on the poetic character of Job and on linguistic problems.

510.   Berry, Donald L. "Scripture and Imaginative Literature: Focus on Job." *Journal of General Education* 19 (1967), 119–131.

We can only understand biblical literature in general, and *Job* in particular, if we remember that both literary and form criticism must be combined in this study. Literary criticism enables us to understand the power of *Job*, while form criticism helps us place its message in the larger context of Israel's prophetic history, since the poet-prophet of Job is showing us Israel in his main character.

511.   Beuken, W.A.M., ed. *The Book of Job*. Leuven (Leuven UP), 1994.

Twenty-eight essays from a 1993 colloquium on *Job*. Several are literary-critical: E.J. Van Wolde, "Job 42, 1–6: The Reversal of Job";

D.J.A. Clines, "Why Is There a Book of Job and What Does It Do to You if You Read It?"; L.J. de Regt," Implications of Rhetorical Questions in Strophes in Job 11 and 15"; E. Talstra, "Dialogue in Job 21: 'Virtual Quotations' or Text Grammatical Markers?"

512. Blumenthal, David R. "A Play on Words in the Nineteenth Chapter of Job." *VT* 16 (1966), 497–501.

The word "skin" in 19:20 and 26 has no etymology, but has cognates in Phoenician and Arabic. It suggests punning on "disgrace" or "abuse." This and a secondary pun in verses 20 and 22 illuminate the structure of chapter 19 as a kind of chiasm.

513. Coogan, Michael David. "Job's Children," in Tzvi Abusch, et al., eds., *Lingering Over Words: Studies in Ancient Near Eastern Literature in Honor of William L. Maran* (Atlanta: Scholars P, 1990), pp. 135–147.

Literary analysis reveals that the prologue is "closely if not perfectly linked to the central poetic sections ... and the epilogue to the prologue, though there are no allusions in the epilogue to the dialogue. Final form is an "artfully-constructed composite ... of original independent parts." Because Job shows no grief over his children, and almost no references to them, the dilemma remains unsolved.

514. Cotter, David W. *A Study of Job 4–5 in the Light of Contemporary Literary Theory.* Atlanta (Scholars P), 1992.

Formalist literary theory, especially of poetics of Roman Jacobsen applied to Job 4–5, concentrating on rhetorical and structural devices and thematic unity. The crucial importance of parallelism in studying HBP.

515. Course, John E. *Speech and Response. A Rhetorical Analysis of the Introductions to the Speeches of the Book of Job (Chapters 4–24).* Washington, DC (Catholic Biblical Association of America), 1994.

Rhetorical analysis of the speech introductions in *Job* 4–24 clearly demonstrates a variety of meaningful connections with previous introductions and speeches, and with the prologue. This is especially true for the first cycle of speeches, less so for the second and third. Sometimes we see a "stylistic feature of delayed reaction" to a speech before the immediately preceding one. The introductions, however, "do not share a common, predictable structure." The links are integral and substantive, and therefore do not appear to be the work of a later editor.

516.   Curtis, John Briggs. "Word Play in the Speeches of Elihu (Job 32–37)." *PEGL* 12 (1992), 23–30.

The skilled and clever word play in Elihu's speeches shows the author of this portion of *Job* to be a masterful artist at characterization. Thus the Elihu speeches do not represent a letdown from the artistry of the rest of *Job*.

517.   Dailey, Thomas F. "The Aesthetics of Repentance: Re-Reading the Phenomenon of Job." *BTB* 23 (1993), 64–70.

"In light of the phenomenological hermeneutics of Paul Ricoeur, the narrative development of the book of Job can be read in successive stages ... [offering] anew perspective on Job's paradoxical repentance." In a first reading, we find an "artistic emplotment"; next, we see Job's repentance "as the metaphorical high point of his theo-linguistics."

518.   Dailey, Thomas F., OSFS. *The Repentant Job. A Ricoeurian Icon for Biblical Theology.* Lanham (UP America), 1994.

Explanation of the phenomenological hermeneutics of Paul Ricoeur, especially narrativity, poetics, and appropriation. Application to *Job*: its "literary configuration and sapiential characterization ... suggests that the book be read as a 'theo-novella'...." The significance of chapters 38–41; Job's silence in 40:4–5 is a "sapiential interiority," a deliberate silence. A repentant Job "serves as an 'icon' of what it means to be a sage." In the context of ancient Wisdom literature, Job's change of stance "indicate[s] that spiritual experience is ... necessary in the pursuit of wisdom."

519.   Dailey, Thomas F., OSFS. "The Wisdom of Divine Disputation? On Job 40.2–5." *JSOT* 63 (1994), 105–119.

A new translation of *Job* 40:2–5 supports the argument that Job is not so much capitulating to the omnipotence of God as offering a "sophisticated epistemological play." Reading this passage in the light of Ricoeur's hermeneutical phenomenology enables us to see Job here as a "heroic sapiential figure." It is true that God corrects Job's objective, rational inquiry, but this "theolinguistic summit" is reached "only by way of a spiritual interaction with the very source of wisdom."

520. Davis, Ellen F. "Job and Jacob: The Integrity of Faith," in #83, pp. 203–224.

Job's integrity and its two fundamental meanings: that of the book and of the man. It is a central, but previously unexplored, theme of the book. "It is a major task of the poem to deepen and complicate the meaning of that key term, ["blameless,"] and thus bring the audience and Job himself to a new sense of what it means to be a person of integrity."

521. Dell, Katherine J. *The Book of Job as Sceptical Literature*. Berlin and NY (Walter de Gruyter), 1991. (*BZAW* 197.)

By a narrow definition, *Job* is not a wisdom book. It contains a "striking variety" of different genres in different chapters—genres which seem to be deliberately misused. Thus "parody" is the most appropriate generic classification. The supposed inconsistencies in Job are fundamental to the author's sceptical and ironic intentions, his deliberate suspension of traditional wisdom categories.

522. Di Lella, Alexander, O.F.M. "An Existential Interpretation of Job." *BTB* 15 (1985), 49–55.

Definition of "existential interpretation." The principal function of the book of *Job* is "to demonstrate dramatically and forcefully that doubt as to the correctness of religious affirmations concerning ultimate reality is a sign of mature faith." Such doubt "is neither reckless nor irreligious, but rather can be ... welcomed with enthusiasm and hope by contemporary believers...."

523. Freedman, David Noel. "The Book of Job," in William Henry Propp et al., eds., *The Hebrew Bible and Its Interpreters* (Winona Lake: Eisenbrauns, 1990), 33–51. [Expanded from *Bible Review* 4 (1988).]

The dialogue "fills the gap between the conclusion of the second test imposed on Job and his restoration and reward at the end of the story.... [It] is a continuation of the testing, ... a third effort on the part of Satan to bring Job down." Job in resisting this effort alters the definition of righteousness from the one God and Satan had agreed on in the prologue.

524. Fullerton, Kemper. "Double Entendre in the First Speech of Eliphaz." *JBL* 49 (1930), 320–374.

The first speech of Eliphaz "is one of the most carefully thought-out and artistic speeches in the book." Eliphaz's limitations, despite his good intentions, and his speech, like the Prologue, "reveals a double character.... The subtlety of it lies in ... the irony and innuendo of the author at the expense of Eliphaz and of the orthodox reader whose position he represents."

525.   Geller, Stephen A. "'Where Is Wisdom?': A Literary Study of Job 28 in Its Settings," in Jacob Neusner, et al., eds., *Judaic Perspectives on Ancient Israel* (Philadelphia: Fortress P, 1987), pp. 155–188.

Relationship between form and content in the Hymn to Wisdom. Its purpose is to create "a feeling of swelling awe at the divine wisdom manifest in nature [which can] overcome the pain of suffering.... This answer to suffering is "consonant with wisdom's focus on nature rather than history...."

526.   Gladson, Jerry A. "Job," in #20, pp. 230–244.

Job is "one of the Bible's superb examples of the symbiotic interaction of the beauties of language and the drama of the human encounter with God...." The problem of genre; unity, theme, and plot in Job; its extensive irony and style.

527.   Gowan, Donald E. "Reading Job as a Wisdom Script." *JSOT* 55 (1992), 85–96.

"... it appears that there may have existed in the ancient Near Eastern mind something we may call a 'wisdom script,' a set of expectations as to what should be included in any story about wisdom. If so, ... the book may be read as a creative use of the wisdom script, turning it into an attack on wisdom, and not only accounting for the otherwise puzzling appearance of Elihu, but also clarifying our reading of chapter 28 and the speeches of the Lord."

528.   Gray, John. "The Book of Job in the Context of Near Eastern Literature." *ZAW* 82 (1970), 251–269.

The extensive affinities of the Book of *Job* with "the sophisticated sapiential tradition of Mesopotamia." The texts of this tradition "suggest ... that the author of the Book of Job had at least available a more sophisticated prototype than the popular folktale" which it is usually assumed he drew on for the Prologue and Epilogue.

529.   Handy, Lowell K. "The Authorization of Divine Power and the Guilt of God in the Book of Job: Useful Ugaritic Parallels." *JSOT* 60 (1993), 107–118.

Satan in Job can be understood as part of "an ancient Syria-Palestine divine character" who works for, not against, God.

529a. Hoffman, Yair. "Ancient Near Eastern Literary Conventions and the Restoration of the Book of Job." *ZAW* 103 (1991), 399–411.

Because the argument of *Job* is anti-dogmatic, the author "was forced into a search for non conventional compositional solutions, but could not completely free himself from the theological and literary conventions of his environment." Thus his compositional solutions could not be satisfactory, and we should be willing to cope with his imperfections, not try to "improve" them.

530. Hunter, Alastair G. "Could Not the Universe Have Come into Existence 200 Yards to the Left? A Thematic Study of Job," in Robert P. Carroll, ed., *Text as Pretext. Essays in Honour of Robert Davidson* (Sheffield: JSOT P, 1992), pp. 140–159.

The central sequence of dialogues forming the core of *Job* and the development of their themes. The structure of the book undermines Job's starting point and leads him "to a new perception of the relationships involved." Literary-psychological analysis shows that *Job* describes a "psychological journey from solitary righteousness (1.1) to a proper understanding of religion as a celebration of the community of men and women and God together (42, 10–11). It is this, rather than the idea of suffering, that is the theme of *Job*.

531. Irwin, W.A. "An Examination of the Progress of Thought in the Dialogue of Job." *JR* 13 (1933), 150–164.

How Job's thought develops in the course of his dialogue with the friends, and how Job's demand for an intermediary derives from pagan fertility god myths. This results in a turn in the author's solution to the mysteries of meaning and suffering: God's remoteness demands an intermediary.

532. Irwin, William A. "Poetic Structure in the Dialogue of Job 4." *JNES* 5 (1946), 26–39.

The subtle artistic form of *Job* and the ways in which its poetic structure may be identified. The strophes "organize themselves into stanzas. As in most Hebrew poetry, the couplet is predominant, but the frequency of the triad is, nonetheless, to be noted." The "astonishing uniformity" of the structure of *Job*.

533.   Irwin, William H. "Conflicting Parallelism in Job 5,13; Isa
       30,28; Isa 32,7." *Biblica* 76 (1995), 72–74.

       "These three examples demonstrate the difficulty that on occa-
       sion arises in attempting to represent the meaning of a text when
       its surface and deep structure do not coincide. It seems a peculiar-
       ity of Hebrew poetic style that the second member of parallel pair
       may occupy the slot normally reserved for the suffix referring to
       the first member of the pair."

534.   Kurzweil, Baruch. "Job and the Possibility of Biblical
       Tragedy," in Arthur A. Cohan, ed., *Arguments and Doc-
       trines: A Reader of Jewish Thinking in the Aftermath of the
       Holocaust* (Philadelphia: Harper and Row, 1970), pp. 323–
       344.

       Job, and biblical narrative in general, lacks the requisites for
       tragedy for several reasons: the biblical hero "does not remain the
       captive of the self"; the narrative itself has no place for "value rela-
       tivism,"—i.e., for different truths equal in worth and importance;
       and its truths are sacral, not secular and subjective.

535.   Lugt, Pieter Van Der. *Rhetorical Criticism and the Poetry of the
       Book of Job* [*OTS* 32]. Leiden (E.J. Brill), 1995.

       History of investigation into the stropic structure of *Job*. Sys-
       tematic analysis of the structure and theme of each speech; design
       of the speech cycles and the role of 25–26 and 27–28 as closing
       speech of the second and opening speech of the third cycles.
       "Introduction to the Design of Biblical Poetry."

536.   Mettinger, Tryggve. "Intertextuality: Allusion and Vertical
       Context Systems in Some Job Passages," in Heather A.
       McKay and David J.A. Clines, eds., *Of Prophets' Visions
       and the Wisdom of Sages* (Sheffield: JSOT P, 1993), pp. 257–
       280.

       "... our understanding of the Book of Job can be fruitfully in-
       formed by the insights and perspectives of the modern study of in-
       tertextuality." The Job speech in chapter 7 shows that the portrayal
       of God is a subversion of Psalm 8, while *Job* 16:7–17 parodies a
       whole genre: the psalms of lament. *Job* 19:6–12 likewise deliber-
       ately uses the siege metaphor of Lamentations 3. This "meta-
       morphic" use of wisdom literature occurs especially in the
       speeches of Job.

537.   Miller, James E. "Structure and Meaning of the Animal Discourse in the Theophany of Job (38,39–39,30)." *ZAW* 103 (1991), 418–421.

The importance of understanding the structure and method of the theophany for grasping the book's answer to the problem of theodicy. The animal discourse is a chiasm; the absence of man in this discourse underlines that, from God's perspective, "man may be seen as a bit player in the food chain...."

538.   ODell, David. "Images of Violence in the Horse in Job 39:18–25." *Prooftexts* 13 (1993), 163–173.

In the violent qualities of the horse image the violence suffered by Job has "undergone in the theophany a subtle but meaningful critique. The absence of all utility and moral measures ... suggest that violence can come as unexpectedly and undeservedly as did the Sabeans and Chaleans, and as tragically as in the death of Job's children."

539.   Owen, John. "The Book of Job," in *The Five Great Skeptical Dramas of History* (Freeport: Books for Libraries, 1972; rpt of 1896 edition), pp. 107–167.

Comparison and contrast of Job with ancient Greek drama. Argument and themes of Job. The daring nature of the book's speculations, given the strictures of ancient Hebrew religion. How ancient Hebrew readers might have reacted to hearing it read. Similarities to, and differences from, Goethe's *Faust*.

540.   Pardes, Ilana. "Conclusion," in #88, pp. 144–156.

"Despite their marginality ... Job's wife and daughters have the power to shed a different light on the Book of Job." Job's wife "avoids taking truths for granted, ... [and] lays bare the problematic presuppositions of given belief systems." Like other key female figures in the HB, she reveals its sometimes antipatriarchal bent.

541.   Porter, Stanley E. "The Message of the Book of Job: Job 42:7b as Key to Interpretation?" *Evangelical Quarterly* 63 (1991), 291–304.

The hitherto unacknowledged importance of *Job* 42:7b (and 48) in interpreting the book. Application of Fish's reader-response theory to this verse, which is ambiguous since we cannot tell to which previous words of Job it refers.

542.   Pyper, Hugh. "The Reader in Pain: Job as Text and Pretext," in Robert P. Carroll, ed., *Text as Pretext: Essays in Honour of Robert Davidson* (Sheffield: JSOT P, 1992), pp. 234–255.

Muriel Spark's novel, *The Only Problem* (1984), in which the protagonist is a reader of *Job*, as illustration of the pain and distress readers can feel in the face of the suffering they read about. Ways in which readers of *Job* "try to evade, assuage or endure the pain of reading." These include attempts to re-arrange the text, ignoring the epilogue or other crucial parts, and resolving incoherencies artificially. Job's anguish is that of the survivor, and so is the reader's. "Part of the pain of the reader is the knowledge of the vicarious nature of the reader's pain."

*   Reed, Walter L. *Dialogues of the Word. The Bible as Literature According to Bakhtin.*

See #6.

543.   Reed, Walter L. "Dimensions of Dialogue in the Book of Job: A Typology According to Bakhtin." *Texas Studies in Literature and Language* 34 (1992), 177–196.

How Bakhtin's concept of the dialogic nature of utterances can shed light on *Job*, both in itself and in relation to the rest of the HB. *Job* stages a struggle between two opposing types of discourse: the unitary and the diversifying tendencies (represented in modern terms by the literary-aesthetic vs. the historical-critical readings of biblical books). Since *Job* offers a critique of law and prophecy, it enters as a whole book into dialogue with the rest of the HB, as well as with earlier Near Eastern laments and theodicies. *Job* "re-asserts the importance of other voices, other languages than one's own religious dialect." Reprinted in expanded form in #6.

544.   Skehan, Patrick W. "Stropic Patterns in the Book of Job." *CBQ* 23 (1961), 125–142; rpt *Studies in Israelite Poetry and Wisdom* (Washington, DC: Catholic Biblical Association, 1971), pp. 96–113.

"... stropic structure is so completely integral to the poems in *Job* that any literary analysis of the book which does not come to grips with this feature is thereby a failure." This analysis offers insights into the composition of other Wisdom books, e.g., Proverbs, and "provides a measuring rod for the integrity of the text...."

545. Smick, Elmer B. "Semeiological Interpretation of the Book of Job." *WTJ* 48 (1986), 135–149.

Reviews work on *Job* from *Semeia* 7 and 19, finding some of it lacking either because it tends to be selective in choosing parts of a text (e.g., only chapter 38 of the theophany) or because it tends to exalt the "absolute text" at the expense of the author.

546. Stevenson, William Barron. *The Poem of Job. A Literary Study with a New Translation*. London (The British Academy), 1947.

Contents and character of the book; development of the poem; rhythm, assonance, structure, and style; connections with Wisdom and folklore.

547. Warner, Martin. "Job versus His Comforters: Rival Paradigms of 'Wisdom,'" in *Philosophical Finesse: Studies in the Art of Rational Persuasion* (Oxford: Clarendon P, 1989), pp. 105–151.

"The book's central appeal, then, is to the pattern of experience in adversity of a man of steadfast integrity; it presents this pattern in such a way as imaginatively to evoke and develop it, and to the extent that it succeeds it may be said to have persuasive power."

548. Williams, James G. "On Job and Writing: Derrida, Girard, and the Remedy-Poison." *SJOT* 7 (1993), 32–50.

How literary methods have opened up the Bible in new ways. These methods were a reaction against history and an attempt to deal with the text as an objective entity. How this can be a mistake. Neither Job nor Oedipus probably existed, but then the question is, to what do they refer? Derrida's "deconstructive metaphor of writing as a way of elucidating Job's witness to his own victimization...." The model proposed by René Girard as a way of criticizing and extending Derrida.

* van Wolde, Ellen. "A Text-Semantic Study of the Hebrew Bible, Illustrated with Noah and Job."

See #210.

See also #11, 38, 71, 72, 75, 78, 96, 97, 104, 145, 384, 465, 549.

PROVERBS

549.   Bellis, Alice Ogden. "The Women of the Wisdom Literature and the Song of Songs," in #64, pp. 191–205.

    "The Wisdom literature contains much that is problematic for feminists but also much that is the source of hope." Most disturbing are the "strange" woman in *Proverbs*, and the dichotomy between good and bad women. On the other hand, Wisdom is important to feminists; many of them find the women of *Job* positive, and of course regard *Song of Songs* as "one of the most feminist of the books of the Hebrew Bible."

550.   Helm, Knut M. "Coreferentiality Structure and Context and Proverbs 10:1–5." *JTT* 6 (1993), 183–209.

    Groups of individual proverbs in the second collection can be considered as coherent discourse. To find this coreferentiality right at the beginning of the collection has "far-ranging consequences." The function of the two opposite kinds of characters in this discourse.

551.   Hildebrandt, Tim. "Proverbial Strings: Cohesion in Proverbs 10." *GTJ* 11 (1990), 171–185.

    Proverbs 10–22 is not a haphazard collection of sentences, but cohesively ordered, with the "proverbial string" as large compositional unit. Four such strings are visible in *Proverbs* 10, with bonding through catchwords, rhetorical devices, themes, sound echoes, and shared syntactic constructions.

552.   Leeuwen, Raymond C. Van. "Liminality and Worldview in Proverbs 1–9." *Semeia* 50 (1990), 111–144.

    The "root metaphors" of *Proverbs* 1–9 "are not to be confined to notions of the 'way' (Habel) or of 'Woman Wisdom' (Camp) but rather the larger metaphoric system and polarity of Wisdom/Folly, Good/Pseudo Good, Life/Death together with the underlying notion of limits and boundaries created and carved by Yahweh as part of the order of creation."

553.   Leeuwen, Raymond Van. "Proverbs," in #20, pp. 256–267.

    Proper reading of *Proverbs* requires attention to the immediate and "long distance" contexts of individual passages. "For all its diversity origin, genre, and point of view ... there is a significant coherence to Proverbs." Outline of the nine "main structural components of this literary mosaic...." The "eloquent brevity" of its style, which "distills ambiguity into concise, potent imagery."

554. McCreesh, Thomas P., OP. *Biblical Sound and Sense. Poetic Sound Patterns in Proverbs 10–29.* Sheffield (JSOT P), 1991.

The study of sound patterns is an integral part of the study of OT Hebrew poetry, despite common critical opinion that its sound patterns were too few or insignificant to warrant investigation. Explanation of methodology and terminology, linking sound patterns, correlation, tagging sound patterns (including imagery and syntactic/semantic markers). All of these techniques applied to those proverbs using repetition or word play. Sound patterns are without doubt characteristic of all OT poetry.

555. Storøy, Solfrid. "On Proverbs and Riddles. Polar Word Pairs and Other Poetical Devices, and Words for 'Poor and Needy' in the Book of Proverbs." *SJOT* 7 (1993), 270–284.

Polar word pairs and other poetic devices "are decisive in the proverbial literature of the O.T...." Hebrew words for "poor" and "needy" as examples illustrated these devices.

556. Whybray, R.N. "The Structure and Composition of Proverbs 22:17–24:22," in #17, pp. 83–96.

There is agreement among scholars that *Proverbs* 22–24 has some sort of literary relationship to the Egyptian *Instruction of Amenemope.* However, given the disparateness of the Proverbs material in these chapters, "its alleged dependence as a whole on *Amenemope* in any way must be regarded as questionable."

See also #77, 87, 97, 111, 145, 164, 261, 465.

RUTH

557. Bellis, Alice Ogden. "Subversive Women in Subversive Books: Ruth, Esther, Susanne, and Judith," in #64, pp. 206–226.

"Most modern readers miss the subversive points being made, because we are not part of the ancient culture out of which these books arose." *Ruth,* e.g., is "subversive of every narrow reading of biblical law, especially biblical laws that oppress." Esther is "a much stronger, more positive character than she might at first appear to modern readers."

558.   Bernstein, Moshe J. "Two Multivalent Readings in the Ruth Narrative." *JSOT* 50 (1991), 15–26.

Two facets of *Ruth* "wherein in the author utilizes two different sorts of literary 'ambiguity': ... *double entendre* language in ch. 3, and ... multivalent meaning in the wedding blessing in ch. 4.... [H]ow these variations on the theme of multiple meaning function within the narrator's artistic framework."

*   Darr, Katheryn Pfisterer. *Far More Precious Than Jewels. Perspectives on Biblical Women*.

See #114.

559.   Gow, Murray D. *The Book of Ruth. Its Structure, Theme, and Purpose*. Leicester (Apollos/Intervarsity Press), 1992.

Literary analysis of the surface structure, themes, theology, purpose and provenance of *Ruth*. It is an artistic unity, authored by someone with a "humane and enlightened outlook," especially toward women, who was also a devout Yahwist. Its author could have been the prophet Nathan from David's lifetime.

560.   Grant, Reg. "Literary Structure in the Book of Ruth." *B Sac* 148 (1991), 424–441.

The plot of *Ruth* is "comic/monomythic"; as such it manifests four literary structural elements as it moves from tragedy to anti-romance to comedy to romance. Discovery of these patterns enhances appreciation "for the aesthetic beauty of God's inspired text," and is a source of truth in itself.

561.   Holbert, John C. "The Bible Becomes Literature: An Encounter with Ruth." *WW* 13 (1993), 130–135.

The value of reading *Ruth* from a literary perspective, and of approaching the entire Bible that way.

562.   Jobling, David. "Ruth Finds a Home: Canon, Politics, Method," in #82, pp. 125–139.

The different effects on the reader of the fact that the Septuagint places *Ruth* between *Judges* and *I Samuel*, whereas the Masoretic does not. How the beginning of *I Samuel* reads differently if we regard it in relation to what comes before it, rather than after it. *Ruth* as "canonical alternative, or shortcut," from the days of judges to the days of kings. Like *Genesis* 38, *Ruth* demonstrates the possibility of a non-Exodus alternative, and makes a subtle argument for virilocol marriage—thus the ambiguous attitudes of feminists toward *Ruth*. How various critics have tried to solve these problems.

563. Landy, Francis. "Ruth and the Romance of Realism, or Deconstructing History." *JAAR* 62 (1994), 285–317.

How various traditional and literary-critical readings of *Ruth* can be simultaneously possible. It is both a romantic and a realistic book, though close readings reveal "fissures and nonsequiturs," making a "disintegrative reading" of the text. How these paradoxes and tensions are revealed in the crucial scene on the threshing floor in chapter 3. The story remains focused on Boaz, denying our attempts to understand Ruth's subjectivity.

564. Luter, A. Boyd, and Richard O. Rigsby. "The Chiastic Structure of Ruth 2." *Bulletin for Biblical Research* 3 (1993), 49–58.

Despite much published work on Ruth in recent years, there is little which combines the exegetical and the structural. How the chiastic structure of chapter 2 "transfers the key ideas ... from the realm of subjective interpretation into that of objective authorial intention.... [W]hat may appear to be good luck or blind chance (2:3) in the believer's life may well be divine favor (2:12) providentially mediated through other servants of the Lord (2:3, 13, 18–20)."

565. McCarthy, Carmel, and William Riley. "The Book of Ruth: Faithfulness Against the Odds," in #120, pp. 55–83.

Ruth is a "love story of the classical type," opening in loss but ending in restoration. Its plot, structure, clever characterization, style, theme, and their relationship to theology. The Davidic connection of the book. How the story still appeals to a modern audience.

566. Pardes, Ilana. "The Book of Ruth: Idyllic Revisionism," in #88, pp. 98–117.

The book of *Ruth* revises the Rachel-Leah story (*Genesis* 30): rivalry between co-wives giving way to a harmonious sharing of the same man. Yet both stories share a reassurance to males that female bonding does not threaten either crops or genealogy. *Ruth* "maintains ... a delicate balance between same and other, where the other, through its very otherness, 'builds' the House of Israel."

*   Rashkow, Ilona N. *Upon the Dark Places. Anti-Semitism and Sexism in English Renaissance Biblical Translation.*

See #201.

567.   Sheehan, John F.X. "The Word of God as Myth: The Book of Ruth," in Richard J. Clifford, S.J., and George W. MacRae, S.J., eds., *The Word in the World* (Cambridge: Weston CP, 1973), pp. 35–46.

"All of these elements together, then ..., the threshing floor, the time of the grain harvest, the sexual union of the two leading characters (and in the locale of the threshing floor at that) [and the movement from sorrow to joy] certainly point up ... a fertility cult motif."

568.   Staples, W.E. "The Book of Ruth." *AJSL* 53 (1937), 145–157.

The extensive connections with a fertility cult in *Ruth* including proper names. For ancient Hebrews, this cult became the basis for a theory of world order. *Ruth* is filled with these motifs.

569.   Tischler, Nancy M. "Ruth," in #20, pp. 151–164.

Ruth is a "small jewel of a folk tale, ... an elegantly wrought classic version of the rags-to-riches story, ... told from the point of view of women." The book as five-act drama. The good and bad of recent feminist criticism of the Bible. *Ruth* as unique among biblical books for its expression of the feminine point of view.

See also #71, 111, 132, 201.

SONG OF SONGS

570.   Astell, Ann W. *The Song of Songs in the Middle Ages.* Ithaca and London (Cornell UP), 1990.

"Examines medieval reader response—both interpretive and imitative—to the Song of Songs," from Origen on. How the twelfth century's "different concept of holiness and of human na-

ture" provided an altered cultural context for reading the Song. "...
medieval readers saw the literal Song as inseparable from its gloss
and felt the rhetorical appeal engendered by that two-in-oneness."

*   Bellis, Alice Ogden. "The Women of the Wisdom Literature
and the Song of Songs."

See #549.

571.   Brenner Athalya. *A Feminist Companion to Song of Songs.*
Sheffield (Sheffield Academic P), 1993.

Twenty-one essays, of which fifteen are reprints; of these fifteen,
eight are literary-critical and described in Minor I: #s 221, 991, 999,
1347, 1353, 1372, 1378, and 1388. Of the six remaining essays which
are new in the volume: A. Brenner surveys issues in feminist criticism of the HB; Brenner summarizes the essays in the volume and
the literary-critical issues they raise; M. Deckers offers a Greima-
sian, structural analysis centered on the Hebrew word *nepes*
(being, vitality); Francis Landy modifies his criticism of the work
of P. Trible; J.W. Whedbee offers a comic reading centering on
"paradox and parody"; A. Brenner briefly summarizes the images
of women in *Song of Songs.*

572.   Carr, G. Lloyd. "*Song of Songs,*" in #20, pp. 281–295.

Review of theories of *Song of Songs* as allegory, as drama, as love
poetry. Its vocabulary is unusual, but its structure shows "a single
hand at work—... the hand of a master craftsman." The key to its
structure is chiasmus.

573.   Elliott, Mark W. "Ethics and Aesthetics in the Song of
Songs." *TB* 45 (1994), 137–152.

The message of *Song of Songs* on the nature of human loving is
"found in its choice of metaphors for that activity." These
metaphors refer not to the body but the whole self. Thus we realize that we should view sexual experience as "something ... which
... reminds us of our belonging to the created order and so summons us out of ourselves."

574.   Elliott, Sister M. Timothea, R.S.M. *The Literary Unity of the
Canticle.* Frankfurt am Main (Peter Lang), 1989.

Poetic analysis reveals a number of major elements of style
which unify the book and argue for a single author. Its six-part
structure is not stages of a story or acts of a drama, but more the
logic of love where certain situations or motifs are continuously

repeated while the love relationship gradually develops. Spring-time is the unifying metaphor, and the author betrays a Yahwist theology.

575.   Emmerson, Grace I. "The Song of Songs: Mystification, Ambiguity and Humour," in #17, pp. 97–111.

Debates over structure of, and imagery in, the *Song of Songs*. "To recognize the Song as Wisdom literature ... is to find a key to its interpretation. Whereas Job and Ecclesiastes look at the dark side of life, the Song celebrates its joys and delights.... To try to search out a particular historical setting, whether factual or fictional, is to ... divert attention from the reader's response...."

576.   Grober, S.F. "The Hospitable Lotus: A Cluster of Metaphors. An Inquiry into the Problem of Textual Unity in the Song of Songs." *Semitics* 9 (1984), 86–112.

The ways in which the author creates "confluences of images" in *Song of Songs* supports those who argue that the text is a unified structure. Specifically, the semantic associations generated by the work's metaphors produce a "literary texture" with structural and thematic coherence.

577.   Landy, Francis. "In Defense of Jakobson." *JBL* 111 (1992), 105–113.

Response to Zevit (*JBL* 109 [1990], 385–401). Summarizes ap-proach to poetics, defends how a Jakobsonian analysis of *Song of Songs* might read.

578.   Murphy, Roland E., O. Carm. *The Song of Songs. A Commen-tary on the Book of Canticles ...*, ed. S. Dean McBride, Jr. Minneapolis (Fortress P), 1990.

Topics covered include literature of love in ancient Near Eastern texts; the literary character and structure of *Song of Songs*; its composition and style (including topic, language, and prosody). Arguments for its unity are not entirely convincing, though we may argue for a dialogic structure, and therefore a unity based on this structure. And, "with the exception of Ecclesiastes, no other book of the Bible so amply displays verbal and thematic repeti-tions."

579.   Pardes, Ilana. "'I Am a Wall, and My Breasts Are Like Tow-ers': The Song of Songs and the Question of Canoniza-tion," in #88, pp. 118–143.

In addition to the usual reasons to be puzzled at the *Song of Songs'* inclusion in the HB, we should also note its antipatriarchal bent, its "tendency to deviate from conventional representations of love in the Bible." Perhaps here most of all Bakhtin's notion of a heteroglot text applies, that the Song was included. The tension between chastity and sexual freedom helped its cause as well.

580.   Schmidt, Nathaniel. "Is Canticles an Adonis Litany?" *JAOS* 46 (1926), 154–164.

While *Song of Songs* probably cannot be considered such a litany, clearly the author derived some of his conceits and imagery from popular ancient Near East pagan festivals, possibly also from customs at agrarian and marriage feasts.

See also #71, 111, 145, 384, 454.

QOHELETH

581.   Fredericks, Daniel C. "Life's Storms and Structural Unity in Qoheleth 11.1–12.8." *JSOT* 52 (1991), 95–114.

Investigates "whether a structural combination of one of the most exegetically challenging sections in Ecclesiastes (1 1.7–12.8) with a section that has received less attention (11.1–6) might produce a better reading.... Such a combination is suggested by the unity of 11.1–12.8 which is shown through its themes and certain rhetorical devices."

582.   Genung, John Franklin. *Words of Koheleth*. Boston and New York (Houghton, Mifflin and Co), 1904.

Translation of the book, preceded by a "study of the literary and spiritual values" of Qoheleth's word. Includes commentary on its Greek spirit, "motive and method," characteristics of its style.

583.   de Jong, Stephan. "A Book on Labour: The Structuring Principles and the Main Theme of the Book of Qoheleth." *JSOT* 54 (1992), 107–116.

Qoheleth has a logical structure whose main principle is "the alternation of observation and instruction complexes." The difference between these complexes "is shown by an analysis of some principal stylistic and semantic features of both complexes. The proposed division sheds light on the main theme of the book: human labour."

584. de Jong, Stephan. "Qoheleth and the Ambitious Spirit of the Ptolemaic Period." *JSOT* 61 (1994), 85–96.

Qoheleth appears to have been written for the sons of the Jewish Hellenistic aristocracy, in order to make them "critically aware of the reality in which they were going to work: a promising ... world which, however, was hiding many traps and frustrations." Its structure is determined by two types of text: observation complexes and instruction complexes. "The main theme of [the former] ... is the frustration of human labour."

585. Ryken, Leland. "Ecclesiastes," in #20, pp. 268–280.

Despite the doubts of earlier critics, "the basic strategy of Ecclesiastes is relatively simple, and literary analysis can provide clear pathways through the book." Its theme of the God-centered life is a "virtual summary of the biblical world view, and it possesses a "tightly organized" dialectical structure. This dialogue is between the positive and negative views of life, with the positive about equally balancing the negative. The writer gives his collection of proverbs a "narrative thread, a lyric and poetic cast, and a story element of satire and protest."

586. Templeton, Douglas A. "A 'Farced Epistol' to a Sinking Sun of David. *Ecclesiastes* and *Finnegans Wake*: The Sinoptic View," in Robert P. Carroll, ed., *Text as Pretext: Essays in Honour of Robert Davidson* (Sheffield: JSOT P), pp. 282–290.

Scripture often parodies scripture, which in turn should remind us that we should read scripture parodically. It is a "mode of appropriation of texts, a mode of literary criticism." Further, all reading is appropriation, re-writing the text, or it could not become our text. Laughter is transcendental for us humans, creatures who are neither devils nor angels.

See also #71, 72, 77, 96, 107, 145, 164, 200, 465.

LAMENTATIONS

*   Dobbs-Allsopp, F.W. *Weep, O Daughter of Zion: A Study of the City-Lament Genre in the Hebrew Bible.*

See #369.

*   Ferris, Paul Wayne, Jr. *The Genre of the Communal Lament in the Bible and the Ancient Near East.*

See #468.

587.   Heater, Homer. "Structure and Meaning in Lamentations." *B Sac* 149 (1992), 304–315.

The structure of *Lamentations* in relation to content and message. Its structure is based on the "split alphabet" principle, with a progression in emotional intensity reinforced by changes in the acrostic patterns.

588.   Renkema, J. "The Meaning of the Parallel Acrostics in Lamentations." *VT* 45 (1995), 379–382.

The author of *Lamentations* "applied the literary form of parallel acrostic as a visualization of the responsive coherence between the (strophes of the) poems. The strophes ... form song responsions: ... in one way or another the identical letter strophes form on the same (letter) level external parallelisms, identical, additional or antithetical, in language and content."

See also #164, 384, 468, 536.

ESTHER

589.   Bal, Mieke. "Lots of Writing." *Poetics Today* 15 (1994), 89–114.

Esther as a work "where words and images converge, where the visual and the verbal, fate and agency, Providence and plotting come together." Visual and verbal "representations of self-reflexion in the story of Esther" and in two Rembrandt paintings which can be used as a gloss on the biblical book. *Esther*'s feast is a "feast of writing, with its relation to Purim revealed in the tension between writing and randomness, agency and luck, or lot."

*   Bellis, Alice Ogden. "Subversive Women in Subversive Books: Ruth, Esther, Susanne, and Judith."

See #557.

590.   Craig, Kenneth M., Jr. *Reading Esther: A Case for the Literary Carnivalesque.* Louisville (Westminster/John Knox P), 1995.

Analysis of *Esther* as an early but nevertheless genuine example of Bakhtin's "literary carnivalesque." The book originates in folk culture, and further its crucial scenes take place exactly where Bakhtin's theory predicts all carnivalesque stories will. Its "collective gaiety" belongs to the serio-comical genre.

*   Darr, Katheryn Pfisterer. *Far More Precious Than Jewels. Perspectives on Biblical Women.*

See #114.

591.   Fox, Michael V. *Character and Ideology in the Book of Esther.* Columbia (U of South Carolina P), 1991.

The "surface clarity and vividness" of character portrayal in *Esther* "are the products of a sharp and subtle craft ... conveying a surprisingly sophisticated—in some ways strikingly modern— view of person, nation, and religion." Characterization in context of other artistic and conceptual concerns of the writer, especially his attempt to "import ... ideas about realities outside the book."

592.   McCarthy, Carmel, and William Riley. "The Book of Esther: Banquet Tables are Turned," in #120, pp. 84–111.

Esther as a tale which acts to relieve anxiety by "giving fears flesh and blood," playing out internal conflicts on an objective stage. Its intricate plot yet simple story line, use of fear and reversal as two basic building blocks, and contrasts in characterization. It should be neither historicized nor politicized but enjoyed and learned from for its portrayal of human conflict.

593.   McClarty, Wilma. "Esther," in #20, pp. 216–229.

Esther is written with a strong feminine bias. Its "complex interplay of narrative elements intrigues and informs...." Plot, characterization, setting, and theme in the narrative.

594. Noss, Philip A. "A Footnote on Time: The Book of Esther." *BTr* 44 (1993), 309–320.

Structural and rhetorical time in *Esther*, and its various uses in the author's design of the plot, including the use of titles and "Homeric device of epithets" as developers of plot. How these two kinds of time plotting underline themes of the book.

* Schildgren, Brenda Deen. "A Blind Promise: Mark's Retrieval of Esther."

See #762.

595. Stefanovic, Zdravko. "'Go At Once': Thematic Reversals in the Book of Esther." *The Asia Journal of Theology* 8 (1994), 163–171.

The book of *Esther* contains "a number of theme reversals closely tied to the overall structure of the book. These reversals are carefully organized in order to present the major reversal of the book which has its turning point in the threefold statement of 6:10." Most frequently recurring motifs are "banquet" and "edict," both being used to portray the reversals artistically.

See also #762.

DANIEL

596. Arnold, Bill T. "Wordplay and Narrative Techniques in Daniel 5 and 6." *JBL* 112 (1993), 479–485.

Examples of metaphoric and autoanaclastic, paronomasia as subtle literary devices that "also bear significant theological content." In *Daniel* 5, this wordplay creates an irony "to contrast the arrogance of human rebellion with the omnipotence of God's response." *Daniel* 6 likewise uses the same devices to underline an interesting theological theme: the irony of Daniel's enemies assuming that what is his greatest strength is in fact his greatest weakness.

597. Avolos, Hector I. "The Comedic Function of the Enumerations of Officials and Instruments in *Daniel* 3." *CBQ* 53 (1991), 580–588.

The recurrence of lengthy lists in *Daniel*, especially in chapter three, "are an integral technique in the author's satire on pagan culture and behavior." In particular, Bergson's theory of comedy "provides a very plausible explanation for the function of the iterations of enumerations in *Daniel* 3."

598.   Burkholder, Byron. "Literary Patterns and God's Sovereignty in Daniel 4." *Direction* 15, #2 (Fall 1987), 45–54.

"... how the literary and structural features of *Daniel* 4 are important means of teaching the dual theme of God's sovereignty and human responsibility." Imagery and parallel structures as literary means to this end.

599.   Collins, John J. *Daniel. A Commentary on the Book of Daniel*, ed. Frank Moore Cross. Minneapolis (Augsburg Fortress P), 1993.

General literary-critical observations about the book as a whole; genre and setting of the tales and the visions. Structure and unity of each identifiable narrative unit: Nehuchadnezzar's dream, the fiery furnace, Nehuchadnezzar's madness, Belshazzar's feast, the lions' den, the beasts, etc.

600.   Di Lella, Alexander A. "Strophic Structure and Poetic Analysis of Daniel 2:20–23, 3:31–33, and 6:26b–28," in Giovanni Claudio Bottini, ed., *Studia Hierosolymitana III: Nell' Ottavo Centenario Francescano (1182–1982)* (Jerusalem: Franciscan PP, 1982), pp. 91–96.

Analysis of those part of Aramaic *Daniel* which the author judges to be poetry, wording to cola structure, alliterative, patterns, etc.

601.   Fewell, Danna Nolan. *Circle of Sovereignty: Plotting Politics in the Book of Daniel*. 2nd ed. Nashville (Abingdon), 1991.

How politics "governs the plot and motivates the characters" in *Daniel*. A reader-response and deconstructive literary reading of the book which "looks for undercurrents, meanings that subvert many of the traditional readings of the book." *Daniel* is ultimately ironic, because the kingdom of God as *Daniel* envisions it never comes to pass. Revision of essay listed as Minor I, #1455.

602.   Prinsloo, G.T.M. "Two Poems in a Sea of Prose: The Content and Context of Daniel 2.20–23 and 6.27–28." *JSOT* 59 (1993), 93–108.

The function of these two poetic passages in the Aramaic section of *Daniel* within their narrative framework. This framework is concentric, with the poetic passages occupying the center of the chiasm, highlighting the theological point that only through God can wisdom be attained. The poetry foregrounds theme, heightens tension, delays narrative pace in order to heighten awareness of the message.

*   Shoulson, Jeffrey S. "Daniel's Pesher: A Proto-Midrashic Reading of Genesis 40–41."

     See #238.

603.   Sims, James H. "Daniel," in #20, pp. 324–336.

The history of arguments over whether *Daniel* is a true prophetic book. It does have "affinity with the literary prophets," and also has affinities with apocalyptic. Even its celebrated "inaccuracies" are an integral part of its literary technique. *Daniel* is a "sophisticated literary unit ... in a final shape that is aesthetically satisfying, thematically clear, and yet, finally, open-ended and mysterious."

604.   Vorster, W.S. "Texts with an Apocalyptic Perspective," in #81, pp. 166–185.

The "apocalyptic-eschatological Apocalyptic texts as products of a subculture," i.e., a "crisis literature." "Because such texts are concerned with metaphysical realities, symbolic language and concealing codes play a prominent part." Their main function is rhetorical.

605.   Wolters, Al. "Untying the King's Knots: Physiology and Wordplay in Daniel 5." *JBL* 110 (1991), 117–122.

The puzzling phrase in 5:6 may refer to the sphincter muscles of the bladder and anus in a burlesque humor intended to "underscore the sovereignty of the Israelite God." The use of wordplay in achieving this effect.

606.   Woodard, Branson L., Jr. "Literary Strategies and Authorship in the Book of Daniel." *JETS* 37 (1994), 39–53.

Authorial voice in *Daniel* 1–6 as evidence for both Danielic authorship and textual unity of the book as a whole. Evangelical scholarship should investigate the relationship between historiography and the literary imagination in Daniel. The "multiple dynamics" present where fact and imagination intersect, and the "artful sophistication and didactic power" of the book of *Daniel*.

607.   Woude, A.S. Van Der. *The Book of Daniel in the Light of New Findings*. Leuven (Leuven UP), 1993.

Thirty essays exploring new evidence and arguments regarding *Daniel*. Several essays in English, French, and German on literary-critical problems and three others illustrating "literary and socio-logical approaches" to the book. Connections with deutero-*Isaiah* and Aramaic literature.

See also #118, 124.

EZRA-NEHEMIAH

608.   Green, Douglas. "Ezra-Nehemiah," in #20, 206–215.

Though these two books "are best understood ... as a unified work," "differently nuanced readings" of the books are possible. Major themes, character treatment, style (especially "subversive style") in the books.

609.   Japhet, Sara. "The Relationship between Chronicles and Ezra-Nehemiah," in [J.A. Emerton, ed.] *Congress Volume Leuven 1989* (Leiden: E.J. Brill, 1991), pp. 298–313.

There is no compelling evidence that the author of *Chronicles* was the same as the author of *Ezra-Nehemiah*. On the contrary, various forms of literary differences show that the author of one "could not have been the author of the other." Nor can we on any literary evidence accept a "Chronistic school" as common authors.

610.   Kraemer, David. "On the Relationship of the Books of Ezra Nehemiah." *JSOT* 59 (1993), 73–92.

Agrees with Eskenazi that literary-critical methodology is more appropriate for *Ezra-Nehemiah* because it is a literary formulation more than a historical record. However, her decision to regard it as one book is a mistake, since, among other reasons, the books ex-hibit "important ideological differences." The structures, themes and motifs of *Ezra* and *Nehemiah* demonstrate this difference as well.

611. Richards, R.R. "National Reconstruction and Literary Creativity in Ezra-Nehemiah: A Black South African Perspective." *OTE* 7 (1994), 277–301.

The tripartite literary form of *Ezra-Nehemiah* preserves and presents historical memory (images) of national reconstruction in the second temple period. Ideological strands in the narrative which give it its thematic unity, and how they relate to the author of the article as a black male academic in South Africa.

612. Vanderkam, James C. "Ezra-Nehemiah or Ezra and Nehemiah?," in Eugene Ulrich et al., eds., *Priests, Prophets and Scribes ... in Honour of Joseph Blenkinsopp* (Sheffield: JSOT P, 1992), pp. 55–75.

That *Ezra* and *Nehemiah* are separate works by different authors can be demonstrated by stylistic analysis, thematic analysis, and use of sources.

See also #104, 164.

CHRONICLES

* Burns, John Barclay. "Solomon's Egyptian Horses and Exotic Wives."

See #340.

613. Graham, M. Patrick. "Aspects of the Structure and Rhetoric of 2 Chronicles 25," in M. Patrick Graham et al., eds., *History and Interpretation: Essays in Honour of John H. Hayes* (Sheffield: JSOT P), pp. 78–89.

The structure of the Chronicler's narrative is unlike his source in *II Kings,* a "tightly woven narrative with a concentric arrangement, whose components are clearly related to one another." Different historical and theological emphases are the result, in a narrative "replete with irony" about Amaziah.

* Japhet, Sara. "The Relationship between Chronicles and Ezra-Nehemiah."

See #609.

614.   Johnstone, William. "Solomon's Prayer: Is Intentionalism
        Such a Fallacy?" *ST* 47 (1993), 119–133.

> Review of the recent debate in literary criticism over E.D.
> Hirsch's theory of authorial intention. Examination of *II Chronicles*
> 6 for evidence of its author's intention reveals Solomon's prayer as
> the center of the author's presentation of Solomon in chapters 1–9.
> Reasons for this intention and how the text induces the reader to
> respond to this intention.

615.   Kalimi, Isaac. "Literary-Chronological Proximity in the
        Chronicler's Historiography." *VT* 43 (1993), 318–338.

> Two main types are recognizable: (a) where the author creates
> proximity between two unconnected events recorded in Samuel
> and Kings; and (b) where he "exploits an already-existing literary
> proximity ..., transforming it into topical-chronological proximity."
> In (a) he creates such proximity between cult reform, passover cel-
> ebration, and Josiah's clash with Necho; in (b) he makes use of *II
> Kings* 12–13 to create literary-chronological proximity between
> Sennacherib's campaign against Judah and his assassination in
> Nineveh.

616.   Pratt, Richard L., Jr. "First and Second Chronicles," in #20,
        pp. 193–205.

> Why the literary approach to books such as these is relevant and
> important. Links between literature and ideology in *1 and 2
> Chronicles*. Characterization of royalty; plot features and structures
> in these narratives.

See also #340, 365, 609.

THE NEW TESTAMENT

Books

617. Bailey, James L., and Lyle D. Vander Brock. *Literary Forms in the New Testament. A Handbook.* Louisville (Westminster/ John Knox P), 1992.

Explanation and illustration of two major sources of NT literary forms: Pauline letters (including diatribe, chiasm, argumentation, paraenesis, household codes, creeds) and the gospels and *Acts* (including aphorism, parable, pronouncement and miracle stories, hymns, and genealogies). Definition of each form, "value for interpretation," and select bibliography of criticism of each form.

* Barr, David L. *New Testament Story: An Introduction.*
   See #63.

618. Black, David Alan, ed. *Linguistics and New Testament Interpretation. Essays on Discourse Analysis.* Nashville (Broadman P), 1992.

Fourteen essays outlining the method of discourse analysis, and applying it to specific NT books and passages, analyzed as #716, 806, 648, 990, 735, 839, 871, 1003, 1013, 1014, 1050, 1106, 1108, 1117.

619. Cameron, Averil. *Christianity and the Rhetoric of Empire. The Development of Christian Discourse.* Berkeley, Los Angeles, Oxford (U California P), 1991.

Christian discourse, from the NT in the first century through the theologians in the fourth century, appealed because it was well suited to the cultural conditions of the empire, because its rhetoric and other literary methods were more nearly like those of the surrounding pagan writing than early Christians were—or some

modern NT scholars are—prepared to admit. It "worked through
the familiar, appealing from the known to the unknown." Its figu-
ral character and use of myth as story were two of these important
elements.

620.   Cotterell, Peter, and Max Turner. *Linguistics and Biblical Interpretation.* Downers Grove, IL (InterVarsity P), 1989.

Basic principles of linguistics applied to numerous biblical passages (almost all NT): semantics, discourse meaning, lexical semantics, sentences and sentence clusters (illustrated by *Hebrews* 2),
discourse analysis (illustrated by *2 Samuel* 13), conversation
analysis, and non-literal language (illustrated by *I Corinthians* 11).

621.   Kurz, William S., S.J. *Farewell Addresses in the New Testament.*
Collegeville, Minneapolis (Liturgical P), 1990.

"Farewell addresses were a common genre in the Hellenistic
world, and had both Greco-Roman and biblical forms." How the
two forms were similar and different. NT examples closer to OT
than Greco-Roman. They would have had a "special impact" on
contemporary readers. Examples analyzed in detail: *Acts* 20, *Luke*
22, *John* 13–14, and *John* 15–17.

622.   McKnight, Edgar V., and Elizabeth Struthers Malbon, eds.
The New Literary Criticism and the New Testament. Sheffield
(Sheffield Academic P) and Valley Forge (Trinity P Inter-
national), 1994.

Fourteen essays by as many critics presenting "a sampling of the
rich variety of critical methodologies employed in contemporary
literary study of the New Testament." Analyzed separately as
#637, 751, 820, 938, 742, 832, 1011, 1039, 1132, 884, 914, 640, 728,
631.

623.   Moore, Stephen D. *Poststructuralism and the New Testament.
Derrida and Foucault at the Foot of the Cross.* Minneapolis
(Fortress P), 1994.

How Derrida's project "has always been in a muted dialogue
with theology ...," and how poststructuralism can defamiliarize
the NT, and specifically its theological ideas. Thus poststructuralism "would be historical criticism's id, the seat of its strongest
antiauthoritarian instincts," able to free it from its tendency "to
genuflect before the icons it had come to destroy." Examples are
from *John* and *Pauline* letters.

624. Porter, Stanley E., and Thomas H. Olbricht, eds. *Rhetoric and the New Testament. Essays from the 1992 Heidelberg Conference*. Sheffield (JSNT P), 1993.

Twenty-seven essays by as many scholars, eight of which deal with "rhetoric and questions of method" on the NT in general; the remaining nineteen analyze specific books or passages in one or more gospels, letters, or *Acts*. These twenty-seven essays analyzed separately below as #61, 636, 644, 647, 679, 807, 813, 852, 948, 949, 971, 974, 975, 981, 982, 984, 998, 1005, 1009, 1025, 1027, 1032, 1046, 1057, 1064, 1066, 1092.

625. Pregeant, Russell. *Engaging the New Testament. An Interdisciplinary Introduction*. Minneapolis (Fortress P), 1995.

A "modified canonical approach" to systematic study of the NT in the classroom, also employing redaction, existentialist, psychological, and literary (including structuralist, rhetorical, and reader-response) methods of criticism. Part One: Before the NT; Part Two: The Gospels and *Acts*; Part Three: The Pauline Corpus; Part Four: *Hebrews*, the General Letters, and *Revelation*.

* Reed, Walter L. *Dialogues of the Word: The Bible as Literature According to Bakhtin*.

See #6.

626. Schneiders, Sandra M. *The Revelatory Text: Interpreting the New Testament as Sacred Scripture*. San Francisco (Harper), 1991.

The necessity of an integrative hermeneutic of the NT, one which combines theological, ideological, historical and literary concerns in new and creative ways. The worlds behind the text, of the text, and before the text, and how each relates to the "revelatory text" itself. Application in a feminist interpretation of *John* 4, which reveals much traditional exegesis of the Samaritan woman to be inadequate to her meaning in the Johannine community.

627. Seeley, David. *Deconstructing the New Testament*. Leiden (E.J. Brill), 1994.

Explanation of how Derridean deconstruction fits in with biblical studies, even those from the distant past. Separate chapters applying the method to each of the four gospels and to Paul's letters. Deconstruction "is able to highlight differences between and within biblical texts...." It leads necessarily to historical investigation, since "its patient but relentless pulling apart of a text's strands must raise the question of where those strands come from."

628.   Tuckett, Christopher. *Reading the New Testament: Methods of Interpretation*. Philadelphia (Fortress), 1987.

Chapters explaining various forms of historical criticism, and chapters on NT and structuralism, and "other approaches," i.e., canon criticism, and literary criticism. The historical-criticism method "remains vitally important in interpreting the N.T.," while we allow the insights of the other methods.

629.   Watson, Duane F., ed. *Persuasive Artistry: Studies in N.T. Rhetoric in Honor of George A. Kennedy*. Sheffield (JSOT P), 1991.

Seventeen essays on rhetorical approaches to the New Testament analyzed separately as #407, 789, 703, 784, 865, 676, 671, 896, 966, 993, 1001, 1033, 1030, 1044, 1042, 1085, 643.

Articles

630.   Beardslee, William A. "Robert Alter's View of Hebrew Narrative from the Perspective of New Testament Studies," in *Margins of Belonging: Essays on the New Testament and Theology* (Atlanta: Scholars P, 1991), pp. 81–88.

Why Alter's work "opens important vistas on unfinished work in New Testament studies." This lies primarily in his concept of "composite artistry," as well as in characterization, plot, the type-scene, and the pace of narration. The controversy over supposed oral stages in the origination of NT material, as evidenced by the difference between Alter's and Werner Kelber's approaches to orality.

631.   Beardslee, William A. "What Is It About? Reference in New Testament Literary Criticism, " in #622, pp. 367–386.

The problematic separation of fact and value in traditional NT historical criticism, and the failure of newer, literary criticism of the NT to show much concern for reference. How consideration of *1 Corinthians* 15 demonstrates the complexity of reference in NT study, and its connection with value.

*   Berger, Klaus. "Rhetorical Criticism, New Form Criticism
        and New Testament Hermeneutics."

        See #679.

632.   Black, David Alan. "Translating New Testament Poetry," in
        Black, ed., *Scribes and Scripture: New Testament Studies in
        Honor of J. Harold Greenlee* (Winona Lake: Eisenbrauns,
        1992), pp. 117–127.

        The nature of poetic form, and illustrations of it in the NT, es-
        pecially passages from *Hebrews* 1, *II Timothy* 2, *Philippians* 2. The
        necessity of understanding the difference between poetry and
        prose, and thus of knowing the difference in the NT.

633.   Boers, Hendrikus. "Polarities at the Roots of New Testa-
        ment Thought," in Charles H. Talbert, ed., *Perspectives on
        the New Testament: Essays in Honor of Frank Stagg* (Macon:
        Mercer UP, 1985), pp. 55–75.

        Semantic/structuralist and related narratological analysis of the
        NT shows that "the contradiction between faith and works is at
        the root of New Testament thought." This is a sign of richness, not
        weakness, which in turn means that the NT "should not be taken
        as a rule of faith, in the sense of a doctrine, but as a religious
        framework within which the Christian is called upon to under-
        stand herself or himself."

634.   Botha, J. "The Ethics of N.T. Interpretation." *Neotestamentica*
        26 (1992), 169–194.

        This ethics compels us to take reading seriously—i.e., the lin-
        guistic, literary, and rhetorical nature of the text must be honored,
        in addition to its social dimension. Such literary study must pre-
        cede concern about God, society, history, or the self, which are
        "text-extrinsic" matters.

635.   Botha, J. Eugene. "Style in the New Testament: The Need
        for Serious Reconsideration." *JSNT* 43 (1991), 71–87.

        Speech act theory can help bring the study of the style of the NT
        up to date, "with other developments in linguistics and literary
        theory."

636.   Di Marco, Angelica-Salvatore. "Rhetoric and Hermeneu-
        tic—On a Rhetorical-Pattern: Chiasmus and Circularity,"
        in #624, pp. 479–491.

The widespread use of chiasmic patterns in the NT, and a defense of the time and effort spent by critics analyzing those patterns. Why the lack of uniform terminology for these patterns is not a drawback or a weakness in critical analysis.

637.   Donahue, John R. "Redaction Criticism: Has the *Hauptstrasse* Become a *Sackgasse*?," in #622, pp. 27–57.

In its modified tradition history form, redaction criticism "is still vital in studies of Q and John Perrin's prediction of its transformation into 'genuine literary criticism' has been more than fulfilled." Yet its fundamental goals "remain a significant part of most contemporary biblical criticism."

638.   Malbon, Elizabeth Struthers, and Janice Capel Anderson. "Literary-Critical Methods," in Elisabeth Schüssler Fiorenza, ed., *Searching the Scriptures, Volume One: A Feminist Introduction* (New York: Crossroad, 1993), pp. 241–254.

Recent NT literary methods described from a feminist perspective: how literary studies are practical in American departments of English and Comparative Literature; narrative criticism of the Gospels; reader-oriented approaches, including recent feminist rhetorical criticism of Pauline letters.

639.   Malherbe, Abraham J. "Hellenistic Moralists and the New Testament." *ANRW* 26.1 (1992), 267–333.

Review of the history of scholarly treatment of the former's influence on the latter, especially on Paul's letters. Recommendations for future study in this area, including remedying the neglect of Latin writers as sources of knowledge about Hellenistic philosophy, and of the ways in which philosophy was vulgarized in the first century.

640.   McKnight, Edgar V. "A Sheep in Wolf's Clothing: An Option in Contemporary New Testament Hermeneutics," in #622, pp. 326–347.

Interpretation of the Bible by the "Radical Reformers" and the reading of literature by feminists "are similar at the formal level.... Both are consciously concerned with texts for ideological reasons ... both must read against the grain of the dominant reading.... Both are 'evangelistic' in that they have a utopian dream that their community will expand to include everyone. The reorientation of hermeneutics in general may be informed, then, by the reading of the Radical Reformers and their descendants and by contemporary feminists."

641. Melick, Richard R., Jr. "Literary Criticism of the New Testament," in David S. Dockery, et al., eds., *Foundations for Biblical Interpretation* (Nashville: Broadman and Holman Publishers, 1994), pp. 434–453.

Reasons for the rise of interest in literary criticism of the Bible. Categories of literary criticism: reader response, rhetorical criticism, and structuralism. Application to the NT of genre considerations, rhetorical criticism, and structuralism. The advantages and dangers of a literary approach to scripture.

642. Oakes, Peter. "Epictetus (and the New Testament)." *VE* 23 (1993), 39–56.

"... Epictetus provides about the best window into the kind of first century Stoic world-view which will have lain prominently in the background of many ... who constituted an important part of the early Church, [thus] ... the importance of understanding Epictetus' teaching extends beyond Paul's letters to most of the NT."

643. Pogoloff, Stephen Mark. "Isocrates and Contemporary Hermeneutics," in #629, pp. 338–362.

Ancient Greco-Roman culture treated words "in a way which might seem bizarre to modern positivist historical critics, but a way which bears remarkable similarity to NT hermeneutics in the wake of Heidegger, Wittgenstein, and Godamer." "The specificity of the rhetorical situation ... is not dissolved by hermeneutics, but emphasized."

644. Robbins, Vernon K. "Rhetoric and Culture: Exploring Types of Cultural Rhetoric in a Text," in #624, pp. 443–463.

Cultural rhetorical analysis of the NT becomes possible if we "begin to discuss the bi-cultural nature in New Testament texts using a framework of dominant, subcultural and countercultural rhetoric.... This will be a revalued and reinvented rhetoric that will lead us forward into regions of analysis we have not yet undertaken."

645. Ryken, Leland. "The Literature of the New Testament," in #20, pp. 361–375.

Debate over the questions of genre, degree of "literariness" of
the NT, and of its unity. Why it seems unliterary at first glance,
and why we must think of its genres not as gospel, letter, etc., but
as "proverb, satire, parable, encomium, and visionary writing"—
i.e., those genres that appear within the NT. It is also literary because it "incarnate(s) its meaning in the form of images, characters,
and events," combines convention and innovation, and exhibits a
literary quality of discourse.

646.   Seeley, David. "Poststructuralist Criticism and Biblical
        History," in Robert Detweiler, ed., *Art/Literature/Religion:
        Life on the Borders* (Chico: Scholars P, 1983), pp. 157–171.

How Derrida fits into the philosophical tradition since Kant, and
how deconstructionist reading of a text works. Example of a deconstructionist reading of *Colossians* 1:15–20. A "thumbnail sketch"
of the discipline, related to NT studies, shows the importance of
intertextuality as a natural outcome of deconstruction.

647.   Thurén, Lauri. "On Studying Ethical Argumentation and
        Persuasion in the New Testament," in #624, pp. 464–478.

The need "for a rhetorical perspective and an analysis of argumentative structures, when studying specific motifs or larger ideological entities" in the NT. To accomplish this, we must first clarify
how persuasion functions at the text level, then analyze the argumentation "with help of modern theories and with Taulmin's
model, emphasizing the role of rhetorical situations, devices and
strategy." How these steps can lead us motifs, topoi, and finally
the ideological level.

648.   Tuggy, John C. "Semantic Paragraph Patterns: A Funda-
        mental Communication Concept and Interpretive Tool,"
        in #618, pp. 45–67.

There are six basic paragraph patterns or semantic genres: hortatory, procedural, expository, narrative, emotional, and descriptive;
all reflect the author's intended effect on his audience. Examples
from all four gospels and a number of letters.

THE GOSPELS

649. Aichele, G., and J.A. Smit. "Two Fantasies on the Death of Jesus"; "Some Remarks on ..."; "Reply to 'Remarks on Two Fantasies.'" *Neotestamentica* 26 (1992), 485–505.

Elements of the fantastic in the gospels' accounts of Jesus' suffering, death, and resurrection. The developing gospel tradition tended to eliminate these elements. Smit: Aichele's article is itself a fantasy by collapsing all indeterminacies as "fantastic," and interpreting them all from postmodernist perspective.

650. Anderson, Øivind, and Vernon K. Robbins. "Paradigms in Homer, Pindar, the Tragedians, and the New Testament," in Vernon K. Robbins, ed., *The Rhetoric of Pronouncement* (*Semeia* 64, 1993), pp. 3–31.

Although early Christians resisted using incidents and people common to Mediterranean society in their own writings, their use of paradigmatic argumentation nevertheless shows "amazing similarities" with its use in Mediterranean culture. While scholars have amply demonstrated this fact for NT letters, they have not yet done so for the gospels. They need to investigate the gospels in the context of Homer, Pindar, Plato, Plutarch, and the tragedians.

651. Burnett, Fred W. "Characterization and Reader Construction of Characters in the Gospels," in Dr. Barry L. Callen, ed., *Listening to the Word of God: A Tribute to Dr. Boyce W. Blackwedder* (Anderson, IN: Warner P, 1990), pp. 69–88.

Surveys issues most in need of resolution for studying characterization in gospels: characterization fiction; the most appropriate genre with which the gospels may be compared; and the debate about characterization in classical and Greco-Roman literature. Characterization is a continuum "on which even secondary characters may momentarily achieve "individuality." Thesis applied briefly to characterization of Peter in Matthew.

*   Burnett, Fred W. "Characterization and Reader Construction of Characters in the Gospels."

See #695.

652.   Burnett, Fred W. "Exposing the Anti-Jewish Ideology of Matthew's Implied Author: The Characterization of God as Father." *Semeia* 59 (1992), 155–191.

"The concept of the implied author [exposes] ... the way the narrative's discourse [positions the reader] ... to side with the character Jesus against the character 'the Jews' so that 'they' become a negative topos for reading the entire narrative. Matthew's implied author is a semantic effect which manipulates its readers (real or implied) [to exclude] ... 'the Jews' from the most basic symbol of Jewish existence: God as their parent."

653.   Burridge, Richard A. *What Are the Gospels? A Comparison, with Graeco-Roman Biography.* Cambridge UP, 1992.

The gospels are not unique, but share many generic features with Greco-Roman biographies. They diverge occasionally, but no more than do individual Greco-Roman biographies, given the relative looseness of the pagan generic categories. The hermeneutical implications of this view.

654.   Chance, J. Bradley. "Fiction in Ancient Biography: An Approach to a Sensitive Issue in Gospel Interpretation." *PRS* 18 (1991), 125–142.

The issue is not whether there are fictitious elements in the gospels, but how we explain them. "The study of ancient biography makes clear that Christians were not alone in their refusal to 'draw the line' between fact and fiction in their narratives.... [F]iction was a fact of ancient biography...."

654a.   Dean-Otting, Miriam, and Vernon K. Robbins. "Biblical Sources for Pronouncement Stories in the Gospels." *Semeia* 64 (1993), 93–115.

"Gospel writers used biblical material in various ways in developing their stories," including abbreviations in settings of chreia expansion, omission of clauses in chreia elaboration, and recitation of law and narrative that intermingle key words with words from the NT discourse. "Biblical materials may serve either as 'artistic' or 'inartistic' proofs depending on their function in a story."

655.   Dewey, Joanna. "Feminist Readings, Gospel Narrative and Critical Theory." *BTB* 22 (1992), 167–173.

Feminist readings of the gospels exist for, or are added to, historical/theological, formalist literature, reader-response, and structuralist readings. Since feminist criticism is non-androcentric, it "shows that the methods giving apparently stable results are ... radically open. Feminist criticism serves ... to relativize meaning, [and] ... focuses interest on questions of ... whose interests does a particular text or interpretation serve."

656. Fitzgerald, John. "The Ancient Lives of Aristotle and the Modern Debate about the Genre of the Gospels." *RQ* 36 (1994), 209–221.

The biographical tradition about Aristotle "displays many of the same tendencies and functions as the Gospels as well as some important differences. This suggests that the recent trend toward viewing the Gospels as a subtype of Hellenistic biography is warranted and that additional study of Greco-Roman biographies should enhance our understanding of the canonical Gospels."

657. Frein, Brigid Curtin. "Fundamentalism and Narrative Approaches to the Gospels." *BTB* 22 (1992), 12–18.

Fundamentalists and narrative critics "prefer synchronic, inductive approaches to biblical texts ... [and] agree on the inadequacy of historical criticism." However, the underlying assumptions of narrative criticism "make it unacceptable to fundamentalists" in that narrative criticism argues that the text is open to multiple interpretations, whereas fundamentalists insist a text can have only one meaning. Illustrations from the gospels.

658. Gardner, Helen. *The Limits of Literary Criticism. Reflections on the Interpretation of Poetry and Scripture.* London (Oxford UP), 1956.

How development in 20th-century literary criticism led to different readings of scripture from those provided by 19th-century literary critics, often for the worse. "I cannot feel satisfied with a literary criticism which substitutes for the conception of the writer as 'a man speaking to men' the conception of the writer as an imagination weaving symbolic patterns to be teased out by the intellect, and ... ends by finding significance in what the work suggests rather than in what it says, and directs our imaginations towards types and figures rather than towards their actualization."

* Heil, John Paul. *Jesus Walking on the Sea. Meaning and Gospel Functions of Matthew 4:22–33, Mark 6:45–52 and John 6:15b–21.*

See #707.

659.   de Lang, Marijke H. "Gospel Synopses from the 16th to the
        18th Centuries and the Rise of Literary Criticism of the
        Gospels," in Camille Focant, ed., *The Synoptic Gospels:
        Source Criticism and the New Literary Criticism* (Leuven:
        Leuven UP, 1993), pp. 599–607.

> The emergence of literary criticism of the gospels in the work of
> Lessing and Griesbach "originated as a reaction to the hypercriti-
> cism of the deists. The historical events ... narrated in the Gospels,
> first had to be subjected to radical historical criticism before the
> discrepancies and the similarities between the Gospels would be-
> come the subject of serious literary-critical investigation."

660.   McCracken, David. "Character in the Boundary: Bakhtin's
        Interdividuality in Biblical Narratives." *Semeia* 63 (1993),
        29–42.

> Character in individual terms is an inadequate concept, since it
> is formed in relationship to others. This relationship is best
> thought of as a threshold or boundary, where character is "re-
> vealed in dialogic interaction at a moment of crisis." The "relative,
> surprising freedom" of biblical characters who are in contact with
> readers, author, and each other. Since in the Gospels, "character
> encounters in Jesus the possibility of offense, ... the discourse of
> the gospels is scandalous and eccentric...."

661.   McCracken, David. *The Scandal of the Gospels. Jesus, Story,
        and Offense.* New York and Oxford (Oxford UP), 1994.

> The "complex of traps-snares-stumbling blocks-offenses-scan-
> dals ... is an essential part of the Jewish and Christian Bibles"—
> especially in the gospel narratives. To read the Gospels properly,
> we need to resist the temptation to "domesticate it to nullify its
> dangerous power." Kierkegaardian and Bakhtinian notions of
> "scandal" as applied to the gospels.

662.   Mohr, Martin, and Mary Hull Mohr. "Interpreting the Text
        and Telling the Story." *Dialog* 21 (1982), 102–106.

> The implications for hermeneutics "of the significant gap be-
> tween the literary and biblical critic's understanding of the gospel
> narrative." The tendencies of recent hermeneutics to view scrip-
> ture as story "allow the biblical scholar to continue refining a
> historical understanding of the man Jesus, while ... freeing the Je-
> sus-story to enter the domain of literary discourse."

663. Moloney, Francis J. "Narrative Criticism of the Gospels." *Pacifica* 4 (1991), 181–201.

The roles of, and interchange between, real readers, implied reader and implied author of the gospels, and how these determine the "lasting value and classical status" of the gospels.

664. Number deleted.

665. Parsons, Mikeal C. "What's 'Literary' About Literary Aspects of the Gospels and Acts?" *SBLSP* (1992), 14–39.

Review of the work of the "Literary Aspects" group since its start in 1981. Significant change has occurred in those years through the advent of poststructuralist approaches, as well as feminism, reader-response, etc. How the author's own ethnic heritage impinges on his interpretations. The importance of the "cultural-literary" approach in enabling the critic to get outside his own assumptions.

666. Petersen, Norman. "Can One Speak of a Gospel Genre?" *Neotestamentica* 28, #3 (1994), 137–158.

There is no gospel genre as such, since internal literary differences preclude this. Likewise, none of the canonical gospels is a biography. Rather, we should define them in terms of plot types. Thus, *Luke-Acts* is historiography, and *Matthew* a manual of discipline or community rule. *Mark* is of the concealment-recognition plot-type, and *John* bears significant similarities to Mark.

667. Placher, William C. "Gospels, Ends: Plurality and Ambiguity in Biblical Narratives." *Modern Theology* 10 (1994), 143–163.

The gospels themselves implicitly address the question of the relation of their narrated world and "our world." We can recognize the narrative strategies used to accomplish this task "only if we respect the narrative logic of the individual Gospels," rather than conflating them into one story.

668. Powell, Mark Allan. "What Is 'Literary' about Literary Aspects?" *SBLSP* (1992), 40–48.

The need for methodological interdependence in literary criticism of the Bible is as great as ever today. Traditional historical and newer literary methods are not as far apart as were first believed, so narrative critics should not try to distance themselves from, say, redaction critics.

669.   Resseguie, James L. "Defamiliarization and the Gospels."
        BTB 20 (1990), 147–153.

        Defamiliarization—the creative distortion of ordinary percep-
        tion for purpose of renewing "the reader's diminished capacity for
        fresh perception"—is a literary device popularized by Victor
        Shklovsky,the Russian formalist. Its frequency and function in the
        gospels.

670.   Robbins, Vernon K. "Progymnastic Rhetorical Composition
        and Pre-Gospel Traditions: A New Approach," in Camille
        Focant, ed., *The Synoptic Gospels: Source Criticism and the
        New Literary Criticism* (Leuven: Leuven UP, 1993), pp.
        111–147.

        Definition of socio-rhetorical criticism and its differences be-
        tween both historical criticism and new literary criticism. The
        rhetorical or "writing" culture of the ancient world, and especially
        the "progymnasmata" (preliminary exercises) of first-century
        rhetorical treatises as clues for gospel critics. The importance of
        argumentation, the contexts of utterance, and of the whole culture-
        transmitting tradition of the ancient world for understanding the
        gospels.

671.   Robbins, Vernon K. "Writing as a Rhetorical Act in Plutarch
        and the Gospels," in #629, pp. 142–168.

        How we understand the act of writing which produced the story
        as it comes to us. Within a rhetorical culture, a written document
        was "a recitation that should be performed anew rather than a
        verbal text that should be copied verbatim.... The similarities and
        variations in wording in both Plutarch and the NT Synoptic writ-
        ers should make it obvious to us that the guiding principle behind
        their transmission of stories and sayings is recitation composi-
        tion."

672.   Segovia, Fernando F. "The Journey(s) of Jesus to Jerusalem.
        Plotting and Gospel Intertextuality," in Adelbert Devaux,
        ed., *John and the Synoptics* (Leuven: Leuven UP, 1992), pp.
        535–541.

        Definitions in literary theory of intertextuality. The journey-of-
        the-hero motif common in ancient narrative, and its function in the
        gospels. Its use is much more important in the synoptics than in
        John, while the substitute in *John* is repeated visits to Jerusalem.
        The influence of this journey motif on the plots of each gospel.
        How Jerusalem functions as the thematic climax of the journey-

ing/teaching of Jesus. Possible explanations of the similarities among the gospels.

673. Swartley, William M. *Israel's Scripture Traditions and the Synoptic Gospels. Story Shaping Story*. Peabody (Hendrickson Publishers, Inc.), 1994.

Narrative-compositioned analysis of the ways in which OT faith traditions have "helped determine the context" and "distinctive common structure" of the synoptic gospels. These traditions are the exodus, conquest, temple, and kingship. They occur primarily in sequence in the synoptics; they also overlap and even fuse with each other. How the gospels use and transform the traditions for their own theological purposes.

674. Taylor, R.O.P. "Greek Forms of Instruction," in *The Groundwork of the Gospels* (Oxford: Basil Blackwell, 1946), pp. 75–90.

The importance of chreiai in Greek biographical writing, and their crucial influence on the writing of the gospels. Their function was to aid the presentation of historical material.

675. Theissen, Gerd. *The Miracle Stories of the Early Christian Tradition*, trans. Francis McDonagh, ed. John Riches. Philadelphia (Fortress), 1983.

Part One is a synchronic approach: miracle stories as structured forms. Provides catalog of motifs (e.g., coming of the miracleworker, description of distress, resistance and submission to the demon, recognition of miracle, etc.) and a catalog of themes. Part Three: "Miracle Stories as Symbolic Actions."

676. Vinson, Richard B. "A Comparative Study of the Use of Enthymemes in the Synoptic Gospels," in #629, pp. 119–141.

The use of enthymemes and their similarities and differences; how the writers' use of this argumentative device supports their narrative strategies. Mark uses enthymemes seventy-seven times, *Matthew* 164, *Luke* 165. Tables showing all examples, their location and type.

677. Vorster, William S. "The Function of Metaphorical and Apocalyptic Language about the Unobservable in the Teaching of Jesus," in Theodore W. Jennings, *Text and Logos: The Humanistic Interpretation of the New Testament* (Atlanta: Scholars P, 1990), pp. 33–51.

"... Jesus used metaphoric and apocalyptic language functionally. He did things with words. He tried to resocialize his hearers by offering them a new symbolic universe. In this sense modern theories about language ... help theologians in their attempt to speak meaningfully about the God in whom they believe. That includes the making of new metaphors and the use of metaphorical language about the unobservable."

678.   Wiarda, Timothy. "Simon, Jesus of Nazareth, Son of Jonah, Son of John: Realistic Detail in the Gospels and Acts." *NTS* 40 (1994), 196–209.

One literary feature within many of the narratives of the gospels and Acts is the distinctive use of certain names in direct speech. While these names differ in narrative function, as a group they share two characteristics: they do not have a theological purpose at that point in the narrative, and they are not used by the narrator. "Their use, then, appears to reflect a concern to portray details realistically." This practice is equally observable in the synoptics, *John* and *Acts*.

See also #11, 72, 638, 695, 890.

THE PARABLES

679.   Berger, Klaus. "Rhetorical Criticism, New Form Criticism and New Testament Hermeneutics," in #624, pp. 390–396.

"Hermeneutics is based on rhetoric, because application does not merely rely on theoretical comprehension ..., but mainly on the pragmatic effect (function).... [W]e must carefully analyze [the situation] and try to find out the ... point by which the biblical text can support people in this situation or give them critical guidance." The parables as ideal texts for measuring and understanding the pragmatic effect of NT texts.

680.   Harnisch, Wolfgang. "Language of the Possible: The Parables of Jesus in the Conflict Between Rhetoric and Poetry." *ST* 46 (1992), 41–54.

"The parables of Jesus are configured in such a way that speech-form and subject-matter converge. To take this insight seriously appears unattainable to exegetical research which remains oriented towards the model of analogy.... Should theology not consider, for example, that literary critics resolutely refuse to take the forms of speech of the fable and the parable as belonging to the category of the similitude...?"

681.   Hedrick, Charles W. *Parables as Poetic Fictions. The Creative Voice of Jesus.* Peabody (Hendrickson), 1994.

Analysis of the Parables as literary narratives in the context of first-century Palestine culture "is crucial to their historical understanding." The place to begin reading the Parables is not by regarding them as metaphor/symbol; rather, only "inside the story ... [may] discoveries about oneself and the world ... be made." Readings of selected parables as poetic factions: *Luke* 10; *Matthew* 13 (*Thomas*: logion 107–113); *Luke* 12 (*Thomas*: logion 63); the Sower (Synoptics and *Thomas*); *Luke* 18.

682.   Hester, James D. "Socio-Rhetorical Criticism and the Parable of the Tenants." *JSNT* 45 (1992), 27–57.

Socio-Rhetorical criticism of this parable (*Matthew* 21, *Mark* 12, *Luke* 20) helps strip away the foreign interpretation provided by early character communities, revealing that its intention was to "expose systems of group and class relations within the Jewish communities of first-century Palestine with respect to the theme of 'land' and 'inheritance.'"

683.   Miller, J. Hillis. "Parable and Performative in the Gospels and in Modern Literature," in *Tropes, Parables, Performatives: Essays on Twentieth-Century Literature* (Durham: Duke UP, 1991), pp. 135–150.

While it ought not to be difficult to distinguish between sacred and secular parables, in practice the distinction blurs. Parabolic interpretation becomes almost bewilderingly paradoxical as we realize how those who need them most are by definition most incapable of interpreting them. Questions about the extent to which Jesus' parabolic language is performative.

684.   Sandifer, D. Wayne. "The Humor of the Absurd in the Parables of Jesus." *SBLSP* (1991), 287–297.

Jesus used humor and even obviously absurd images in his parables deliberately as a rhetorical tool to force his hearers to a decision. To miss the humor is to miss part of the message.

685.   Scott, Bernard Brandon. *Jesus, Symbol-Maker for the Kingdom.* Philadelphia (Fortress), 1981.

The implications of a literary-structuralist model for analyzing Jesus' language outside the parables, and of the parables themselves as performances. "... How Jesus' language as a system of signs effects meaning in the parables as individual performances." How his "sayings and deeds result from the same organizing symbolic world as [his] parables...."

686.   Sider, John W. "The Parables," in #20, pp. 422–435.

Critics of the parables should test their theories inductively by the texts themselves. We should begin with analogy—"the most significant common denominator in all the parabolai." To label them as "story" is therefore misleading; they are rather "elaborated story-parables" or story-analogies with a context that cannot be ignored. Interplay of image and text in the parables, as shown in *Luke* 10.

687.   Thoma, Clemens, and Michael Wyschogrod, eds. *Parable and Story in Judaism and Christianity.* NY and Mahwah (Paulist), 1989.

Ten essays, of which six are literary-critical: David Flusser on Parable of Talents and Aesop; David Stern on Wicked Husbandmen and Rabbinic parables; Aaron Milovec on Wicked Husbandmen and anti-Judaism in *Luke*; Frank Kermode on new literary interpretations of David and Bathsheba and of several gospel narratives; Paul Michel on a linguistic/figurative speech approach to parables; Romano Peña on narrative dimensions of Paul's letters.

INDIVIDUAL GOSPELS

MATTHEW

688. Adam, A.K.M. "Matthew's Readers, Ideology, and Power." *SBLSP* (1994), 435–449.

While Matthew may not be innocent of anti-Semitism, we as readers must accept our role in perpetuating anti-Jewish readings of Matthew because such readings are all too attractive to us. "Our historical context does indeed provide constraints which limit our interpretations. On the other hand, our contexts also provide us with resources with which to resist."

689. Allison, Dale C. "Anticipating the Passion: The Literary Reach of Matthew 26:47–27:56." *CBQ* 56 (1994), 701–714.

Various parables between individual events in various parts of chapters 1–25 and 26–28 demonstrate how the entire narrative "leans toward" its climax. Examples include the executions of John and Jesus (14:3–12 and 27:46–61); turning the other cheek (5:38–42 and 27:32); the afflictions of missionaries (10:17–23 and 26:45–27:1); the transfiguration and crucifixion (17:1–8 and 27:27–56); and the teaching on true service (20:20–28). All these display the rhetorical strategy of borrowing language from the passion narratives.

690. Anderson, Janice Capel. *Matthew's Narrative Web: Over, and Over, and Over Again.* Sheffield (JSOT P), 1994.

Narrative and reader response analyses of *Matthew* as a narrative and as a web of verbal repetition that helps create the tale. In a complex sense, the evangelist, the narrative, and the reader of *Matthew* all spin this web. Examination of verbal repetition, narrative and reader-response criticism in light of recent work on aurality, orality, and literacy. Importance of understanding first-century aural conventions for reading *Matthew* (or any gospel).

691. Barta, Karen A. "Mission in Matthew: The Second Discourse as Narrative." *SBLSP* (1988), 527–535.

Based on the structuralist distinction between "story" and "discourse," "a dramatic story of mission life unfolds within the

Second Discourse by means of a careful arrangement of traditional Jesus-sayings and sayings of Jesus as key moments which are peculiar to Matthew.... There is actually a plot ... that unfolds within the discourse as part of the story that not only breathes life into these traditional teachings but quickens the gospel as a whole."

692. Bauer, David R. "The Major Characters of Matthew's Story." *Interpretation* 46 (1992), 357–367.

Since Matthew is a story, we may assume the author uses his characters to communicate with the reader. Since Jesus is the central figure, all the characters will be seen in relation to him, whether they be hostile or friendly.

693. Black, C. Clifton II. "Depth of Characterization and Degrees of Faith in Matthew." *SBLSP* (1989), 604–623.

Review of Kingsbury's assessment of the characters in Matthew. Reconsideration of the subject in light of recent developments in literary theory concerning characterization and how it affects our understanding of Matthew's theological uses of characterization.

*   Blount, Brian K. "A Socio-Rhetorical Analysis of Simon of Cyrene: Mark 15:21 and Its Parallels."

See #785.

694. Boring, M. Eugene. "The Convergence of Source Analysis: Social History, and Literary Structure in the Gospel of Matthew." *SBLSP* (1994), 587–611.

While Matthew's use of Q, his adaptation of sources for his particular community, and the resulting structure of his gospel are all familiar matters to interpreters of the first gospel, seeing them as interwoven provides new perspectives on Matthew. The chiastic structure of the gospel (already found in rudimentary form in his sources) derives from all three elements.

695. Burnett, Fred W. "Characterization and Reader Construction of Characters in the Gospels." *Semeia* 63 (1993), 1–28.

Characters as both constructs and effects of the reading process. If the former, a character tends to dissolve into segments of textual indicators; if the latter, a character may seem to transcend the text. Degrees of characterization in the gospels, from "agent" to "type" to "character." Peter in *Matthew* as an example of a type who "achieves a higher degree of characterization than the disciples do as a group."

696.   Carter, Warren. "Kernels and Narrative Blocks: The Struc-
        ture of Matthew's Gospel." *CBQ* 54 (1992), 463–481.

        The current impasse over the structure of Matthew may be re-
        lieved by F. Matera's analysis of the plot [Minor I, #1743]. How-
        ever, his identification of kernels and narrative block seems un-
        convincing. A better alternative might be to recognize "a whole
        host of other internal structural devices." The key is the focus on
        kernels, satellites, and narrative blocks.

697.   Charette, Blaine. *The Theme of Recompense in Matthew's
        Gospel.* Sheffield (JSOT P/Sheffield Academic P), 1992.

        Composition criticism applied to the study of how the themes of
        reward and punishment function to other Matthean themes. Espe-
        cially reiteration of significant terms and phrases, juxtaposition of
        topics, use of inclusion to connect sections of the gospel.
        Matthew's extensive dependence on the HB's ideas of recompense,
        rather than on the other gospels of which he was presumably
        aware.

698.   Davies, Margaret. *Matthew.* Sheffield (JSOT P), 1993.

        Commentary emphasizing reader-response approach to this
        qgospel, with a review and critique of dominant reader-response
        theories. How *Matthew* differs from modern historical narratives,
        and what the narrative of Matthew implies about the world the
        characters inhabit.

699.   Donaldson, Terence L. "The Mockers and the Son of God
        (Matthew 27.37–44): Two Characters in Matthew's Story
        of Jesus." *JSNT* 41 (1991), 3–18.

        Literary theory of plot development and character, especially of
        N. Friedman's concept of the three possible changes (fortune,
        moral character, or knowledge), leads us to better understanding
        both of Matthew's plot of fortune, and of Jesus as central character
        in reconciling two conflicting concepts of divine sonship.

700.   Edwards, Richard A. "Characterization of the Disciples as a
        Feature of Matthew's Narrative," in F. Van Segbroeck, et
        al., eds., *The Four Gospels 1992: Festschrift Frans Neirynck*
        (Leuven: Leuven UP, 1993), Vol. 2, pp. 1305–1323.

        The characterization of the disciples in *Matthew* 4:18–22 and
        8:18–27 is "only beginning to expand." The importance of the dis-
        tinction between implied and real reader, which "helps to clarify

the very importance of the world of the narrative." Context and flow of narrative in *Matthew*. "Limiting the analysis to the hypothetical implied reader results in a much clearer recognition of the amount of material that the real reader can attach to the story."

701.   Garland, David E. *Reading Matthew: A Literary and Theological Commentary on the First Gospel*. NY (Crossroad), 1993.

Section-by-section, rather than line-by-line, commentary, highlighting especially role of the narrator and reader(s) of *Matthew*.

703.   Grams, Rollin. "The Temple Conflict Scene: A Rhetorical Analysis of Matthew 21–23," in #629, pp. 41–65.

The rhetorical features of *Matthew* 21–23 make an interesting study. Overview of Matthew's rhetoric. Presence of two inclusios demonstrates that *Matthew* 21–23 is a christological unit. The unity and power of this scene discovered through rhetorical criticism, which other methods often ignore. Its place in the whole gospel. How rhetorical criticism "honors Scripture's authority in its concern with the text as it is and ... the author's intentions."

*   Hedrick, Charles W. "Miracle Stories as Literary Compositions: The Case of Jairus's Daughter."

See #772.

704.   Heil, John Paul. "The Blood of Jesus in Matthew. A Narrative-Critical Perspective." *PRS* 18 (1991), 117–124.

Jesus' blood has an additional meaning: the Jews' search for vengeance is what makes possible the very sacrifice which saves mankind. They paradoxically invoke his atoning blood upon themselves.

705.   Heil, John Paul. *The Death and Resurrection of Jesus: A Narrative-Critical Reading of Matthew 26–28*. Minneapolis (Fortress), 1991.

The "intricate and dynamic design" of these chapters. The rhetorical effect on the reader of the "alternating and progressive sequence of contrasting scenes," and how that effect produces the "meaning latent in the text...." Such a reading "enables us ... to experience the dynamic process of communication involved in the intricate structures formed by these Matthean scenes."

706. Heil, John Paul. "Ezekiel 34 and the Narrative Strategy of the Shepherd and Sheep Metaphor in Matthew." *CBQ* 55 (1993), 698–708.

The "subtle rhetorical progression" in references to Jesus as a shepherd in *Matthew*. The "narrative strategy of Matthew's shepherd metaphor is guided and unified by *Ezekiel* 34 which supplies the reader with some of its terms and with all of its concepts and images."

707. Heil, John Paul. *Jesus Walking on the Sea. Meaning and Gospel Functions of Matthew 14:22–33, Mark 6:45–52 and John 6:15b–21*. Rome (Biblical Institute P), 1981.

Relationships of the three sea-walking epiphanies to the rest of their respective gospels. The "importance and uniqueness" of these epiphanies for the theological, christological and ecclesiological interpretation of each gospel.

708. Heil, John Paul. "The Narrative Roles of the Women in Matthew's Genealogy." *Biblica* 72 (1991), 538–545.

If we take seriously the structural positions and the sequence in which the implied reader experiences their naming, we reveal the similarities and differences among the women named in *Matthew's* genealogy, and get at their thematic functions.

709. Humphries-Brooks, Stephenson. "Spatial Form and Plot Disruption in the Gospel of Matthew." *Essays in Literature* 20 (1993), 54–69.

Matthew is myth, not fiction. The text is "a hybrid form that unifies a linear, episodic, causal-sequential biography with spatial, non-sequential, associative modes of representation. The experience of reading *Matthew* may therefore become a way of reappropriating a lost aspect of critical consciousness ... as myth.... *Matthew* takes seriously its own representational character and makes its reading strategy a matter not of entertainment and pleasure, but of life and death."

710. Jones, John Mark. "Subverting the Textuality of Davidic Messianism: Matthew's Presentation of the Genealogy and the Davidic Title." *CBQ* 56 (1994), 256–272.

How Matthew's Jesus "reconstructs the OT paradigm of Messiaship.... Matthew utilizes typology in his subversive narrative in order to hint that the antitype does not simply fulfill or replace the type but in some cases may actually destroy it." Thus, "Matthew's narrative is liberating because it overturns the textuality of Davidic messianism."

711.   Kea, Perry V. "Writing a bios: Matthew's Genre Choices and Rhetorical Situation." *SBLSP* (1994), 574–586.

Treatments of gospel genre as biography must recognize that "ancient literary theory had very little to say about biography," and that the ancient genre of biography was flexible. Ancient pagan practices of characterization and of presenting the life and the teachings compared to Matthew's practices. "Matthew's choice of a bios indicates that torah is not the voice of authority in his community, but the voice of Jesus is."

712.   Kingsbury, Jack Dean. "The Plot of Matthew's Story." *Interpretation* 46 (1992), 347–356.

The plot of *Matthew* is one of conflict between Jesus and the religious authorities, arranged by Matthew through several literary devices to rise toward a climax in Jerusalem: placement of conflict, "confrontational" narrative tone, focus of all the incidents on questions of authority, compression of incidents into a short span of two days; and portrayal of a hostile atmosphere.

713.   Kingsbury, Jack Dean. "The Rhetoric of Comprehension in the Gospel of Matthew." *NTS* 41 (1995), 358–377.

The main way in which Matthew describes his characters is through the literary strategy of the "rhetoric of comprehension"— intended to show "whether, or to what extent, they ... understand [Jesus] ... aright and respond by, receiving, him and 'doing' God's will as he teaches it." Matthew's purpose then becomes to lead the reader to so understand and respond.

714.   Kingsbury, Jack Dean. "The Significance of the Cross within the Plot of Matthew's Gospel," in Camille Focant, ed., *The Synoptic Gospels: Source Criticism and the New Literary Criticism* (Leuven: Leuven UP, 1993), pp. 263–279.

How and to what effect Jesus' conflict with the authorities "reaches its resolution in the cross and resurrection and its culmination in the cross" in the unfolding plot of *Matthew*. The scene on the cross plays a crucial role in two respects in the plot: it resolves the conflict with the religious authorities as well as being the place where the entire gospel story culminates. The themes associated with this plot function.

715. Kodjak, Andreij. *A Structural Analysis of the Sermon on the Mount.* Berlin, New York, and Amsterdam (Mouton de Gruyter), 1986.

Paradigmatic and syntagmatic analysis of *Matthew* 5–7. Structuralism "broadens the concept of art." The Sermon on the Mount communicates on both primary and secondary levels of language. It has a "unique secondary language and therefore can be approached as an artistic text." Appendices comparing to Luke's "Sermon on the Plain" and the parable of the Sower (*Matthew* 13, *Luke* 8).

* LaVerdiere, Eugene, S.S.S. "The Lord's Prayer in Literary Context."

See #822.

716. Lowe, J.P. "Reading a Text as Discourse," in #618, pp. 17–30.

Explanation of discourse analysis, illustrated with examples from *Matthew* 19, *John* 3, *Colossians* 2–3. Why discourse and structural analysis are not coextensive.

717. Nau, Arlo J. *Peter in Matthew: Discipleship, Diplomacy, and Dispraise.* Collegeville, MN (Liturgical P), 1992.

Both redaction and rhetorical criticism of *Matthew* demonstrate that the author's seemingly inconsistent portrayal of Peter is the result of his editing into his gospel traditions about Peter which Matthew does not personally espouse. Rather, he was "applying the rubrics of a mature form of 'encomiastic' dispraise" in order to "neutralize Peter's traditional prominence within the Antiochan community," the goal being to present Jesus as unrivaled head of the new church.

718. Nortjé, L. "Matthew's Motive for the Composition of the Story of Judas's Suicide in Matthew 27:3–10." *Neotestamentica* 28, #1 (1994), 41–51.

Matthew's intention is not to report how Judas died so much as "to provide a particular version of the story in order that the more important motifs of the rest of the gospel can be contained in it." Through these motifs Matthew "wants to indicate who is responsible for Jesus' death": the chief priests and elders.

719. Orton, David E. "Matthew and Other Creative Jewish Writers," in #17, pp. 133–140.

Matthew "fits in very well within the character of much of ... a great deal of creative Jewish writing going on in the first century...." Comparison of *Matthew* to "a wide range of ... Jewish literature, all of it scribal and much of it apocalyptic, adds bright colour to our picture of his literary art and his religious standpoint."

720.   Patte, Daniel. "Bringing Out of the Gospel-Treasure What Is New and What Is Old: Two Parables in Matthew." *Quarterly Review* 10, #3 (Fall 1990), 79–108.

Three possible readings for each of two chapters in *Matthew*: 18 and 20. Why "any text has several coherent dimensions that can be the basis of different consistent interpretations." We need not reconcile them, simply be aware that they "present different dimensions of the text." Each reading addresses questions ignored by the other readings.

721.   Powell, Mark Allan. "Direct and Indirect Phraseology in the Gospel of Matthew." *SBLSP* (1991), 405–417.

Literary analysis of the "discourse component of characterization" in *Matthew* demonstrates that the author provides reliable information for characterization of Jesus and of his disciples, but of the religious leaders only when it is indirect. "In this way, Matthew highlights the duplicity of the religious leaders and guides the reader to recognize the deceptive way in which hypocrites may try to hide their real nature."

722.   Powell, Mark Allan. "Expected and Unexpected Readings in Matthew: What the Reader Knows." *The Asbury Theological Journal* 48 (1993), 31–51.

How real readers who wish to place themselves in the role of Matthew's implied reader must function. What the implied reader is expected to know about other, pre-Matthean texts, and the need to set aside knowledge which implied readers could not have had.

723.   Powell, Mark Allan. "The Plot and Subplots of Matthew's Gospel." *NTS* 38 (1992), 187–204.

Reviews previous work on the plot of *Matthew*. A better conclusion is that the gospel not only has a "discernible and logical plot," but "significant subplots concerning the religious leaders and Jesus' disciples" which add depth to the main plot. Only the main plot is resolved favorably.

724. Powell, Mark Allan. "Toward a Narrative-Critical Understanding of Matthew." *Interpretation* 46 (1992), 341–346.

"The implications of taking seriously this narrative character of the Gospel are profound." Explanation of the narrative analysis of *Matthew* in terms of narrative rather than redactor, implied reader rather than community, and plot rather than structure.

*   Robbins, Vernon K. "Using a Socio-Rhetorical Poetics to Develop a Unified Method: The Woman Who Anointed Jesus as a Test Case."

See #792.

725. Scott, Bernard Brandon. "The Birth of the Reader: Matthew 1:1–4:16,11 in John T. Carroll, et al., eds., *Faith and History: Essays in Honor of Paul W. Meyer* (Atlanta: Scholars P, 1990), pp. 35–54.

The beginning of *Matthew*, as with beginning of all the gospels, cannot be ignored, because it provides clues to how that book is to be read, especially to point of view. Narratological analysis of the role of the genealogy, birth narrative, post-birth events. Ideology, focalization, and theme in these narratives. *Matthew* describes not the birth of Jesus but of the reader, the narrator constructing an "ideological map by which the reader is to make sense of the story that follows."

726. Scott, Bernard Brandon, and Margaret E. Dean. "A Sound Map of the Sermon on the Mount." *SBLSP* (1993), 672–725.

Semantic analysis of *Matthew* 5–7, emphasizing the signifier, or the sign's physical aspect—a matter often neglected in biblical criticism. In a rhetorical world, "reading is *recitatio* and writing is for the purpose of *recitatio*" with sound as the "primary receptive clue." This analysis leads to modification of plot outline based on writing/reading model.

727. Stanton, Graham N. "MATTHEW: *BIBΛΟΣ, ΕΥΑΓΓΕΛΙΟΝ*, OR *BIOΣ*?," in F. Van Segbroeck, et al., eds., *The Four Gospels 1992: Festschrift Frans Neirynck* (Leuven: Leuven UP), vol. 2, pp. 1187–1201.

The importance of the literary genre of *Matthew* for its interpretation. His "first readers and listeners responded to his writing quite instinctively as a type of Graeco-Roman biography....

Matthew's use of extended discourses and his frequent topical arrangement of material are both found in many ancient biographies. However, as a result of paying more attention to the storytelling techniques of modern novelists than to the methods of ancient biographers, narrative critics have emphasized the "storyline" and plot of Matthew at the expense of doing justice to his five extended discourses. Like many ancient biographers, Matthew was concerned to give particular prominence to the sayings of Jesus."

728.   Via, Dan O. "Matthew's Dark Light and the Human Condition," in #622, pp. 348–366.

Investigation of *Matthew* 6:22–23 in terms of "an anthropological question: what does the darkened light of Matthew 6.22–23 tell us about human being in principle ... and about the actual human condition[?]" Consideration of three structural levels: the grammatical–logical–philosophical, the metaphorical, and the narrative, how they reinforce one another, and the resulting pessimistic picture of the human condition.

729.   Wainwright, Elaine Mary. *Towards a Feminist Critical Reading of the Gospel According to Matthew.* (BZNW 60.) Berlin and New York (Walter de Gruyter), 1991.

Definition of feminist biblical hermeneutics. Application to *Matthew* "must [begin with] ... the restoration of the stories of women to the gospel text" using narrative and reader-response criticism in a "hermeneutics of suspicion and remembrance." The androcentric perspective of Matthew. Chapters of specific women characters included within the text or within the formation of the text, on women in Matthew's narrative world and in the Matthean communities.

730.   Weaver, Dorothy Jean. "Power and Powerlessness: Matthew's Use of Irony in the Portrayal of Political Leaders." *SBLSP* (1992), 454–466.

How *Matthew* portrays such leaders as Herod, Pilate, and the Jewish authorities ironically by contrasting their earthly power to their powerlessness in the face of the truth about and of Jesus.

731.   Whittle, Amberys R. "Matthew," in #20, pp. 376–386.

Review of major theories of the structure and rhetoric of *Matthew*. The gospel's use of irony, paradox, and inversion; the importance of discourse material; principles of Matthean characterization and plot dynamics. All these make traditional approaches inadequate, and invite a literary one.

See also #63, 71, 111, 651, 681, 682, 806, 822, 834.

MARK

732.   Anderson, Janice Capel, and Stephen D. Moore, eds. *Mark and Method: New Approaches in Biblical Studies.* Minneapolis (Fortress P), 1992.

"... to introduce students and teachers to new approaches in the interpretation of the Gospels, using the Gospel of Mark as a case study." Introduction: history of interpretation of *Mark.* Malbon: Narrative Criticism; Fowler: Reader-response criticism; Moore: Deconstruction [reworked excerpts from *Mark and Luke in Post-structural Perspective*, see #753]; Anderson: Feminist criticism; Rhoads: Social criticism.

733.   Augustine, John H. "Mark," in #20, pp. 387–397.

The episodic plot, literary form, rhetorical strategies including irony, and the importance of the initiation motif.

734.   Beardslee, William A. "Narrative and History in the Post-Modern World. The Case of the Gospel of Mark," in *Margins of Belonging: Essays on the New Testament and Theology* (Atlanta: Scholars P, 1991), pp. 89–100.

How *Mark* has fared in humanistic research and analysis of the last century and a half, as well as in theological interpretation. The "striking" consensus that *Mark* is a "remarkably coherent narrative." The work of Rhoads and Michie, Kermode, Frei, among other literary critics. How the "task that lies beyond Mark as fiction" may be formulated.

735.   Black, David Alan. "Discourse Analysis, Synoptic Criticism, and Markan Grammar: Some Methodological Considerations," in #618, pp. 90–98.

How discourse analysis can make the internal workings of a text explicit. Specifically, it cannot support the contention that

Matthew and Luke corrected Mark's grammar. Instead, this can be shown through the study of style through choice.

736.   Broadhead, Edwin K. "Jesus the Nazarene: Narrative Strategy and Christological Imagery in the Gospel of Mark." *JSNT* 52 (1993), 3–18.

Christological titles are literary elements "participating in particular narrative worlds and narrative strategies." Mark's image of the Nazarene and its subsequent complication with other titles as a literary strategy suggests a pattern for future investigation of this question.

737.   Broadhead, Edwin K. *Teaching with Authority. Miracles and Christology in the Gospel of Mark.* Sheffield (JSOT P), 1992.

Re-evaluation of the miracle traditions, through highlighting "the narrative identity and the christological focus of the Gospel of Mark," in order to reconsider the role played by miracle stories in the characterization of Jesus. A "narrative morphology" of Markan miracle stories, as well as their "narrative syntax" and thematic genres.

738.   Bryan, Christopher. *A Preface to Mark: Notes on the Gospel in Its Literary and Cultural Settings.* NY, Oxford (Oxford UP), 1993.

Asks what kind of text *Mark* would have been seen to be by its author and first audience. Its likely identity as a Hellenistic life of Christ, and as a work intended to be heard rather than read by an audience, though it is not oral traditional literature in the full sense. Its "remembrance of the living voice was decisive for its trustworthiness."

739.   Camery-Hoggatt, Jerry. *Irony in Mark's Gospel: Text and Subtext.* Cambridge UP, 1992.

Markan irony, both verbal and dramatic, is intentional, forming an integral factor in the Gospel's overall strategy of composition. Polyvalent functions of narrative elements for serving different rhetorical strategies. "... the core of the ironies lies in the tension between exclusionary strategies and veiled revelations," so that, while the characters cannot understand the full meaning of the events in which they participate, the reader can.

740.   Danove, Paul L. *The End of Mark's Story. A Methodological Study.* Leiden (E.J. Brill), 1993.

Structuralist analysis of *Mark*. Plot in Aristotle and contemporary theorists. Proposal for a "narrative grammar" and a "phenomenological model of narrative communication" for a coherent method of narrative analysis. Narrative structures, implied reader, rhetoric, and irony in *Mark*. Such analysis lessons the importance of the negative portrayal of the disciples, and recognizes irony as one of Mark's most important tools.

741. Davidsen, Ole. *The Narrative Jesus. A Semiotic Reading of Mark's Gospel*. Aarhus (Aarhus UP), 1993.

Explanation of semiotic method, and its general application to the gospels in general, and Mark in particular. Narrative exegesis of Jesus in three modes: wonder worker, proclaimer, and savior. The narrative genre of the first; the narrative's cognitive dimension in the second; "the narrative Jesus as savior" in the third. Relationship between narrativity and historicity in *Mark*.

742. Dewey, Joanna. "The Gospel of Mark as an Oral–Aural Event: Implications for Interpretation," in #622, pp. 145–163.

Orality and literacy in antiquity; characteristics of oral narratives and methods of oral composition. How a first-century listening audience would have experienced Mark recited aloud and the differences that makes in our interpretation of *Mark* because we are then not dealing with a work that began its existence in writing. The necessity of recognizing the instability of an oral text. Thus, our *Mark* "represents one version among many.... [W]e do not know how typical it is, and ... we do not know which audience it reflects at what time."

743. Dewey, Joanna. "Mark as Aural Narrative: Structures as Clues to Understanding." *Sewanee Theological Review* 36 (1992–93), 45–56.

We have stopped trying to understand *Mark* as a print narrative whose purpose is to convey information, and begun to see it as a powerful oral/aural narrative which engages its audience in a story of humor and pathos. How the characteristics of such a narrative reveal its richness of meaning.

744. Dewey, Joanna. "Mark as Interwoven Tapestry: Forecasts and Echoes for a Listening Audience." *CBQ* 53 (1991), 221–236.

Mark does not have a single, linear structure of discrete sequential units "but rather is an interwoven tapestry or fugue made up of multiple overlapping structures and sequences, forecasts of what is to come and echoes of what has already been said.... [S]uch a nonlinear recursive compositional style is characteristic of aural narrative...."

745.   Dewey, Joanna. "Oral Methods of Structuring Narrative in Mark." *Interpretation* 43 (1989), 32–44.

Mark "was composed in writing for a listening audience," which suggests that we need to take the dynamics of orality more seriously in interpreting that gospel. It exhibits both "oral methods of connecting individual episodes and a very high degree of consistency among the episodes." This means he was probably building on existing oral narrative tradition rather than connecting disparate episodes for the first time.

746.   Fowler, Robert M. *Let the Reader Understand: Reader-Response Criticism and the Gospel of Mark.* Minneapolis (Fortress), 1991.

About the experience of reading *Mark*, rather than about the gospel itself, though "we have always talked about our experience of reading *Mark*'s Gospel but have usually done so under the guise of talking about the intentions of the evangelist...." To recognize this is to shift from story to discourse. Defines reader-response criticism; analyzes narrator's explicit commentary and implicit, "rhetoric of indirection," ambiguity, and outlines the history of its interpretation.

747.   Hamerton-Kelly, Robert G. *The Gospel and the Sacred. Poetics of Violence in Mark.* Minneapolis (Augsburg Fortress P), 1994.

A reading of *Mark* "through the lens of René Girard's theory of violence and the sacred." Successive discussions of "sacred violence and sacred space" in chapters 11 and 12; "disclosure of the sacred" in chapters 13–16; "the poetics of place ... and the scapegoat" in 1–3; "poetics of faith" in 4–10; and general discussions of time and space, and the gospel and the sacred.

*   Hauge, Hans. "The Sin of Reading: Austin Farrer, Helen Gardner and Frank Kermode on the Poetry of St. Mark."

See #33.

748.   Heil, John Paul. *The Gospel of Mark as a Model for Action.* Mahwah (Paulist P), 1992.

Scene-by-scene interpretation of Mark's story of Jesus "with emphasis upon the response of the implied reader to each scene." Its meaning and its value for Christians today can be elicited "by considering Mark's dramatic narrative as a dynamic process of communication between its author and audience, calling forth definite and active responses applicable to the life of that audience." General presuppositions of Mark's implied reader.

749.   Johnson, Steven R. "The Identity and Significance of the Neaniskos in Mark." *Forum* 8 (1992), 123–139.

Since a key theme of *Mark* is "the identification of baptism with death and resurrection," and since "the future proclamation of the *neaniskos* anticipated in Mark is in part the actual writing of Mark.... [T]he gospel in turn gains authority and persuasive power from the location of the implied author in the narrative."

750.   Juel, Donald H. *A Master of Surprise. Mark Interpreted.* Minneapolis (Fortress P), 1994.

We need a rhetorical strategy for reading *Mark* which rejects the disinterested approach in favor of one which readmits referentiality and religious interest, since texts must not just contain truths, but also fulfill needs. The crucial importance of the concept of the implied audience in interpreting *Mark*.

751.   Malbon, Elizabeth Struthers. "The Major Importance of the Minor Characters in Mark," in #622, pp. 58–86.

Minor characters around Mark's Jesus are to be judged only by their response to Jesus. Many of them act as exemplars and "communicate to the implied audience that anyone can be a follower of Jesus," though "no one finds it easy." The importance of knowing "where a minor character is in the unfolding narrative of the Markan gospel," as well as where they are in relation to other characters.

752.   Meagher, John C. *Clumsy Construction in Mark's Gospel. A Critique of Form- and Redaktionsgeschichte.* New York and Toronto (The Edwin Mellen P), 1979.

Mark's "uneven performance, characterized by stumbling and awkward narratives, full of anticlimaxes, unexplained variations in texture, laconic abbreviations intermixed with inefficient ramblings," and various sorts of "ordinary bumblings." "We see no particularly great talent for storytelling in *Mark*, but rather "great ordinariness" in narrative technique. As a result, we must recognize that we cannot make sense of the gospel without taking these matters into account.

753.   Moore, Stephen D. *Mark and Luke in Poststructuralist Perspective. Jesus Begins to Write.* New Haven and London (Yale UP), 1992.

A deconstructive literary reading of *Mark* and *Luke*, derived primarily from the work of Derrida and de Man. "I am eager to reply to the Gospels in kind, to write in a related idiom.... I prefer to respond to ... a narrative text narratively, producing a critical text that is a postmodern analogue of the premodern text that it purports to read."

754.   Myers, Ched. *Binding the Strong Man: A Political Reading of Mark's Story of Jesus.* Maryknoll, NY (Orbis Books), 1988.

A "socioliterary reading" of *Mark*, integrating literary criticism, "socio-historical exegesis," and "political hermeneutics" to argue that *Mark* is a "manifesto of radical discipleship." This is preferable to a purely literary-critical reading, because literary criticism tends to ignore or minimize historical/political context of a narrative.

755.   Ong, Walter J. "Text as Interpretation: Mark and After," in John Miles Foley, ed., *Oral Tradition in Literature: Interpretation in Context* (Columbia: U of Missouri P, 1986), pp. 147–169.

Definition of what it means to interpret verbal utterance (whether oral performance or text). Problems created by distance between the pre-Markan oral tradition and the "later inspired textual kerygma...." How Werner Kelber attempts to define and deal with this issue. One of Mark's major themes—the disciples' failure to comprehend Jesus—advertise[s] the discontinuity of oral sayings and text." The persistence of orality in Christian tradition down to our own day.

756.   Oyen, Geert Van. "Intercalation and Irony in the Gospel of Mark," in F. Van Segbroeck, et al., eds. *The Four Gospels 1992: Festschrift Frans Neirynck* (Leuven: Leuven UP, 1992), vol. 2, pp. 949–974.

"The Markan 'sandwich technique' or intercalation is one of the forms of duality 'which is more concerned with the structuring of the gospel.'" It has long been recognized as a characteristic of Mark's narrative style. How T. Shepherd's Andrews University dissertation (1991) furthers the discussion of the connection between irony and intercalations in *Mark*, and the cautions we should observe about creating too big a gap between implied and real readers of the gospel.

757. Petersen, Norman R. "'Literarkritik,' the New Literary Criticism and the Gospel According to Mark," in F. Van Segbroeck, et al., eds., *The Four Gospels 1992: Festschrift Frans Neirynck* (Leuven: Leuven UP, 1992), vol. 2, pp. 935–948.

Starting with narration can provide insights into Mark's sources and his editing of them. How source, form, and redaction criticisms will have to be rethought as a result of starting with narration criticism, and the order in which these methods must be used.

758. Powell, Mark Allen. "Toward a Narrative-Critical Understanding of Mark." *Interpretation* 47 (1993), 341–346.

Explanation of what narrative critics look for in a gospel, and how this differs from historical criticism. Application of its techniques to several specific problems in *Mark*: effects in terms of their function within the narrative; the function of the abrupt ending as example of unresolved conflict.

759. Reid, Robert S. "When Words Were a Power Loosed: Audience Expectation and *Finished* Narrative Technique in the *Gospel of Mark*." *QJS* 80 (1994), 427–447.

The "expectation of architectonic parallelism as a compositional technique of persuasion in Hellenistic narrative emplotment ... and two narrative complexes from ... *Mark* as case examples of this ... narrativist's assumption of audience awareness of these genre constraints as the necessary condition of his compositional technique." The two cases are *Mark* 1:16–2:14 and 15:40–16:8, which demonstrate how Mark manipulated his audience to force them to act.

760. Rhoads, David. "Jesus and the Syrophoenician Woman in Mark. A Narrative-Critical Study." *JAAR* 62 (1994) 343–375.

The hearer experiences this story "in the context of a developing plot, in interaction with characters who have been introduced ... and in light of the larger designs of the kingdom." Mark's use of recurring type-scenes; stylistic devices including two-step progression and parallelism; characterization; settings; all show the episode as integral to the fabric of Mark's narrative. The likely rhetorical impact of this story as a "boundary-crossing narrative."

761.   Robbins, Vernon K. *New Boundaries in Old Territory. Form and Social Rhetoric in Mark*, ed. David B. Gowler. New York (Peter Lang), 1994.

Ten previously published essays (1973–1990) tracing the growth of Robbins' socio-rhetorical criticism. First three employ redaction criticism; of the remaining seven, four analyzed in Minor I as #s 1576, 1803, 1804, and 1840, and three are from *NTS* 33 ("The Woman Who Touched Jesus' Garment"), *Reliêf* 24 [Norway] ("Rhetorical Argument About Lamps and Light...."), and Paul Flesher, ed., *Studies in Judaism* ("Interpreting the Gospel of Mark as a Jewish Document in a Greco-Roman World").

762.   Schildgren, Brenda Deen. "A Blind Promise: Mark's Retrieval of Esther." *Poetics Today* 15 (1994), 115–131.

Mark's account of John the Baptist's death is a "neglected but provocative retrieval" of *Esther*. It constitutes his "creation of a canon of precursor readings to which he attached his own narrative": an attempt to achieve cultural continuity with the Hebraic tradition. Mark uses *Esther* to "render the celebration of God's intercession on behalf of Israel, as paradoxical in the corrupt era of the Herodian tetrarchy."

763.   Shiner, Whitney Taylor. *Follow Me! Disciples in Markan Rhetoric*. Atlanta (Scholars P), 1995.

The character of the disciples "through an analysis of analogous characters found in literature from approximately the same period as the Gospels." These are: Xenophon's *Memorabilia*, Iamblichus' *Pythagorean Life*, Philostratus' *Life of Apollonius*, and *The Wisdom of Ben Sira*. The disciples "do not maintain a single, stable rhetorical function throughout the Gospel [because] ... Mark's presentation of Jesus so dominates his Gospel that it is questionable whether he intended any coherent characterization of the disciples.

763a.   Smith, Stephen H. "A Divine Tragedy: Some Observations on the Dramatic Structure of Mark's Gospel." *Nov T* 37 (1995), 209–231.

Mark "was probably conscious of composing a work formally and structurally akin to tragic drama, and ... he intended it to be presented to a specific audience in the manner of a closet drama....

In this way, he was able not only to preserve his message in all its radical newness, but to ensure that ... its dynamism would emerge from the oral presentation itself."

764. Stock, Augustine, O.S.B. *The Method and Message of Mark.* Wilmington (Michael Glazier), 1989.

A commentary on *Mark* based on the argument that the gospel shows a five-part concentric structure: Wilderness (1:1–13), Galilee (1:14–8:26), The Way (8:26–10:52), Jerusalem (10:53–15:41), Tomb (15:42–16:8). These are marked off by four hinge or transition passages: 1:14–15, 8:22–26, 10:46–52, and 15:40–41.

765. Tate, W. Randolph. "Eco-ing Mark." *EL* 20 (1993), 129–144.

Mark's "tendency to create openness on the semantic level through structures of openness at the narrative level." Further complicating it is his "notable use of parataxis on the syntactical level...." Through these devices *Mark* creates not only a naive reader but a second-level, semiotic reader who finds himself in the same predicament as the disciples. It is a "mysterious labyrinth" where "the beginning never points to the end, but the end always points back to the beginning."

766. Taylor, David Bruce. *Mark's Gospel as Literature and History.* London (SCM Press, Ltd.), 1992.

In the gospels, experience and the "imaginary world of aspiration" meet. How the literary and historical aspects of *Mark* may be analyzed so as to reveal this union of fact and aspiration. Section-by-section commentary on structure, likely accuracy or inaccuracy of traditions behind key verses, and intentions of Mark (and the other gospel writers) as author(s) in their work.

767. Telford, William R. "Mark and the Historical-Critical Method: The Challenge of Recent Literary Approaches to the Gospel," in Camille Focant, ed., *The Synoptic Gospels: Source Criticism and the New Literary Criticism* (Leuven: Leuven UP, 1993), pp. 491–502.

Historical criticism is in decline because, at least in its redactional variety, it is in tension with itself, trying to be both diachronic and synchronic. The role played in Markan studies in recent years by composition, reader-response, and structuralist (both rhetorical and narrative) criticisms. Their value for biblical critics, their challenge to historical criticism, and their main weaknesses as methods.

768.   Thompson, Mary R., S.S.M.N. *The Role of Disbelief in Mark: A New Approach to the Second Gospel.* NY and Mahwah (Paulist P), 1989.

Holistic literary reading of *Mark* which reveals its negations and failures and negative results—all of which is kept in tension with the affirmative level. This is its unifying artistic principle—keeping the negative level as complete and compelling as the affirmative.

769.   Tolbert, Mary Ann. "How the Gospel of Mark Builds Character." *Interpretation* 47 (1993), 347–357.

Mark fashions all of his character portrayals (regardless of their historicity) to promote his goal of persuading his readers to action. Like pagan Greco-Roman narrators, Mark is not interested in readers identifying with characters, but rather with our understanding and recognition of the message which the characters embody.

770.   Williams, Joel F. *Other Followers of Jesus. Minor Characters as Major Figures in Mark's Gospel.* Sheffield (Sheffield Academic P), 1994.

How *Mark* develops his characterization of minor characters, and how this development influences the reader. Given the importance of *Mark*'s theme of discipleship, we need to know what he does with these lesser characters who follow Jesus. How *Mark* uses them to issue both an invitation and a warning.

See also #15, 63, 71, 340.

Mark 1–8

771.   Delorme, Jean. "Text and Context: 'The Gospel' According to Mark I: 14–18," in Theodore W. Jennings, ed., *Text and Logos: The Humanistic Interpretation of the New Testament* (Atlanta: Scholars P, 1990), pp. 273–287.

The resistance various texts offer to being used outside their originating culture. Some, like *Mark* 1, are innovative, not escaping their culture but at least contesting or surpassing it. "The context allows historical commentary on such texts [though] it does not furnish the key to them."

*   Dwyer, Timothy. "Prominent Women, Widows, and Prophets: A Case for Midrashic Intertextuality."

     See #341.

772.   Hedrick, Charles W. "Miracle Stories as Literary Compositions: The Case of Jairus's Daughter." *PRS* 20 (1993), 217–233.

"Mark's brief story ... that obscures the young girl's actual condition, challenges the piety of Matthew and Luke. Mark's narrator simply did not confirm—or deny—Jesus' diagnosis of the young girl's condition, and thereby Mark's story reaffirms the mysteries of life and death." The ambiguities and mysteries in Mark's version which lead to this reader response.

*   Heil, John Paul. Jesus *Walking on the Sea. Meaning and Gospel Functions of Matthew 14:22–33, Mark 6:45–52 and John 6:15b–21.*

     See #707.

773.   Heil, John Paul. "Reader-Response and the Narrative Context of the Parables about Growing Seed in Mark 4:1–34." *CBQ* 54 (1992), 271–286.

"... the growth parables in *Mark* 4 function as embedded metaphorical narratives which not only recapitulate the success despite failure of Jesus' ministry that the implied reader has already experienced in the previous narrative, but also point to inevitable future success despite failure for both Jesus and his disciples."

774.   Iersel, B.M.F. Van. "Concentric Structures in Mark 1:14–3:35 (4:1), with Some Observations on Method." *BI* 3 (1995), 75–98.

Mark 1:14–3:35 as a chiasm with its concentric/thematic center at 2:18–22. Such concentric structure probably originated in the needs of a semi-literate, listening audience for the gospels. How the criteria help us identify the macro- and micro-structures of *Mark*.

775.   Iersel, Bas van. "Concentric Structures in Mark 2,1–3,6 and 3,7–4,1: A Case Study," in Camille Focant, ed., *The*

Synoptic Gospels: Source Criticism and the New Literary Criticism (Leuven: Leuven UP, 1993), pp. 521–530.

Study of the function of concentric structures in antiquity leads us to modify the arguments of earlier critics about their appearance in *Mark*. We must thus develop new criteria for recognizing and analyzing them, e.g., that of "easily recognizable repetitions," since their function is to "structure the reading and hearing process by distinguishing between segments."

776. Keegan, Terence J., O.P. "The Parable of the Sower and Mark's Jewish Leaders." *CBQ* 56 (1994), 501–518.

While *Mark* presents the conflict with the Jewish leaders as a unified plot, the story clearly distinguishes two separate groups of leaders. These distinct groups "serve to illustrate types of conflict with the disciples and to heighten the rhetorical effect of the gospel."

777. Malbon, Elizabeth Struthers. "Echoes and Foreshadowings in Mark 4–8: Reading and Rereading." *JBL* 112 (1993), 211–230.

"Mark's Gospel presents its hearer/reader with echoes and fore-shadowings ... —in the process of hearing or reading and rehearing or rereading—the narrative.... Listening and looking more closely for Mark's echoes and foreshadowings in chaps. 4–8 will give us a richer understanding of Mark's narrative (story and discourse) and the relation between Mark's author (real and implied) and reader (implied and real)."

778. Parrott, Rod. "Conflict and Rhetoric in Mark 2:23–28," in Vernon K. Robbins, ed., *The Rhetoric of Pronouncement* (*Semeia* 64), pp. 117–137.

Mark 2:25–28 is a *chreia* elaboration, though with a change in the order of the normal one "due to the conflict in which the Pharisees are seeking to destroy Jesus." Such elaboration "was employed in the early community to provide self-definition and support."

779. Robbins, Vernon K. "Beelzebul Controversy in Mark and Luke: Rhetorical and Social Analysis." *Forum* 7 (1991), 261–277.

Such analysis reveals significant differences between these two versions: Mark's account "exhibits a centric flow of social interaction toward Jesus ... in a social environment where boundaries ... are considerably confused." Luke's Jesus, on the other hand, "evokes the power of God's kingship to gain access to possessions for the purpose of distributing them to others...." Luke's Jesus, further, shows "optimism about persuasion ... [reflecting] an attainment area high in Jewish culture with access to the lower echelons of elite Hellenistic-Roman culture."

780. Salyer, Gregory. "Rhetoric, Purity, and Play: Aspects of Mark 7:1–23," in Vernon K. Robbins, ed., *The Rhetoric of Pronouncement* (*Semeia* 64), pp. 139–169.

Rhetorical analysis of *Mark* 7 reveals *chreia* elaboration of the type discussed by Hermogenes and Theon, with epideictic rhetoric "concerned primarily with censure of Pharisees and scribes." Deconstruction enhances the marginalized, shattering the center and dissolving its power; "Jesus exposes the center (the temple coalition) as a margin." These methods and socio-ideological analysis "can be complementary in offering a meaningful interpretation of a pronouncement story."

781. Sankey, P.J. "Promise and Fulfilment: Reader-Response to Mark 1.1–15." *JSNT* 58 (1995), 3–18.

The "dynamic between expectation and fulfilment in the experience of reading Mark 1.1–15." *Mark* creates a misfit between promise and fulfilment which in turn "increase[s] the reader's creative role in finding coherence" in the narrative. This is a "highly creative tension" which "forces the reader to struggle to iron out inconsistencies."

782. Sibinga, J. Smit. "Text and Literary Art in Mark 3:1–6," in J.K. Elliott, ed., *Studies in New Testament Language and Text* (Leiden: E.J. Brill, 1976), pp. 357–365.

Illustrations of proportion, symmetry, and correspondence in *Mark* 3:3–5 through precisely numerical chiasms.

Mark 9–16

783. Aichele, George. "Fantasy and Myth in the Death of Jesus." *Cross Currents* 44 (1994), 85–96.

"The Christian myth of Jesus as the divine savior is confronted and subverted by the elements of the fantastic in Mark's story of the death of Jesus. The narrative is fantastic because it resists mythic identity and believability, and instead it disrupts the illusions of realism. Myth and fantasy are fundamentally opposed; Mark rejects the myth of Jesus."

784.   Black, C. Clifton. "An Oration at Olivet: Some Rhetorical Dimensions of Mark 13," in #629, pp. 66–92.

How Kennedy's rhetorical analysis helps us with the knotty problems of *Mark* 13. It is not an apocalypse, but is eschatologically oriented. The rhetorical unit that is *Mark* 13; the rhetorical situation and problem. Its invention and style show it to be epideictic address. It in fact flouts many rhetorical norms though showing "directness, depth, and rhetorical sophistication."

785.   Blount, Brian K. "A Socio-Rhetorical Analysis of Simon of Cyrene: Mark 15:21 and Its Parallels," in Vernon K. Robbins, ed., *The Rhetoric of Pronouncement (Semeia* 64), pp. 171–198.

Mark 15:21, *Matthew* 27:32, and *Luke* 23:26 "from the point of view of the recitation of the 'narrative' ... in Theon's *Progymnasmata.*" These stories take on new meanings when seen as parts of a larger, single story. The material is epideictic rhetoric: readers of *Matthew* and *Mark* are "encouraged to praise and admire Simon's actions," whereas in *Luke* readers censure the Jewish community which does not respond positively to Jesus.

786.   Broadhead, Edwin K. *Prophet, Son, Messiah. Narrative Form and Function in Mark 14–16.* Sheffield (JSOT P), 1994.

Narrative analysis of chapters 14–16 unveils the nature and purpose of the Gospel of *Mark* as deriving from proclamation of Jesus' messianic life, death and resurrection. Emphasis on characterization and on the "context and dynamics of the narrative portrait of Jesus in Mark 14–16." *Mark* "places before the reader this world of strategies and portraits, of persuasion and polemic ... a paradoxical christological complex built upon an intricate narrative strategy and a crucial interrelationship with the larger narrative."

787.   Heil, John Paul. "The Progressive Narrative Pattern of Mark 14,53–16,8." *Biblica* 73 (1992), 331–358.

In *Mark* 14:53–16:8, the "intricate narrative structure" allows the implied audience to experience "an architecture in motion" of "contrastingly framed" scenes which determines how they are to respond to and interpret Jesus' death, burial, and resurrection.

788. Hester, J. David. "Dramatic Inconclusion: Irony and the Narrative Rhetoric of the Ending of Mark." *JSNT* 57 (1995), 61–86.

The "elaborate system of ciphers, characterization and plot movements within *Mark* 16.1–8 suggests the possibility of intended narrative incompletion." The "intended rhetorical suspension of narrative dynamics forces the actual reader to enter into the story to finish it." We then "rescue" the story "without the explicit help of the implied author or implied reader."

789. Levison, John R. "Did the Spirit Inspire Rhetoric? An Exploration of George Kennedy's Definition of Early Christian Rhetoric," in #629, pp. 25–40.

Summary of Kennedy's definition; relevant aspects of the Jewish world that produced early Christian rhetoric; evaluation of Kennedy's interpretation of his two key texts: *Mark* 13:9–13, and *I Corinthians* 1:22–2:13. "Kennedy's definition of radical Christian rhetoric does in fact draw too radical a distinction between the Spirit and rhetoric, between Christian preaching as proclamation and Christian preaching as persuasion."

790. Malbon, Elizabeth Struthers. "The Poor Widow in Mark and Her Poor Rich Readers." *CBQ* 53 (1991), 589–604.

Multiple readings of passages, e.g., *Mark* 12:41–4, occur because there are many readers and many contexts. We can prefer one reading to others while still recognizing the worth of other readings if we can resist our temptation to clarify everything.

791. Robbins, Vernon K. "The Reversed Contextualization of Psalm 22 in the Markan Crucifixion: A Socio-Rhetorical Analysis," in F. Van Segbroeck, et al., eds., *The Four Gospels 1992: Festschrift Frans Neirynck* (Leuven: Leuven UP, 1992), vol. 2, pp. 1161–1183.

The "possibility that the intertextual boundaries for interpretation of the Markan account of the crucifixion and resurrection should be expanded beyond Jewish and Christian literature." The "conversation ... in a possible cultural network of significations" among *Psalm* 22, Dio Chrysostom's description of a ritual mocking and abuse of a prisoner at an annual Mediterranean festival, and *Mark* 15.

792.   Robbins, Vernon K. "Using a Socio-Rhetorical Poetics to Develop a Unified Method: The Woman Who Anointed Jesus as a Test Case." *SBLSP* (1992), 302–319.

Evaluation of a number of recent literary analyses of this incident (which appears in all four gospels), including those by Mack, Tolbert, Tannehill; of social-scientific treatments by Malina and Neyrey; of ideological interpretation by Fiorenza and Myers. Analysis of areas of agreement and disagreement. The crucial importance of all brands of criticism to engage in team work to establish the first century gospel context, rather than continuing academic turf wars.

793.   Telford, William R. "The Pre-Markan Tradition in Recent Research (1980–1990)," in F. Van Segbroeck, et al., eds., *The Four Gospels 1992: Festschrift Frans Neirynck* (Leuven: Leuven UP, 1992), vol. 2, pp. 693–723.

How historical and literary criticism, especially reader-response, structuralism, and narrative criticism of *Mark* have developed during the 1980's. Which problems have achieved consensus, and which ones have eluded consensus. The strengths and weaknesses of each method demonstrate that literary criticism forces us to modify, but not abandon, the historical-critical method. Issues remaining include the genre debate, orality vs. textuality, and Markan creativity.

794.   Tippens, Darryl. "Reading at Cockcrow: Oral Reception and Ritual Experience in Mark's Passion Narrative." *EL* 20 (1993), 145–163.

The ending of *Mark* is necessary and hopeful, liminal as is the cock's crowing. We need to remember "the Gospel's oral, didactic, and ritual reception within a living community," by putting ourselves in the place of the early Christian community. Its cultic setting makes good sense when we consider certain episodes. Peter as "threshold person" in the narrative.

See also #682.

LUKE-ACTS

795. Alexander, Loveday. *The Preface to Luke's Gospel. Literary Convention and Social Context in Luke 1.1–4 and Acts 1.* Cambridge (Cambridge UP), 1993.

Luke's models are undoubtedly historical and scientific conventions of Greco-Roman literature. His preface reflects "general socio-cultural aspects of the life of the first-century churches." His designs on his readers and their expectations in the context of the Hellenistic schools.

796. Balch, David L. "Comments on the Genre and a Political Theme of Luke-Acts: A Preliminary Comparison of Two Hellenistic Historians." *SBLSP* (1989), 343–361.

"Luke-Acts is written in the genre of Greco-Roman political historiography, which the author both imitates and drastically revises." The author's awareness and use of the Roman constitution, Dionysius' and Strabo's histories.

797. Brodie, Thomas L., O.P. "Luke-Acts as an Imitation and Emulation of the Elijah-Elisha Narrative," in Earl Richard, ed., *New Views on Luke and Acts* (Collegeville: Liturgical P, 1990), pp. 78–85.

"... of all the models and sources used by Luke ... the most foundational was the main body of the Elijah-Elisha story.... This was the component around which all the components would be adapted and assembled." Thus the overall plan of *Luke-Acts* is based on the Elijah-Elisha narrative, rather than primarily on Greco-Roman biographies.

798. Chance, J. Bradley. "The Jewish People and the Death of Jesus in Luke-Acts: Some Implications of an Inconsistent Narrative Role." *SBLSP* (1991), 50–81.

The Lukan passion narrative portrays the Jewish people as passively non-resistant to their leaders, while the speeches in *Acts* make "no distinction between active conspirators and the passive onlookers and mourners." This "inconsistent narrative role of the people" is puzzling, but can complement the recent work of critics like Dawsey, Sanders, and Tannehill.

799.   Creech, R. Robert. "The Most Excellent Narrates: The Signif-
        icance of Theophilus in Luke-Acts," in Naymond H.
        Keathley, ed., *With Steadfast Purpose: Essays on Acts in
        Honor of Henry Jackson Flanders, Jr.* (Waco: Baylor UP,
        1990), pp. 107–126.

> We can carry the portrait of Theophilus back to the text to un-
> derstand his function as narratee of *Luke-Acts*. He is mediator be-
> tween narrator and real reader, characterizes the narrator more
> precisely, assists the implied author in emphasizing significant
> themes.

800.   Darr, John A. "Discerning the Lukan Voice: The Narrator as
        Character in Luke-Acts." *SBLSP* (1992), 255–265.

> Literary-critical work on Luke's narrator "is yet in its infancy."
> But the conclusions of James Dawsey's valuable *The Lukan Voice*
> are not supported by thoroughgoing reader response analysis of
> the relevant evidence.

801.   Darr, John A. "Narrator as Character: Mapping a Reader-
        Oriented Approach to Narration in Luke-Acts." *Semeia* 63
        (1993), 43–60.

> Reader-response interpretation of the Lucan narrator, based on
> the idea that narrators are specialized kinds of characters, con-
> structed as other characters are by an audience. The need to pay
> close attention to "reader identification, narrative sequence, liter-
> ary context, textual rhetoric, and extratextual repertoires" in doing
> this analysis of narration in *Luke-Acts*.

802.   Darr, John A. *On Character Building: The Reader and the
        Rhetoric of Characterization in Luke-Acts.* Louisville (West-
        minster/John Knox P), 1992.

> Reader-response model for analyzing *Luke-Acts* "attuned to the
> Greco-Roman literary culture of the first century." Guidelines for
> interpreting dramatis personae in *Luke-Acts*, illustrated through
> analysis of John the Baptist, the Pharisees, and Herod the Tetrarch.
> Literary characterization as a function of the dialogue between text
> and reader.

*   Darr, John A. "'Watch How You Listen' (Luke 8.18): Jesus
        and the Rhetoric of Perception in Luke-Acts."
        See #820.

803.   Gowler, David B. *Host, Guest, Enemy and Friend. Portraits of the Pharisees in Luke and Acts*. New York (Peter Lang), 1991.

Characterization in modern literary theory; in ancient narratives. The importance of knowing culturally bound connotations in narratives from other times and places. Elements of continuity and discontinuity between the characterization of the Pharisees in *Luke* and in *Acts*, and how demands of the plot sometimes require unexpected changes in characterization of these figures.

804.   Kurz, William S., S.J. "Intertextual Use of Sirach 48.1–16 in Plotting Luke-Acts," in Craig A. Evans and W. Richard Stegner, eds., *The Gospels and the Scriptures of Israel*. Sheffield (Sheffield Academic P, 1994), pp. 308–322.

Evidence suggests that the plot of *Luke-Acts* was modeled on *Sirach* 48:1–16. The plot line of God's people failing to repent "provides a principle of putting 'order' into the many episodes in the Gospel and Acts"—grounded in the previous rejections of Moses and the prophets.

805.   Kurz, William S., S.J. *Reading Luke-Acts: Dynamics of Biblical Narrative*. Louisville (Westminster/John Knox P), 1993.

Narrative criticism of *Luke-Acts*, aimed especially at shedding new light on such issues as the function of the prologues, kinds of narrators including the "we" sections of Acts; discrepancies in the three versions of Paul's conversion experience; characterization; use of irony and misunderstanding as implicit commentary; implied authors and readers.

806.   Levinsohn, Stephen H. "Participant Reference in Koine Greek Narrative," in #618, pp. 31–44.

How major and minor participants are distinguished in Koine Greek narrative through the "iconicity principle," default and marked encoding, illustrated from *Luke* 15 and 20, *Acts* 5 and 9, and *Matthew* 4.

807.   McDonald, J. Ian H. "Rhetorical Issue and Rhetorical Strategy in Luke 10.25–37 and Acts 10.1–11.18," in #624, pp. 59–73.

Rhetorical analysis of the structure of the parable of the Good Samaritan from *exordium* to *peroratio*. It is a rhetoric of Scripture-using communities, ones "accustomed to parabolic discourse." Peter's speech in Acts as intradiegetic narrative exemplifying deliberative rhetoric. The importance and value of rhetorical analysis for homiletics and religious education, if it is genuinely interactive.

808.   O Fearghail, Fearghus. *The Introduction to Luke-Acts: A Study of the Role of Luke 1,1–4,44 in the Composition of Luke's Two-Volume Work.* Roma (Editrice Pontificio Istituto Biblico), 1991.

Literary analysis shows a major break at *Luke* 4:44/5:1, and the unity of 1:5–4:44. The role of 4:14–44 is as "programmatic anticipation of Jesus' ministry placed in an introductory narrative section." The remarkably similar literary structures of *Luke* and *Acts*. Use of a geographical principle of arrangement for narrative parts of both volumes and its effect. Hellenistic influence on *Luke-Acts*.

809.   Parsons, Mikeal. "The Unity of the Lukan Writings: Rethinking the *Opinio Communis*," in Naymond H. Keathley, ed., *With Steadfast Purpose: Essays on Acts in Honor of Henry Jackson Flanders, Jr.* (Waco: Baylor UP, 1990), pp. 29–53.

The authorial unity of Luke and Acts should not blind us to their lack of unity on other levels, e.g., the generic. At the narrative level they are "independent but interrelated" works. The tendency since Cadbury labelled them "Luke-Acts" has been to miss their distinctive literary features.

810.   Robbins, Vernon K. "The Social Location of the Implied Author of Luke-Acts," in Jerome H. Neyrey, ed., *The Social World of Luke-Acts: Models for Interpretation* (Peabody: Hendrickson, 1991), pp. 305–332.

In *Luke-Acts*, "Major characters, the narrator, and the inscribed author produce previous events as a social product of their audiences.... The implied author produces previous events as a means of establishing and maintaining sets of relationships among various kinds of Christians, Jews and Romans who encounter one another and exchange values, goods, beliefs, and challenges."

811.   Sheeley, Steven M. *Narrative Asides in Luke-Acts.* Sheffield (JSOT P), 1992.

Review of recent research on the subject, and a suggested list of criteria for identifying and analyzing narrative asides. Application of these criteria to "selected ancient narratives and Luke-Acts." Differences between the narrators of *Luke* and of *Acts* may be accounted for either by differences in audiences or subject matter.

Similarities include advancement of the plot or of a theme, intensification of rhetoric, affirmation of authorial reliability and authority, and reader guidance. The distribution of asides generally correlates better with ancient romances and histories than with biographies.

812. Shepherd, William H., Jr. *The Narrative Function of the Holy Spirit as a Character in Luke-Acts*. Atlanta (Scholars P), 1994.

How recent literary-critical work on the Bible has laid the groundwork for studying the Holy Spirit as spirit of prophecy in *Luke-Acts*, and how this work has nevertheless missed the function of the Holy Spirit as a character in the book. Characterization in current narrative theory. "In a community formed by narrative criticism, the Spirit as character may well be said ... to be a creature—jointly created by reader, text, and context in the act of reading."

813. Siegert, Folker. "Mass Communication and Prose Rhythm in Luke-Acts," in #624, pp. 42–58.

The rhythms and sounds of public oratory in the first-century Greco-Roman world, and examples detectable in *Luke*. Application of this knowledge to the prologues of *Luke* and *Acts*, and to the end of *Acts*, reveals evidence of the author's literary ambitions— that he "took pains to create the typical sound of a harangue.... This explains well the rhetorical style of the Lukan Paul, not less than that of the Lukan Peter." Yet in his prologues and hymns, he imitates the Septuagint, thus "choosing at will the language appropriate to the situation."

814. Sterling, Gregory E. *Historiography and Self-Definition. Josephus, Luke-Acts and Apologetic Historiography*. Leiden (E.J. Brill), 1992.

Definition of the genre; history of its development among Greek and Hellenistic Jewish historians. The place of Josephus and *Luke-Acts* in this tradition. What the analysis of *Luke-Acts* as apologetic historiography tells us about the likely date, provenance, and authorship of the book.

815. Sterling, Gregory E. "Luke-Acts and Apologetic Historiography." *SBLSP* (1989), 326–342.

Evidences that *Luke-Acts* belongs to this genre include its insiders' standpoint, emphasis on the antiquity of Christianity, tension

between native traditions and Hellenism, offering of a self-definition of Christianity, and an indirect apologetic strategy.

816.   Tyson, Joseph B. "Torah and Prophets in Luke-Acts: Tem-
        porary or Permanent?" *SBLSP* (1992), 539–548.

The implied reader of *Luke-Acts* may be like certain characters
who appear in the text, namely Godfearers (i.e., non-Jews attracted
to Judaism). If so, this may explain Luke's apparent ambivalence
toward the authority of the Torah and prophets, since Luke seems
to work to pull such readers away from pro-Jewish tendencies.

817.   Wallis, Ethel E. "The First and Second Epistles of Luke to
        Theophilus." *JTT* 5 (1992), 225–251.

Luke-Acts follows the "scheme of a classical prose-poem on a
grand scale": an "overall chiastic literary pattern ... with appropriate lexical rhyme and discourse rhythm." The macrostructure of
Luke-Acts, especially the function of the thirteenth chapter of each
book as a dramatic fulcrum.

See also #852.

LUKE

818.   Brawley, Robert L. "Canon and Community: Intertextuality,
        Canon, Interpretation, Christology, Theology, and Per-
        suasive Rhetoric in Luke 4:1–13.11." *SBLSP* (1992), 419–
        434.

The presence of "implied counter readers" in texts—i.e., readers
"who will read against the norms implicit in the text." In *Luke-Acts*
the devil is such a counter reader. Luke thus "anticipates some
readers who advance views of Jesus, God, and canon comparable
to the devil's." The narrative, though, holds potential for their
conversion.

819.   Brodie, Louis T., O.P. "A New Temple and a New Law."
        JSNT 5 (1979), 21–45.

Luke rewrites the Chronicler, as the Chronicler had once rewrit-
ten *Samuel*. "While Luke's narrative contains several elements of
history ... much of it is not based on history but rather on scripture

and theology. It is largely an artistic composition, a creative rewriting of OT texts."

820. Darr, John A. "'Watch How You Listen' (Luke 8.18): Jesus and the Rhetoric of Perception in Luke-Acts," in #622, pp. 87–107.

"At the level of discourse, Jesus' words about perception serve to program the authorial audience's hearing/reading of Luke's story. The Nazareth episode and the parable of the Sower exhibit some of the primary ways in which this authoritative voice guides readers as they process the text": drawing the reader into the story while breaking down disbelief; controlling intertextual reading; linking perception and "the complex web of ethical values Luke weaves."

821. Frein, Brigid Curtin. "The Literary and Theological Significance of Misunderstanding in the Gospel of Luke." *Biblica* 74 (1993), 323–348.

Luke sees the "inability to comprehend or perceive as part of the divine plan." This failure is an important function of the plot of *Luke* and of its character development. The deliberate ironies of this device for Luke's theme.

822. LaVerdiere, Eugene, S.S.S. "The Lord's Prayer in Literary Context," in Carolyn Osiek, RSCJ, and Donald Senior, CP, eds., *Scripture and Prayer* (Wilmington: Michael Glazier, 1988), pp. 104–116.

History of the interpretation of the Lord's Prayer. A literary approach exploring the prayer in relation to its context in *Matthew* and *Luke*. The ways in which each gospel's use of the prayer epitomizes that gospel as a whole.

* Moore, Stephen D. *Mark and Luke in Poststructuralist Perspective. Jesus Begins to Write.*

    See #753.

823. Noakes, Susan. "Gracious Words: Luke's Jesus and the Reading of Sacred Poetry at the Beginning of the Christian Era," in Jonathan Boyarin, ed., *The Ethnography of Reading* (Berkeley: U California P, 1993), pp. 38–57.

Luke's "ambitious approach to the reading of the Hebrew Scriptures ... is an application of traditional Jewish methods of interpretation made with special urgency within a particular cultural and political framework." Jesus, in Luke's eyes, is in two respects the kind of reader which no other human being can be: he offers the final interpretation of the HB, and he is himself its interpretation. Luke's "scene of reading" is a product of his stand in the controversies of the early church over how the HB was to be read.

824. Tannehill, Robert C. "What Kind of King? What Kind of Kingdom? A Study of Luke." *WW* 12 (1992), 17–22.

If we try to read *Luke* "holistically, as a continuous narrative," we ask "how the beginning sets up expectations and how these initial expectations are realized, not realized, or modified through a process of struggle and conflict." We must understand, that is, the relation of each scene to the rest of the narrative. If we do so, new insights emerge which other methods do not uncover.

825. Travers, Michael. "Luke," in #20, pp. 398–408.

Narrative theology in *Luke*: plot as archetypal quest story, and its characteristic structure. The "Zacchaeus" episode (19:1–10) as the gospel of Luke in microcosm. The gospel "is unified primarily by the presence of the protagonist." Since humans think primarily in narrative, this approach to doctrine is very appropriate.

826. York, John O. *The Last Shall Be First: The Rhetoric of Reversal in Luke*. Sheffield (JSOT P), 1991.

Luke "exhibits a pattern of double or 'bi-polar' reversal which is not as prevalent in the other Gospels." Examination of this literary pattern, its impact on our understanding of Luke's eschatology, and its likely effect on Luke's first-century audience.

See also #63, 71, 1126.

Luke 1–9

827. Coleridge, Mark. *The Birth of the Lukan Narrative. Narrative as Christology in Luke 1–2*. Sheffield (JSOT P), 1993.

Luke 1–2 "set[s] the Lukan narrative in motion and lay[s] the ground for all that follows by articulating in narrative form a vision of both the divine visitation and human recognition of it ... as a way of preparing for the birth of a distinctively Lukan christology." The care with which Luke builds his narrative in chapters 1 and 2, and its essential unity. Techniques of repetition and characterization.

828.   Coleridge, Mark. "In Defence of the Other: Deconstruction and the Bible." *Pacifica* 5 (1992), 123–144.

Biblical criticism needs to engage the claims of deconstruction "with a view to entering into a more vigorous and enriching conversation with the humanities. "That deconstruction is not nihilistic is shown by applying it to Luke's infancy narrative, where God emerges as the ultimate deconstructor of fixed boundaries, and even of Luke's own text.

*   Fortna, Robert T. "Diachronic/Synchronic: Reading John 21 and Luke 5."

See #919.

*   Hedrick, Charles W. "Miracle Stories as Literary Compositions: The Case of Jairus's Daughter."

See #772.

829.   Kolasny, Judette. "An Example of Rhetorical Criticism: Luke 4:16–30," in Earl Richard, ed., *New Views on Luke and Acts* (Collegeville: Liturgical P, 1990), pp. 67–77.

Luke 4:16–30 as a "patterned pericope" of confrontation, rejection, and expansion in spite of rejection. Other such texts found in *Luke* 20 and *Acts* 4, 5, 13, 18, all of which exhibit literary links among each other, as revealed through rhetorical criticism.

830.   Landry, David T. "Narrative Logic in the Annunciatio to Mary." *JBL* 114 (1995), 65–79.

Examination of Jane Schaberg's solution to the questions raised by Fitzmyer and Brown about the narrative logic of the annunciation to Mary in *Luke*. Using "the principles of literary criticism and a construct of an ancient reader," we can see where Schaberg's argument holds up and where it fails. Her reading is preferable to earlier ones from a literary perspective, but is in other ways unlikely. We can preserve the narrative logic of the passage in other ways.

831.   Merritt, H. Wayne. "The Angel's Announcement: A Structuralist Study," in Theodore W. Jennings, Jr., ed., *Text and*

Logos: The Humanistic Interpretation of the New Testament (Atlanta: Scholars P, 1990), pp. 97–108.

Semantic/syntagmatic analysis of the parallels between the stories of the angel's announcement of John's and of Jesus' birth in *Luke* 1; their significance is not usually recognized. How Lévi-Strauss's theory myth fits this chapter, and helps explain the sacred-secular tension and the underlying mythic dilemma of the binary opposition.

832.   Robbins, Vernon K. "Socio-Rhetorical Criticism: Mary, Elizabeth and the Magnificat as a Test Case," in #622, pp. 164–209.

Socio-rhetorical criticism suggests that we need to look carefully outside many of the boundaries within which we customarily interpret the Magnificat. "Then, we need to subject those new boundaries to analysis and to look beyond them for additional insight. How Jesus "picks up on and embellishes the language of reversal Mary introduces...." Thus, Mary does not have the last word in Luke, but a male does.

*   Robbins, Vernon K. "Using a Socio-Rhetorical Poetics to Develop a Unified Method: The Woman Who Anointed Jesus as a Test Case."

See #792.

833.   Sheeley, Steven M. "Following Everything Closely: Narrative Presence in Luke 1–2." *EL* 20 (1993), 100–110.

As careful readers, we search out a picture of the narrator, even though he would probably rather remain on the periphery. Luke's narrator "assume[s] the roles of direction, reporter, and commentator, ... not ... afraid to intrude into the reader's consciousness when necessary." The reader must regard this voice as authoritative.

834.   Shuler, Philip L. "Luke 1–2." *SBLSP* (1992), 82–97.

Luke incorporates Jewish, Matthean and non-Jewish Hellenistic elements into chapters 1–2, "in a manner consistent with Hellenistic encomium literature." He follows the style of *bios* narratives, using the Hellenistic rhetorical device of "comparison." Luke skillfully frames his narrative twice, thereby introducing several important themes. Evidence of the dependence of *Luke* 1–2 on *Matthew* 1–2 must be included in this argument.

835.   Siker, Jeffrey S. "'First to the Gentiles': A Literary Analysis of Luke 4:16–30." *JBL* 111 (1992), 73–90.

Luke 4:16–21 shows chiastic structure, while that of 22–30 is more problematic. 25–27 is the interpretive key to the story, resolving the themes anticipated in 16–24. Emphasizes reversal of traditional expectations about Gentiles, Jesus' prophetic role modeled after Elijah/Elisha as central, and inclusion and the Gentiles stands prior to the Jewish mission.

836.   Silberman, Lou H. "A Model for the Lukan Infancy Narratives?" *JBL* 113 (1994), 491–493.

The presence of two infancy narratives early in *Luke* might be explained by Luke's having used the double readings for Rosh Hashanah as a model. He may have understood *Genesis* 21 and *I Samuel* 1 as proleptic: "Samuel anticipates John; Isaac, Jesus." Luke may thus be recalling a midrashic tradition of Isaac's resurrection.

837.   Staley, Jeffrey L. "'With the Power of the Spirit': Plotting the Program and Parallels of Luke 4:14–37." *SBLSP* (1993), 281–302.

Within the second of the four major plot sequences in Luke (4:13–9:62), Jesus' "programmatic proclamation in Nazareth generates a tripartite narrative subsequence." This can be an example of how social-anthropological and literary criticisms can usefully converse with one another, since the latter "reveals how language functions rhetorically within a narrative world."

838.   Thibeaux, Evelyn R. "'Known to be a Sinner': The Narrative Rhetoric of Luke 7:36–50." *BTB* 23 (1993), 151–160.

Rhetorical criticism of this passage demonstrates three conclusions or themes of the central plot: Jesus' forgiveness of the Samaritan woman and her initiation into the kingdom; Simon's misunderstanding of the kingdom; and Jesus' rhetoric as opening the door to him. Luke's rhetorical strategy of centering on the need for Christians to tell and retell stories of God's work through Jesus. How we might "refigure" *Luke* in our context.

839.   Wendland, Ernst R. "A Tale of Two Debtors: On the Interaction of Text, Cotext, and Context in a New Testament Dramatic Narrative (Luke 7:36–50)," in #618, pp. 101–143.

How careful linguistic study "can help interpret these artistic narratives that are seemingly far removed from us in language, style, and setting.... The story [of *Luke* 7] communicates simulta-

neously on several planes of cognitive and emotive significance.
Why analysis of text, cotext, and context are all necessary.

See also #75, 11, 715.

Luke 10–24

840.   Beavis, Mary Ann. "Ancient Slavery as an Interpretive Context for the N.T. Servant Parables." *JBL* 111 (1992), 37–54.

How references to slavery in ancient Greco-Roman literature, especially biographies of and fables about Aesop, illuminate the parables, including that of the Unjust Steward (*Luke* 16). "Against the background of the Aesopic and Plautine tradition of the slave as clever rascal, certain widely held opinions about the steward parable require reassessment." E.g., the steward is a slave, is unjustly dismissed, genuinely worries about his new freed status, gets revenge on his master by doing what he was fired for. His action is approved of by Jesus because he aligned himself not with the sons of this world (master) but with the sons of light (debtors). It was radical to identify with slaves and not with masters.

*   Blount, Brian K. "A Socio-Rhetorical Analysis of Simon of Cyrene: Mark 15:21 and Its Parallels."
      See #785.

841.   Braun, Willi. "Symposium or Anti-Symposium? Reflections on Luke 14:1–24." *Toronto Journal of Theology* 8 (1992), 70–84.

A "similarity in sympathies and technique" between Lucian's dialogues and this passage in *Luke* is unmistakable. These include shared authorial views of social roles, flagging of symposium conventions and topoi, common terms and themes, analogous moralizing—all of which show up in Lucian's Cynic anti-symposium satires.

842.   Combrink, H.J.B., et al. *Neotestamentica* 22 (1988), 189–484.

Articles by fifteen different critics on *Luke* 12: reading it as part of the travel narrative; ideological, reader response, rhetorical, sociological, black South African, psychological, deconstructive, empirical, and syntactic analyses of this chapter.

843. Crossan, John Dominic. "Structuralist Analysis and the Parables of Jesus. A Reply to D.O. Via, Jr., 'Parable and Example Story ... *Ling. Bibl.* 25/26. 1973, 21–30.'" *LB* 29/30 (1973), 41–51.

Replies to essay listed in Minor I as #1693. We can accept *Luke* 10:30b–35 as a "discrete enclave of story" but still insist that it is a parable and not an example, "a metaphor-story of the Kingdom's advent as a world-shattering event, from the story alone."

844. Devaux, Adelbert. "The Delineation of the Lukan Travel Narrative within the Overall Structure of the Gospel of Luke," in Camille Focant, ed., *The Synoptic Gospels: Source Criticism and the New Literary Criticism* (Leuven: Leuven UP, 1993), pp. 357–392.

The Lukan travel narrative, rightly so called, does not form the second of three parts of the structure of the gospel, "but rather the first of three subsections within the second main part of the Gospel (9,51–24,53)." How *Mark* may have suggested the idea of a travel narrative to *Luke*, and how he reworked *Mark*. These results show that synchronic and diachronic methods can be integrated, but critics using the former must always begin with the latter.

845. Durber, Susan. "The Female Reader of the Parables of the Lost." *JSNT* 45 (1992), 59–78; rpt George J. Brooke, ed., *Women in the Biblical Tradition* (Mellen, 1992), pp. 187–207.

Biblical texts construct the reader as male, so that the hypothesis of a "woman reader" is problematic. This can be illustrated by the 'parables of the lost' in *Luke* 15.

846. Eddy, Gaylyn E. Ginn. "Transformed Values of Honor and Shame in Luke 18:1–14." *PEGL* 12 (1992), 117–129.

Literary and anthropological analysis of these two parables shows how the author leads his readers toward an altered set of cultural values by embodying those values in given characters. Had the characters been differently gendered, this authorial intention would have been negated.

847. Fiorenza, Elisabeth Schüssler. *But SHE Said. Feminist Practices of Biblical Interpretation.* Boston (Beacon P), 1992.

"Strategies of Feminist Biblical Interpretation"; "The Hermeneutical Space of a Feminist Rhetoric of Liberation"; "Practices of Bib-

lical Interpretation." Detailed analyses of Luke 10:38–42 and 13:10–
17. Reading against the grain 'must critically unmask the androcentric and kyriocentric strategies in the text, dislodging the story
from its anti-Jewish rhetorical contextualization in Luke's Gospel
in order to recontextualize it....' "

848.   Fusco, Vittorio. "'Point of View' and 'Implicit Reader' in
        Two Eschatological Texts: Luke 19,11–28; Acts 1,6–8,11,"
        in F. Van Segbroeck, et al., eds., *The Four Gospels 1992:*
        Festschrift Frans Neirynck (Leuven: Leuven UP, 1992), vol.
        2, pp. 1677–1696.

        Relationship between the narrative setting and the actual setting
        of the evangelist and his readers, especially the narrator's point of
        view and his implied reader. What, e.g., did Luke's implied reader
        actually make of the pronouncement concerning the parousia? For
        them, experience of delay could coexist with short-term expecta-
        tion, as for us in the twentieth century it cannot. It seems likely
        that, though Luke had gone further than Paul or Mark toward
        shifting the parousia to an indefinite future, even he had not done
        so totally.

849.   Gowler, David B. "Hospitality and Characterization in Luke
        11:37–54: A Socio-Narratological Approach," in Vernon K.
        Robbins, ed., *The Rhetoric of Pronouncement* (*Semeia* 64), pp.
        213–251.

        Definition of socio-narratological method, especially as it reveals
        a "cultural context of hospitality [which] creates the reading envi-
        ronment for evaluating the characters in this pericope.... The ago-
        nistic setting of this episode is part of a larger narrative strategy
        that clarifies the disputes between Jesus and his opponents
        throughout Luke."

850.   Green, Joel B. "The Problem of a Beginning: Israel's Scrip-
        ture in Luke 1–2." *Bulletin for Biblical Research* 4 (1994), 61–
        86.

        Narratological study of the many echoes of the Abraham story
        of *Genesis* in *Luke* 1–2 convinces us "that the 'beginning' of Luke-
        Acts can be located only in God's purpose as articulated in the
        Scriptures of Israel...." How Umberto Eco's distinction between
        two kinds of reader helps illuminate this interpretive task; specifi-
        cally why Luke's first readers (in first-century Palestine) would
        have sensed most if not all of these allusions, and why we need to
        become more like these "first readers."

851.   Hartman, Lars. "Reading Luke 17,20–37," in F. Van Seg-
       broeck, et al., eds., *The Four Gospels 1992: Festschrift Frans
       Neirynck* (Leuven: Leuven UP, 1992), vol. 2, pp. 1663–
       1675.

Contrary to the unusual assumption, this passage does not
chiefly give information about the future. Rather it "has a mainly
admonitory semantic function, a function which is strengthened
by what is said in ... 18,1–30.... Thus it has ... the same principal
semantic function as so much other 'apocalyptic' material."

852.   Hughes, Frank W. "The Parable of the Rich Man and
       Lazarus (Luke 16.19–31) and Graeco-Roman Rhetoric," in
       #624, pp. 29–41.

The importance of a knowledge of a particular tradition of
Greco-Roman rhetoric as a key to this parable, and to its function
"in the more general scheme of Luke-Acts." This tradition is the
ethopoiïa, which would have enabled the author to compose such a
parable without any historical source at all. How the rhetorical
reading of this parable sheds light on the portrayal of Jews in *Luke-
Acts*.

853.   Kitzberger, Ingrid Rose. "Love and Footwashing: John 13:1–
       20 and Luke 7:36–50 Read Intertextually." *BI* 2 (1994),
       190–206.

Three intertextual readings of *John* 13:1–20 and *Luke* 7:36–50
starting from a feminist hermeneutic, and focused on reader-response (reading as an experience, effects of texts on readers, and
finally reflection on the reading process). Intertextuality may be
both between written texts and as dialogue between written texts
and the reader's life-experience. How the female reader illuminates Jesus' acts of love in these passages, "liberating [the] potential inherent in the Jesus-tradition ... to bear its fruits."

854.   Kloppenborg, John S. *"Exitus Clari Viri*: The Death of Jesus
       in Luke." *Toronto Journal of Theology* 8 (1992), 106–120.

Plato's *Phaedo* and its Greco-Roman imitators, e.g., Cato the
Younger and Seneca, in their accounts of the deaths of famous
men, were studied widely in Hellenistic elementary education.
The way in which *Luke* has emphasized Jesus' last words, as a de-
parture symposium, noble and composed manner of death, and
treatment of friends, all point to the influence of this pagan genre
on the gospel.

855.   Kozar, Joseph Vlcek. "Absent Joy: An Investigation of the
       Narrative Pattern of Repetition and Variation in the Para-
       bles of Luke 15." *Toronto Journal of Theology* 8 (1992), 85–
       94.

       Luke controls our understanding of his parables through repeti-
       tion—both its occurrence and (once our expectations are aroused)
       through the failure of repetition. Both Pharisees and readers are to
       heed the "pattern of repetition and variation" and to "ratify Jesus'
       welcome of the lost." The parables of *Luke* 15 "invite audiences to
       embrace, and so replicate, the pattern of rejoicing over the lost
       who are found."

*   Kurz, William S., S.J. *Farewell Addresses in the New Testament*.
       See #621.

856.   *Neotestamentica* 22, #2 ["Literary Approaches to Luke 12"].

       Fifteen essays on various aspects of *Luke* 12, including analyses
       of its ideology, point of view, reader-response, rhetorical structure,
       and readings from sociological, psychological, deconstructive,
       empirical and syntactical viewpoints. Authors include H.J.B.
       Combrink, A.G. van Aarde, Wilhelm Wuellner, P.J. Hartin, and
       D.J. Smit.

*   Phillips, Gary A. "Sign/Text/Différance. The Contribution
       of Intertextual Theory to Biblical Criticism."
       See #44.

857.   Phillips, Gary A. "'What Is Written? How Are You Read-
       ing?' Gospel, Intertextuality and Doing Likewise: A
       Writerly Reading of Luke 10:25–37 (and 38–42)." *SBLSP*
       (1992), 266–301.

       The dialogue between Jesus and the lawyer shows "structure
       and balance: double question, double citation and double answer."
       The dialogue between implied author and implied reader at the
       narrational level. "My aim has been to produce an *other*, differen-
       tial reading that exploits the fact of difference among the text's el-
       ements and their relationship. Whereas Luke proposes a textual ...
       reading, I have proposed an intertextual ... one."

858.   Piper, Ronald A. "Social Background and Thematic Struc-
       ture in Luke 16," in F. Van Segbroeck, et al., eds., *The Four*

Gospels 1992: Festschrift Frans Neirynck (Leuven: Leuven UP, 1992), vol. 2, pp. 1637–1662.

The interplay of thematic structure and social background. In the context of chapters 15–18, the repeated concern for the acceptance of Gentile God-fearers provides help in interpreting the parables in chapter 16. Luke "draw[s] out the significance of the [Steward's] benefaction ... as a sign of 'faithfulness,' that is, as truly a deed worthy of repentance and thus of acceptance." Thus also the otherwise puzzling attack on the Pharisees in 16, who "refuse to accept a repenting sinner and refuse to accept a deed worthy of repentance...."

859. Sellew, Philip. "Interior Monologue as a Narrative Device in the Parables of Luke." *JBL* 111 (1992), 239–253.

Six of Luke's parables (two in 12, one each in 15, 16, 18, and 20) use an otherwise rare device of interior monologue, probably as a way of dramatizing "their self-understanding and moral dilemmas with increased psychological depth and empathy." The device has parallels in ancient Greek literature, though it does not otherwise fit with Luke's general mode of discourse.

860. Shirock, Robert J. "The Growth of the Kingdom in Light of Israel's Rejection of Jesus: Structure and Theology in Luke 13:1–35." *Nov T* 35 (1993), 15–29.

Luke 13:1–35 is to be understood as a unit, "tied together structurally and develop[ing] one major theological theme." It explicates the deteriorating relationship between Jesus and the Jews. Literary analysis illuminates Luke's use of Matthew as well as the Jewish/prophetic character of the gospel.

861. Sloan, Ian. "The Greatest and the Youngest: Greco-Roman Reciprocity in the Farewell Address, Luke 22:24–30." *SR* 22 (1993), 63–73.

Luke's construction of the farewell address as reflection of his apparent opposition to Greco-Roman concepts of greatness, and of reciprocity. Instead, Luke's Jesus proposes a kenotic ethic which relaxes rigid Greco-Roman social norms.

862. Soards, Marion L. "A Literary Analysis of the Origin and Purpose of Luke's Account of the Mockery of Jesus," in Earl Richard, ed., *New Views on Luke and Acts* (Collegeville: Liturgical P, 1990), pp. 86–93.

The ways in which Luke has adapted his probable written and oral sources into a "carefully managed plot" where the effect of his narrative technique is "that the apparent victim becomes the one in charge and the apparent authorities become the victims of their own ignorance."

863.   Tannehill, Robert C. "The Lukan Discourse on Invitations (Luke 14,7–24)," in F. Van Segbroeck, et al., eds., *The Four Gospels 1992: Festschrift Frans Neirynck* (Leuven: Leuven UP, 1992), vol. 2, pp. 1603–1616.

How social scientific and literary theories can mutually illuminate biblical passages, while still not exhausting them. The great banquet parable would encourage missionaries "to believe that the banquet will certainly take place, in spite of rejection.... Careful attention to literary composition, supported by a historically informed imagination, may help us to discover more in their work than we initially expected."

864.   Tannehill, Robert C. "The Story of Zacchaeus as Rhetoric: Luke 19:1–10,11," in Vernon K. Robbins, ed., *The Rhetoric of Pronouncement (Semeia* 64), pp. 201–211.

The rhetoric of this passage makes Zacchaeus an interesting character, thus attracting the readers' attention, and getting them involved in his quest—a quest which deepens in significance as the story proceeds. "... the most pointed rhetoric of the story is found in vv. 8–10, in which statements by Zacchaeus and Jesus combine to form an indirect response to the crowd's objection."

865.   Wuellner, Wilhelm. "The Rhetorical Genre of Jesus' Sermon in Luke 12.1–13.9," in #629, pp. 93–118.

It is epideixis. The problems with applying Greco-Roman rhetorical standards in a Jewish culture, with changing genres.

See also #44, 75, 621, 681, 682, 806, 825, 829.

JOHN

866.   Beck, David R. "The Narrative Function of Anonymity in Fourth Gospel Characterization." *Semeia* 63 (1993), 143–158.

In *John*, anonymous characters function differently from those in the synoptics. Anonymity "frees the reader to enter the narrative world of the text." The significant ones in *John* are "those whose encounters with Jesus produce a faith response," including Jesus' mother, the Samaritan woman, the royal official (chapter 4), the lame man (chapter 5), the blind man (chapter 9), and the woman caught in adultery (7:53–8:11). The "beloved disciple" as paradigm of discipleship, as climax of reader participation with the anonymous characters.

867.   de Boer, M.C. "Narrative Criticism, Historical Criticism, and the Gospel of John." *JSNT* 47 (1992), 35–48.

Historical critics of the gospels should welcome narrative criticism as another useful tool, especially since both schools recognize the unity of *John*, and both use "the same author-text-reader model of communication." Narrative critics in turn "cannot evade historical inquiry and considerations."

868.   Braun, Willi. "Resisting John: Ambivalent Redactor and Defensive Reader of the Fourth Gospel." *SR* 19 (1990), 59–71.

"By reopening a closed text the Johannine redactor refuses to absolutize the claims of his precursor. The belated addendum assures the reader that the canonical John is not a closed world, whether narrative or ideological, but a work in conversation with itself. This internal conversation between author and editor, most visible in the gospel's aporia of ending, permits if not invites the reader to approach the text with critical ambivalence."

869.   Brodie, Thomas L. *The Gospel According to John: A Literary and Theological Commentary.* NY and Oxford (Oxford UP), 1993.

We should begin with the literary approach, since historical and theological approaches depend on our sense of the Bible's literary structure. *John* has both a time-based and a space-based structure; though time is the "foundational element" of its literary structure, at times space or geography becomes primary. Ultimately, it combines these two elements to focus on the progress of human life as its "decisive structuring factor." Commentary provides "excurses" on various literary devices in selected passages: 1:1–2;22, 6:25–59, 7:53–8:47, 14.

870.   Brodie, Thomas L. *The Quest for the Origin of John's Gospel. A Source-Oriented Approach.* NY and Oxford (Oxford UP), 1993.

How John followed first-century Greco-Roman literary practices for reworking texts by adapting various biblical passages into a new whole. John made heaviest use of all of *Mark*, parts of *Matthew, Luke-Acts,* and *Ephesians*. He also adapted sections of the Pentateuch, especially *Genesis* and *Exodus*.

871.   Buth, Randall. "Οὖν, Δέ, Καί,, and Asyndeton in John's Gospel," in #618, pp. 144–161.

We should view these four connectors "as reflecting a four-celled matrix composed of two parameters: 'close connection, and significant change.'" These are "pragmatic, structural devices for presenting the continuous flow of sentences and for aiding the reader in processing the information."

872.   Culpepper, R. Alan, and Fernando F. Segovia, eds. *The Fourth Gospel from a Literary Perspective.* (*Semeia* 53). 1991.

Contents: Segovia, Introduction; Segovia on the plot; Jeffrey Staley on character in chapters 5 and 9; Robert Kysar on metaphor in chapter 10; Wilhelm Wuellner on the narrative rhetoric of chapter 11; R. Alan Culpepper on chapter 13; Gail R. O'Day on narrative time in chapters 13–17; Segovia on Jesus' final farewell in chapters 20–21. Responses by Johannes Beutler and Mary Ann Tolbert.

873.   Davies, Margaret. *Rhetoric and Reference in the Fourth Gospel.* Sheffield (JSOT P), 1992.

A "comprehensive reading of the Fourth Gospel": the type of narrative, its theological themes and metaphors, its historical references and reception. Concentration on structuralist and reader response methods, but using them to demonstrate how John integrates history, theology, and aesthetics. How time is structured, possible generic classifications, and the problem of women readers then and now.

874.   Ellis, Peter F. *The Genius of John: A Composition-Critical Commentary on the Fourth Gospel.* Collegeville (Liturgical P), 1984.

Commentary based on the argument that *John* is a unified work by one author, "written according to the laws of parallelism rather than the laws of narrative." *John* has five major parts, each patterned chiastically, "part with part, sequence with sequence, and section with section."

875. Flanagan, Neal. "The Gospel of John as Drama." *The Bible Today* 19 (1981), 264–270.

The way in which the Fourth Gospel "lends itself to instant theatre. Many of its chapters are ... dramatically structured...." Elements of drama in *John* include irony, the "double stage technique," and the "dramatic dynamism of ambiguity, misunderstanding, and clarification."

876. Gibbons, Debbie M. "Nicodemus: Character Development Irony and Repetition in the Fourth Gospel." *PEGL* 11 (1991), 116–128.

Use of repetition and irony in the characterization of Nicodemus shows that John characterized him not negatively but ambiguously. This suggests the author might see him as a symbol of hope that as yet unaligned believer-members might join the Johannine community.

877. Hedrick, Charles W. "Authorial Presence and Narrator in John: Commentary and Story," in James E. Goehring, et al., eds., *Gospel Origins and Christian Beginnings: In Honor of James M. Robinson* (Sonoma: Polebridge P, 1991), pp. 74–93.

Narrative asides that "correct" or "improve" a story are common in ancient literature. The so-called "redaction" of *John* by a later figure "is readily understandable within the conventions of narrative criticism." The difficulty of knowing whether "the authoritative 'telling' is actually more reliable than the showing." It is even possible that the intrusive commentary "is due to the fact that the story that the principal narrator shows ... actually subverts the (implied) author's (later) understanding of the story."

878. Kelber, Werner H. "In the Beginning Were the Words. The Apotheosis and Narrative Displacement of the Logos." *JAAR* 58 (1990), 69–98.

"John's gospel is deeply informed by the double gesture of decentering and logocentrism ... the strategy of deconstructing a sense of presence ... and of repositioning presence in absolute transcendality; and the further strategy of decentering the Logos, while forging a deliberately signifying narrative. In this simultaneity of deconstructionism and metaphysical positivism John suffers the problem of language and metaphysics in search of central presence."

879.   Kilpatrick, G.D. "What John Tells Us About John," in *Stud-
       ies in John, Presented to Professor Dr. J.N. Sevensters on the
       Occasion of His Seventieth Birthday* (Leiden: E.J. Brill, 1970),
       pp. 75–87.

Stylistic and content analysis of *John* shows the author to have
been "a poor man from a poor province," uneducated in Greek
terms with no contact with Greek religious and philosophical
writing of his day. Yet his work shows many affinities with
Philo—probably through the influence of Hellenistic Judaism on
Palestinian Judaism.

880.   Lincoln, Andrew T. "Trials, Plots and the Narrative of the
       Fourth Gospel." *JSNT* 56 (1994), 3–30.

"A survey of the narrative of the Fourth Gospel demonstrates
the pervasiveness and significant positioning of the extended
metaphor of a trial on a cosmic scale. This motif proves illuminating for a closer analysis of the plot in terms of both commission,
complication and resolution, and of an actantial model. The cosmic
lawsuit also colours the narrative's two-storey phenomenon, and
the intertextual echoes of the motif from Isaiah 40–55 suggest a
third foundational scriptural storey which shapes the narrative.
Particularly important in support of Yahweh's claims in the trial
scenes of Isaiah is evidence stressing the correspondence can be
seen to inform the function of the trial motif and its accompanying
theme of truth when they appear in both the opening and the closure of the Fourth Gospel's narrative."

881.   MacRae, George W., S.J. "Theology and Irony in the Fourth
       Gospel," in R.J. Clifford and G.W. MacRae, eds., *The Word
       in the World* (Cambridge: Weston College P, 1973), pp. 83–
       86; rpt #893, pp. 103–113.

What irony in *John* is not: humor or satire, Socratic, tragic, or
metaphysical. Johannine irony is dramatic, and is further part of
an ironic vision—a whole literary outlook. The clearest example is
the trial before Pilate (18:28–19:15), thematic irony throughout the
gospel.

882.   Menken, M.J.J. *Numerical Literary Techniques in John.* Leiden
       (E.J. Brill), 1985.

Analysis of numerical composition allows literary analysis to be
refined and become more concrete. The author of John employed
two basic quantitative techniques: division of a text into parts, and
division "into portions which are present all over the literary unit

and throughout its successive parts...." The former has two basic patterns of relationship. Such analysis helps focus on the center of a passage.

883. Moloney, Francis J., S.D.B. "Who Is 'The Reader' in/of the Fourth Gospel?" *ABR* 40 (1992), 20–33.

A reading of John should mediate between text as mirror and as window "by allowing the mirror of the narrative world of the text to reflect a point of view to the world in front of the text." As real readers, we twentieth-century Christians must find the "unfolding relationship between the implied author and the implied reader in the Johannine Gospel."

884. Moore, Stephen D. "How Jesus' Risen Body Became a Cadaver," in #622, pp. 269–282.

Biblical scholarship is similar to medicine in that it "subjects the written body of Jesus to a rigorous examination." Why this has sometimes been seen as an irreligious act, as has the dissection of cadavers. How Culpepper's Anatomy of the Fourth Gospel does and does not resemble Ceray's Anatomy. How the Gospel of John acts itself as the risen body of Jesus. "Scholar surgeons" of the Bible have a tendency to decline the invitation to ingest the text which they have expertly dissected.

*   Moore, Stephen D. *Poststructuralism and the New Testament. Derrida and Foucault at the Foot of the Cross.*
     See #623.

885. Newman, Barclay M., Jr. "Some Observations Regarding the Argument, Structure and Literary Characteristics of the Gospel of John." *BTr* 26 (1975), 234–239.

John is "closer to a symphonic masterpiece than to a logically ordered argument." Its "extremely complex" structure; its use of inclusio, chiasmus, and irony.

886. Petersen, Norman R. *The Gospel of John and the Sociology of Light: Language and Characterization in the Fourth Gospel.* Valley Forge (Trinity P International), 1993.

The language of *John* is a blend of ordinary, everyday language and a special language used by the Johannine community. Use of synonyms, contrastive style, semantic opposites, and grammatical negations to create this language. Relationship between language and characterization in *John*. Play on double meanings, irony, and figurative versus plain speech. "Semantic referent blurring" in Jesus' language as means of creating effects John seeks. John's contrast between the "disciples of Moses" and those of Jesus, as structures created by the contrast of languages in order to distinguish the Johannine believers from their opponents.

887.   Porter, Stanley E. "Can Traditional Exegesis Enlighten Literary Analysis of the Fourth Gospel? An Examination of the Old Testament Fulfilment Motif and the Passover Theme," in Craig A. Evans and W. Richard Steener, eds., *The Gospels and the Scripture of Israel* (Sheffield: Sheffield Academic P, 1994), pp. 396–428.

Literary critics could benefit from even more interaction with traditional historical criticism of the Bible. Two recent literary-critical studies of *John* illustrate this need. The OT fulfilment motif and the Passover theme converge in chapter 19 of *John*. This convergence "speaks directly to several literary issues, including plot, character and motivation. When both literary and historical factors are considered ... an important theme and motif ... can be appreciated."

888.   Reinhartz, Adele. "Great Expectations: A Reader-Oriented Approach to Johannine Christology and Eschatology." *LT* 3 (1989), 61–76.

The "amenability of the Fourth Gospel to a reader-oriented critical approach...." How John's theological propositions become acceptable to the implied reader. Thus a reader-oriented analysis illuminates not only the inner workings of John, but is also of value "to those with primarily historical and theological concerns."

888a. Reinhartz, Adele. "Jesus as Prophet: Predictive Prolepses in the Fourth Gospel." *JSNT* 36 (1989), 3–16.

The christological significance of the Johannine prolepses. They function "as part of a literary device in which almost every prolepsis has an internal referent." They point to Jesus' unique identity as Son of God.

889.   Reinhartz, Adele. *The Word in the World. The Cosmological Tale in the Fourth Gospel.* Atlanta (Scholars P), 1992.

The "implied reader's construction and utilization of the gospel's story in reading and making sense of the Fourth Gospel as a whole." John's cosmological tale; its role in the narrator's strategy and its effect on the reader. Analysis of 10:1–5 as a "test case of the way in which the implied reader may have used the cosmological tale as an interpretive key." Implications for understanding John's literary technique and the historical situation of the implied audience.

890. Roth, Wolfgang. "Mark, John and Their Old Testament Codes," in Adelbert Devaux, ed., *John and the Synoptics* (Leuven: Leuven UP, 1992), pp. 458–465.

The influence of the Elijah-Elisha narrative (*I Kings* 17–2 *Kings* 13) on the small units within the synoptics; the influence of the move from *Deuteronomy* to *Numbers* as models on the seemingly illogical break between *John* 5 and 6. The genre of the NT gospels "is basically that of literary re-creations of scriptural models, originating in a kind of midrashic activity not unlike the Hellenistic practice of "imitation and thus conceptualizing their Jesus stories as rooted in a scriptural matrix."

891. Ruckstuhl, Eugen. "Johannine Language and Style: the Question of Their Unity," in M. de Jonge, ed., *L'Evangile de Jean* (Leuven: Leuven UP, 1977), pp. 125–147.

Defense of the author's published arguments that differences in Johannine style and vocabulary from chapter to chapter do not demonstrate the existence of non-Johannine material in that gospel. The narrative structures of those chapters show "significant correspondence" with the other chapters.

892. Stibbe, M.W.G. "The Elusive Christ: A New Reading of the Fourth Gospel." *JSNT* 44 (1991), 19–38; rpt #893, 231–247.

"... the elusiveness of Jesus is one of the most striking facets of John's literary art. Indeed, it is this feature which accounts for the excitement of John's plot for the first-time readers." The elusiveness of Jesus as a "key factor in the creation of suspense, movement and tension," and its tendency to encourage rereading.

893. Stibbe, Mark W.G., ed. *The Gospel of John as Literature. An Anthology of Twentieth-Century Perspectives.* Leiden (E.J. Brill), 1993.

Thirteen essays published between 1923 and 1991, of which twelve are literary-critical. Seven of these analyzed in Minor I as #s 1966, 1976, 1985, 2010, 2014, 2018, and 2026. Of the remaining five, two are translations (Hans Windisch, "John's Narrative Style"—1923; R. Alan Culpepper, "John 5.1–18: A Sample of

Narrative-Critical Commentary"—1990), and three are analyzed elsewhere in this volume as #881, 904, 892.

*   Stibbe, Mark W.G. *John as Storyteller: Narrative Criticism and the Fourth Gospel.*

See #932.

894.   Stibbe, Mark W.G. "'Return to Sender': A Structuralist Approach to John's Gospel." *BI* 1 (1993), 189–206.

The usefulness of Greimas' actantial approach for structural analysis of plot sequences of *John*: and for delving into deeper subtleties of *John*'s plot structures in ways accessible to both new readers and scholars. The "open-ended" nature of John's story as revealed by this analysis.

*   Talbert, Charles H. *Reading John: A Literary and Theological Commentary on the Fourth Gospel and the Johannine Epistles.*

See #1112.

895.   Tenney, Merrill C. "The Symphonic Structure of John." *B Sac* 120 (1963), 117–125.

The signs and themes of the Fourth Gospel as forming the elements of a subtle but real "symphonic structure" which creates a coherent, thematic whole.

896.   Thielman, Frank. "The Style of the Fourth Gospel and Ancient Literary Critical Concepts of Religious Discourse," in #629, pp. 169–183.

Puzzling elements of John's style and narrative structure. Study of the relationship between theological content and literary style in antiquity shows that "the unusual features of John's grammar and narrative are intentional.... [T]hey are a product of the evangelist's desire to write in a way appropriate to the mysterious and profound nature of his subject."

897.   Thompson, Marianne Meye. "'God's Voice You Have Never Heard, God's Form You Have Never Seen': The Characterization of God in the Gospel of John." *Semeia* 63 (1993), 177–204.

We need to be aware of the "sophistication with which characters are portrayed in ancient narrative"—e.g., the fact that they are not static or stereotypical, but develop as the narrative proceeds.

Alter's scale of characterization as means of analyzing presentation of God in John. "Although many of the textual indicators of (human) character are present for God in the Gospel, others are missing."

898. Thompson, Marianne Meye. "John," in #20, pp. 409–421.

We must assume that John constitutes a literary whole, that "one can study the text as a whole precisely because it makes good sense and reads well if analyzed in the form in which we now have it...." and that the author's interest is in presenting history and theology "in a readable and artistic fashion." It is, in effect, a "docudrama." Theme, plot, and unity of the gospel; characterization and other narratological features. Brief analysis of *John* 9.

899. Timmins, Nicholas G. "Variations in Style in the Johannine Literature." *JSNT* 53 (1994), 47–64.

How syntactic patterns in the woman taken in adultery pericope can be used as a "stylistic identifier" as a means of "monitoring instances where the style of a text has become embedded in the style of another which has assimilated it." How this can work on the Johannine literature.

900. Wead, David W. "The Johannine Double Meaning." *RQ* 13 (1970), 106–120.

Six possible varieties: those based on Greek alone; based on both Greek and Aramaic; based on Aramaic only; double meaning used in a short pericope or saying; verbs based on ambiguity of mode; and reliance on a figurative sense for fuller expression of meaning.

See also #63, 672.

John 1–10

901. Bailey, Kenneth E. "The Shepherd Poems of John 10." *Near East School of Theology Theological Review* 14 (1993), 3–21.

Recognition of the inverted repetition and Hebrew parallelisms in the "shepherd" sayings of *John* 10 "greatly simplify and clarify" what otherwise can seem meaningless repetition. "These are in fact poems with "finely tuned [rhetoric] full of beauty and rich with theological meaning."

902.   Born, Bryan. "Literary Features in the Gospel of John: An
        Analysis of John 3:1–21." *Direction* 17, #2 (Fall 1988), 3–17.

        Analysis of the implicit commentary in *John*, using Culpepper's
        distinction between the narrator's explicit and implicit commen-
        taries. Techniques include multiple allusions, Jesus' use of misun-
        derstanding by others, irony, and symbolism. These are used in
        John 3 to warn the reader not to confuse superficial and real, to
        enable readers to distinguish what is "above" from what is
        "below," and to form such a bond between author and readers
        that the latter will accept the former's beliefs.

903.   Botha, J. Eugene. *Jesus and the Samaritan Woman: A Speech
        Act Reading of John 4:1–42.* (Suppl. to *NTS* LXV.) Leiden,
        NY, etc. (Brill), 1991.

        Review of previous stylistic studies of *John* shows a static, nar-
        row, grammatical concept unchanged since the 19th century. Must
        deal with it as a "communication of the text, that is, from a prag-
        matic perspective." How implied author of *John* uses language to
        achieve this goal. Readers are subject to constant manipulation
        and "unstabling."

904.   Botha, J. Eugene. "John 4.16: A Difficult Text Speech Act
        Theoretically Revisited." *Scriptura* 35 (1990), 1–9; rpt #893,
        pp. 183–192.

        "... how the speech acts on the level of the character serve to en-
        hance the communication on the level of the interaction between
        implied author and implied readers." How this scene "keep[s] the
        readers involved in the narrative by forcing them into conversa-
        tional implicatures."

905.   Brodie, Thomas Louis, O.P. "Jesus as the New Elisha:
        Cracking the Code." *ET* 93 (1981), 39–42.

        The similarity of Jesus to Elisha reflects a conscious effort by
        John to follow contemporary literary practice. "What Seneca did to
        the dramas of Euripedes, John did to the drama of 2 Kings 5—but
        more so."

905a.   Collins, Matthew S. "The Question of Doxa: A Socioliterary
        Reading of the Wedding at Cana." *BTB* 25 (1995), 100–109.

        "Read in the light of the cultural context and literary setting, the
        Wedding at Cana provides clues for an ironic reading focused on
        the revelation of Jesus' *doxa*.... The literary context of irony in-
        volves the *doxa* of Jesus." The wine shortage suggests its loss, and

Jesus' production of wine results, ironically, not in an increase of his public *doxa* but of his lesser known heavenly *doxa*.

906.　Culpepper, R. Alan. "The Pivot of John's Prologue." *NTS* 27 (1981), 1–31.

The prologue to *John* is a chiasm which pivots on 1:12b—this, rather than 1:14 being "the prologue's climactic affirmation." The crucial importance of "children of God" (1:12b) in the Johannine community.

*　Heil, John Paul. *Jesus Walking on the Sea. Meaning and Gospel Functions of Matthew 14:22–33, Mark 6:45–52 and John 6:15b–21.*

See #707.

907.　Holleran, J. Warren. "Seeing the Light: A Narrative Reading of John 9. I: Background and Presuppositions. II: Narrative Exposition." *ETL* 69 (1993), 5–26, 354–382.

The background and presuppositions for a narrative reading of the chapter, including context, independent as a narrative unit, literary and thematic structure, and narrative features, e.g., plot, characterization, use of space and time, and point of view. "The narrator's ironic perspective works to bring the implied readership into collusion with the ideal point of view emanating from the implied author...." Detailed reading of *John* 9, based on contention developed in earlier work that the chapter consists of seven scenes arranged in a concentric structure. Concentration on motifs and other narrative devices.

908.　Lee, Dorothy A. *The Symbolic Narratives of the Fourth Gospel. The Interplay of Form and Meaning.* Sheffield (JSOT P), 1994.

Examination of six long narratives in John from a literary-critical perspective. These "reveal the complex interplay of form and meaning in the relationship that develops between symbol and narrative ... [revealing] the way in which material reality becomes symbolic of the divine." Analyses of chapters 3, 4, 5, 6, 9, and 11.

909.　Mealand, D.L. "John 5 and the Limits of Rhetorical Criticism," in A. Graeme Auld, ed., *Understanding Poets and Prophets: Essays in Honour of George Wishart Anderson* (Sheffield: JSOT P, 1993), pp. 258–272.

In focusing on such questions as the implied author or ideal implied reader of *John*, too often recent critics have ignored the larger questions of meaning because they lie below the surface where author and reader may be found. The text of John 5 may guide the reader to a relatively determinate meaning, but the text is not wholly determinate; it has gaps, ambiguities, paradoxes, metaphors and symbols. It is not, therefore, as logocentric as it may first seem.

*   Mojola, A. Ototsi. "Theories of Metaphor in Translation: With Some Reference to John 1.1 and I John 1.1."''

       See # 1109.

910.   Moloney, Francis J., S.D.B. *Belief in the Word: Reading the Fourth Gospel: John 1–4.* Minneapolis (Fortress P), 1993.

       Narrative criticism applied to *John* 1–4, concentrating on the way in which an implied reader evolves from the temporal flow of the narrative. Spatial aspect of each chapter precedes discussion of temporal flow, and is followed by summary of the reading. Discovery of the implied reader must not simply reflect the experience of a contemporary reader. The author of *John* shapes an implied reader in order to create in real readers a desire to follow Jesus.

911.   Moloney, Francis J., S.D.B. "Reading John 2:13–22: The Purification of the Temple." *Revue Biblique* 97 (1990), 432–452.

       A narrative-critical reading of this episode suggests "that its canonical form and its present place in the text portray 'the Jews' as failing in faith, and point the reader towards an eventual experience of true faith." How the author shaped an implied reader who could speak to the intended reader (the Johannine community).

912.   Moore, Stephen D. "Are There Impurities in the Living Water that the Johanine Jesus Dispenses? Deconstruction, Feminism, and the Samaritan Woman." *BI* 1 (1993), 207–227.

       How deconstruction dismantles the binary hierarchial oppositions of John's gospel, and enables us to "read against the grain of the biblical authors' intentions in ways that affirm women." For many scholars, "the woman's oblivion to her own need ... is the pivot on which the irony of ... [Jesus and the woman's] dialogue turns. Deeper by far, however, is the irony that Jesus' own need ... is just as great as the woman's."

913.   Painter, John. "Quest Stories in John 1–4." *JSNT* 41 (1991),
        33–70.

        The quest story typology, as evidenced in related synoptic pro-
        nouncement stories and the *chreiai* of Greco-Roman biographies
        and rhetorical texts, "has distinctively shaped the narrative struc-
        ture of the Gospel and especially 1.19–4.54."

914.   Phillips, Gary A. "The Ethics of Reading Deconstructively,
        or Speaking Face-to-Face: The Samaritan Woman Meets
        Derrida at the Well," in #622, pp. 283–325.

        "... deconstruction offers readers [of the Bible] a way to be ethi-
        cally responsible ... to the specific text, to its historical context, to
        its readers—in ways that traditional critique and method are not....
        Deconstruction does this by searching for a subtler understanding
        of the way texts prefer, represent and bring about a different
        opening onto the world...." Recognition of the text as "Other" is
        key. How this method works on *John* 4 as an example of a difficult
        text which challenges us to read more actively than we are used to
        doing.

*   Reinhartz, Adele. *The Word in the World. The Cosmological
        Tale in the Fourth Gospel.*

        See #889.

*   Schneiders, Sandra M. *The Revelatory Text: Interpreting the
        New Testament as Sacred Scripture.*

        See #626.

See also #71, 626, 716, 898.

John 11–21

915.   Black, David Alan. "On the Style and Significance of John
        17." *Criswell Theological Review* 3 (1988), 141–159.

        The narrative technique and chief rhetorical/stylistic effects of
        Jesus' prayer for unity in *John* 17. It is more complexly organized
        than most discourse units in the NT. Repetition of syntactic struc-
        tures, semantic units, and themes help to create cohesion in the
        prayer. Use of homoeoteleuton, alliteration, anaphora, chiasmus,

etc., and frequency of semantic and inverted parallelism. The theological and practical significance of Jesus' prayer.

916. Brawley, Robert L. "An Absent Complement and Intertextuality in John 19: 28–29." *JBL* 112 (1993), 427–443.

John 19:28–29 tropes Psalm 69, since "the incident on the cross is not the meaning of Psalm 69 in its literary and historical context. It is the meaning of Psalm 69 figuratively, metaphorically, yet in fact more "a figure of a figure." It is not allegory, but completion, implying both continuity and discontinuity. It is, however, more than completion, since the "gain in meaning occurs at the expense of a loss of meaning of the precursor." John has suppressed part of Psalm 69 in order to project it onto another level—"a prolepsis of a divine triumph over enemies."

917. Bridges, James J. *Structure and History in John 11: A Methodological Study Comparing Structuralist and Historical Critical Approaches.* San Francisco (Mellen Research UP), 1991.

Although both historical critical and structuralism are "complementary and mutually informative," both suffer from a tendency to "decontextualize" story, failing "to take seriously the holistic narrative configuration of the Gospel of John." Detailed summary of structuralist approach to *John* 11 in the dissertation of John R. Jones and of the historical-critical approach to *John* 11 of Gerard Rochais. We need a "synthetic vision which does justice to the full scope of narrative trajectories and which facilitates the integration of the results of such narrowly-focused analyses into a more holistic engagement with the biblical text."

918. Byrne, Brendan, S.J. *Lazarus. A Contemporary Reading of John 11:1–46.* Collegeville (The Liturgical P), 1991.

Historical criticism combined with literary criticism can illuminate the origins and meaning of the story about Lazarus being raised from the dead by Jesus. The story within the wider pattern of the fourth gospel; its structure and literary form; detailed verse-by-verse commentary, and how the episode in John probably came to be composed. The story functions as a microcosm of the entire gospel of John.

919. Fortna, Robert T. "Diachronic/Synchronic: Reading John 21 and Luke 5," in Adelbert Devaux, ed., *John and the Synoptics* (Leuven: Leuven UP, 1992), pp. 387–399.

The diachronic reading of the question of John 21 in relation to *Luke* 5 can help us "come close to what the gospel originally meant." However, such readings may not still be valid. The advantages of reading the text synchronically—i.e., as coherent in itself as it stands—are that it lets each gospel speak for itself "uncontaminated by questions of historicity...." The disadvantage is that it ignores the obvious fact that the two texts have so much verbatim in common.

920. Giblin, Charles Homer, S.J. "Confrontations in John 18, 1–27." *Biblica* 65 (1984), 210–232.

Analysis of the way John tells a story, e.g., the passion narrative, provides "solid insights" into John's understanding of Jesus. The plot-line, structure, and motifs of this narrative. Ways in which the narrative ties in with the earlier episodes of Jesus' life.

921. Giblin, Charles Homer, S.J. "John's Narration of the Hearing Before Pilate (John 18, 28–19, 16a)." *Biblica* 67 (1986), 221–239.

Pilate's "distinctive role" in the Johannine narrative at this point in the gospel. The two-stage structure of this episode, the parallels between the stages and substages, and the careful building of tension toward a climax. Unlike the synoptic gospel's portrait of Pilate, John's shows a consistency throughout.

922. Hartman, Lars. "An Attempt at a Text-Centered Exegesis of John 21." *ST* 38 (1984), 29–45.

Literary context, organization, characterization, "information flow" as contributors to an understanding of the text through text-linguistics analysis of this chapter. What these may also tell us about the Johannine community behind the fourth gospel.

923. Jasper, Alison. "Interpretative Approaches to John 20:1–18. Mary at the Tomb of Jesus." *ST* 47 (1993), 107–118.

We need to read the story of Mary Magdalene through an approach "which does not afford restricting privileges to one sort of critical stance," e.g., the methodology of Mieke Bal. The resulting picture of Mary is bleak, but enables us to avoid silencing "the nature of her longing for the physical presence of Christ."

* Kitzberger, Ingrid Rose. "Love and Footwashing: John 13:1–20 and Luke 7:36–50 Read Intertextually."

See #853.

*   Kurz, William S., S.J. *Farewell Addresses in the New Testament.*
      See #621.

924. Malatesta, Edward. "The Literary Structure of John 17." *Bib-
      lica* 52 (1971), 190–214.

      The themes of the chapter "are woven together with ... astonish-
      ing variety and subtle repetition, and form ... delicate combina-
      tions...." Its chiastic structure and related stylistic features as re-
      lated to its theme of the glorified Jesus.

925. Moloney, Francis. "The Faith of Martha and Mary. A Nar-
      rative Approach to John 11, 17–40." *Biblica* 7 (1994), 471–
      493.

      John 11 exhibits "a carefully articulated narrative design which
      determines the shape and message of John 11, and links it inti-
      mately with John 12." How awareness of this design alters the
      reader's evaluation of the two women.

926. Du Rand, J.A. "A Story and a Community: Reading the First
      Farewell Discourse (John 13:31–14:31) from Narratological
      and Sociological Perspectives." *Neotestamentica* 26 (1992),
      31–45.

      The discourse is narrated from the perspective of a strong group
      and a strong grid. It is narrated so as to promote the idea that the
      community will exist forever. Similarities between this and the
      farewell discourse in *I John*.

*   Robbins, Vernon K. "Using a Socio-Rhetorical Poetics to
      Develop a Unified Method: The Woman Who Anointed
      Jesus as a Test Case."
      See #792.

927. Rosenblatt, Marie-Eloise, RSM. "The Voice of One Who
      Prays in John 17," in Carolyn Oseik, RSCJ, and Donald
      Senior, CP, eds., *Scripture and Prayer* (Wilmington:
      Michael Glazier, 1988), pp. 131–144.

      The subtle merging of the voices of Jesus, the disciples, and the
      narrator which makes the prayer attributed to Jesus the prayer of
      the Johannine community.

928. Segovia, Fernando F. *The Farewell of the Word: The Johannine
      Call to Abide.* Minneapolis (Fortress), 1991.

The farewell discourse of Jesus "as both artistic and strategic whole, with a unified literary structure and development, as well as unified strategic concerns and aims."

929. Sibinga, J. Smit. "Towards Understanding the Composition of John 20," in F. Van Segbroeck, et al., eds., *The Four Gospels 1992: Festschrift Frans Neirynck* (Leuven: Leuven UP, 1992), vol. 3, pp. 2139–2152.

John 11 and 20 both show the same numerical pattern, and it is a pattern appropriate to the very similar subjects of these two chapters. "In the case of chapter 20, discerning this pattern ... is ... of vital importance for our understanding of the unity and internal structure of this part of the fourth gospel."

930. Staley, Jeffrey L. "Reading with a Passion: John 18:1–19:42 and the Erosion of the Reader." *SBLSP* (1992), 61–81.

The "eroded" reader as a further stage in the development of reader-response theory. How the author's (Staley) autobiography intertwines with the critical discourse on the Johannine passion narrative. "Somehow I would have to integrate myself into the reading in such a way that it would express both the polyvalence of that self and the polyvalence of the text."

931. Staley, Jeffrey L. "Subversive Narrator/Victimized Reader: A Reader Response Assessment of a Text-Critical Problem, John 18.12–24." *JSNT* 51 (1993), 79–98.

Examination of the old problem of this passage: Who interrogates Jesus—Annas or Caiaphas? in the light of reader-response criticism, especially from perspective of a reception history of the passage. This history (and recent source-criticism theories) is evidence of "reader-felt gaps and confusions." When seen in the larger issue of Johannine narrative rhetoric, we realize that the author has deliberately undermined the reader's grasp of the story "in order to lead the reader into a deeper experience of discipleship."

932. Stibbe, Mark W.G. *John as Storyteller: Narrative Criticism and the Fourth Gospel.* Cambridge and New York (Cambridge UP), 1992.

Defines narrative criticism as "practical" or "realistic" criticism of the narrative artistry, unity, genre, and social function of *John* against its historical background. Applies the method in Part One to the whole gospel, in Part Two to John 18–19. John unconsciously saw his story in context of mythos of tragedy.

933.   Stibbe, Mark W.G. "A Tomb with a View: John 11.1–44 in Narrative-Critical Perspective." *NTS* 40 (1994), 38–54.

Narrative analysis of a chapter which "calls out for sustained aesthetic appreciation." It is "artfully structured, with coloured characters, timeless appeal, a sense of progression and suspense, subtle use of focus and no little sense of drama." Form, plot, point of view, structure, characterization, reader response, themes implicit and explicit. The power of Lazarus' silence at the end.

934.   Tolmie, D.F. "A Discourse Analysis of John 17:1–26." *Neotestamentica* 27 (1993), 403–418.

Analysis of the surface structure of *John* 17, with a review of various recent proposals of its structure and their various shortcomings. Semantic relationships among the cola of each section.

935.   Vanhoozer, K.J. "The Hermeneutics of I-Witness Testimony: John 21.20–24 and the 'Death' of the 'Author,'" in A. Graeme Auld, ed., *Understanding Poets and Prophets: Essays in Honour of George Wishart Anderson* (Sheffield: JSOT P, 1993), pp. 366–387.

The anecdote of the Beloved Disciple as invitation to us not only to interpret but to reflect on the interpretive process itself. The extent to which the question about the authorship of chapter 21 becomes a hermeneutical as versus a historical problem. The reader of this or any text must first let the text "fulfill its aim as a work of written discourse," rather than constantly practicing a hermeneutics of suspicion on it.

936.   Wendland, E.R. "Rhetoric of the Word. An Interactional Discourse Analysis of the Lord's Prayer of John 17 and Its Communicative Implications." *Neotestamentica* 26 (1992), 59–88.

Application of three integrated types of discourse analysis: lexical, syntactic-semantic, and architectonic, to poetic structures of *John* 17. Relevance of speech act theory to this analysis. John's technique of "re-familiarization," the rhetorical purpose being to consolidate knowledge as well as to motivate action. The subtle placement and artistry of John's use of the prayer.

937.   Wiarda, Timothy. "John 21.1–23: Narrative Unity and Its Implications." *JSNT* 46 (1992), 53–71.

Various evidences that *John* 21 is a literary unity, and their "important implications for our understanding of the author's purposes." John may have intended the scene as an echo after Jesus' resurrection of a similar one before Jesus' resurrection in *Luke* 5.

See also #621, 881.

ACTS OF THE APOSTLES

938.   Anderson, Janice Capel. "Reading Tabitha: A Feminist Reception History," in #622, pp. 108–144.

An "interpretive reception history" of *Acts* 9:36–42, and the insights such a history offers us from the perspective of feminist criticism. In this case, "an emphasis on the power of God or the Holy Spirit rather than on human authority strengthens the utopian moment for women." Yet, "a single verse can be both oppressive and liberative," which is "why it is important to examine readings from many different subject positions."

939.   Brodie, Thomas Louis, O.P. "The Accusing and Stoning of Naboth (1 Kings 21:8–13) as One Component of the Stephen Text (Acts 6:9–14; 7:58a)." *CBQ* 45 (1983), 417–432.

Luke's dependence on his OT source for story of Stephen is more extensive than hitherto thought, and seems to follow Greco-Roman literary method of paraphrase and imitation rather than the Jewish midrash.

940.   Bulley, Alan D. "Hanging in the Balance: A Semiotic Study of Acts 20:7–12." *ETh* 25 (1994), 171–188.

Examination of the "web of textual relationships which constitute Acts 20:7–12 and ... meanings which are suggested by 'the language itself.'" The importance of the oppositions of light/dark and up/down in creating meaning in Acts 20, and the even more important thematic role played by the window on which Eutychus was seated: it not only points out oppositions in the text, but also highlights "the numerous pivotal points which appear."

941.   Cheung, Alex T.M. "A Narrative Analysis of Acts 14:27–
        15:35: Literary Shaping in Luke's Account of the
        Jerusalem Council." *WTJ* 55 (1993), 137–154.

    This narrative "is an artistically composed whole rather than a
    haphazard patchwork of sources. "It is naturally structured
    around Paul's four mission reports. In the literary design, each re-
    port leads either to dispute or to its resolution. "Such a way of
    telling the story creates suspense and excitement, and induces the
    readers to accept the outcome of the Jerusalem Council...."

942.   Co, Maria Anicia. "The Major Summaries in Acts: Acts 2,42–
        47; 4,32–35; 5,12–16. Linguistic and Literary Relationship."
        ETL 68, #1 (April, 1992), 49–85.

    "Each of the three summaries contains linguistic and thematic
    interconnections which suggest a conscious and careful composi-
    tion by the author," with each summary itself showing an underly-
    ing unity.

943.   Dawsey, James M. "Characteristics of Folk-Epic in Acts."
        SBLSP (1989), 317–325.

    "Acts as literature and Acts as folk narrative exist together in
    tension. The tension ... is well illustrated ... by the opening of the
    book." We have a slow, calm start characteristic of folk narratives,
    and throughout the book no building to a climax and abrupt end.

944.   Fowl, Stephen E. "Who's Characterizing Whom and the
        Difference This Makes: Locating and Centering Paul."
        SBLSP (1993), 537–553.

    Comparison of the portrayals of Paul in *Acts* and the Pauline let-
    ters for the purpose of understanding not the historical Paul but
    Pauline characterization. Paul's self-portrayal in Acts (which of
    course is actually Luke's) is primarily apologetic, whereas in the
    letters it often varies: sometimes ironic, often moral, designed to
    further his own enterprise.

945.   Hamm, Dennis. "Paul's Blindness and Its Healing: Clues to
        Symbolic Intent (Acts 9; 22 and 26)." *Biblica* 71 (1990) 63–
        72.

    Luke treats Paul's blindness and recovery symbolically, "in
    ways that point beyond themselves to themes that run through the
    whole of Luke-Acts." In chapter 9, it is a punitive and healing act
    by God; in 22, it is muted and ambiguous; in 26 it is "transmuted
    [in]to a metaphor describing the end-time missions of Israel, Jesus

and Paul." His narrative tools are ambiguous, ironic language; metaphor; and the symbolic world of Isaiah.

946. Hawthorne, Tim. "A Discourse Analysis of Paul's Shipwreck: Acts 27:1–44." *JTT* 6 (1993), 253–273.

Overview of the typology of the discourse structure of *Acts*, and the author, receiver situation, and participant reference of the text. Details of the discourse structure of *Acts* 27, and how it increases appreciation for its themes and complex organizations.

947. Hilgert, Earle. "Speeches in Acts and Hellenistic Canons of Historiography and Rhetoric," in Ed. L. Miller, ed., *Good News in History: Essay in Honor of Bo Reicke* (Atlanta: Scholars P, 1993), pp. 83–109.

Clearly, Luke's speeches meet the Hellenistic canons of "appropriateness" and "genuine contests." At the same time, Luke's notion of the first canon both resembles and differs from that of Dionysius. The latter defines appropriateness rhetorically rather than historically; at the same time, Luke, like Dionysius, "offers speeches that ... apparently were intended to be credible in terms of what he knew" of his main characters.

* Kolasny, Judette. "An Example of Rhetorical Criticism: Luke 4:16–30."

See #829.

* Kurz, William S., S.J. *Farewell Addresses in the New Testament.*

See #621.

948. Marguerat, Daniel. "The End of Acts (28.16–31) and the Rhetoric of Silence," in #624, pp. 74–89.

In writing the ending of *Acts*, Luke has used a convention found in Homer, Greco-Roman poetry, and Herodotus: the suspended ending. This "rhetoric of silence ... allows Luke to reinterpret the memory of Paul's death through the reversal of the scheme of the trial" and succeeds in "making the conclusive summary ... into a portrait of the exemplary pastor, whereby the realization of the missionary agenda of the book of acts is anticipated."

949. Murphy, James J. "Early Christianity as a 'Persuasive Campaign': Evidence from the Acts of the Apostles and the Letters of Paul," in #624, pp. 90–99.

Acts and Paul's letters show evidence of "a real persuasive campaign in the early church," and thus individual uses of language can be analyzed rhetorically to see how they fit into this purpose. For example, the different terms for the risen Jesus before different audiences (Pharisees, Hellenists, etc.). The success of this campaign as reason to analyze its strategy.

950. Newman, Cary C. "Acts," in #20, pp. 436–444.

The chronological and geographical markers in Acts can fool us into missing the literary character of the work. It shares some connections of several genres, and may be best thought of as "documentary," since that generic label may include seemingly irreconcilable characteristics: accuracy and significant editing, for example. Its two primary literary contexts are the HB and the gospel of Luke. It employs a number of structuring devices, and the sub-genre (as in 9:1–22) of Christophany. "Textual openness and ambiguity" characterize the book, displaying "resolution without closure."

951. Noorda, S.J. "Scene and Summary: A Proposal for Reading Acts 4,32–5,16," in J. Kremer, ed., *Les Actes des Apôtres* (Leuven: Leuven UP, 1979), pp. 475–483.

Summary as a narrative device in Acts must move considerably beyond their content. The coherence of the recognized units in *Acts*, and why 4:32–5:16 should be read as one. Why treatment of "summaries" is superior to treatment of "scenes" in *Acts*.

952. O'Reilly, Leo. "Chiastic Structures in Acts 1–7." *PIBA* (1983), 87–103.

Luke has a "particular penchant" for concentric symmetry. How the rhetorical structures of *Acts* follow Lund's rules about identifying chiasms, despite his own neglect of Luke's writings. The power of chiastic structure in *Acts* 1–7 to reveal and emphasize larger and smaller themes, as well as the book's christology.

953. Parsons, Mikeal C., and Joseph B. Tyson, eds. *Cadbury, Knox, and Talbert: American Contributions to the Study of Acts.* Atlanta (Scholars P), 1992.

Thirteen essays by twelve contributors evaluating the contributions of Henry Cadbury, John Knox, and Charles Talbert to the literary-critical study of *Acts* during this century, plus three separate bibliographies of their work. Two of the essays are responses by Knox and Talbert themselves. The concluding essay argues that the most productive future scholarship on *Acts* will focus on its combination of Hellenistic rhetoric and theological subject matter as an entry into "the context of conflict in first-century Israel to which this testimony was addressed."

954. Rosenblatt, Marie-Eloise, R.S.M. "Recurrent Narration as a Lukan Literary Convention in Acts: Paul's Jerusalem Speech in Acts 22:1–21,11," in Earl Richard, ed., *New Views on Luke and Acts* (Collegeville: Liturgical P, 1990), pp. 94–105.

Acts 22 in light of Gerard Genette's categories of order of event, speed of narration, and repeated narration of a single event, "The shifting point of view in each case [*Acts* 9, 22, 26] is a gradual turning over of the meaning of an event. As a narrative pondering, it is an exercise in reflection" which seems "essentially related to Luke's message about the significance of the apostle's individual life...."

955. Schmidt, Daryl D. "Syntactical Style in the 'We' Sections of Acts: How Lukan Is It?" *SBLSP* (1989), 300–309.

No significant patterns characterize all four "We" sections which cannot be found elsewhere in *Acts*. Thus insufficient evidence exists for arguing that the "We" sections have a separate source.

956. Schweizer, Edward. "Concerning the Speeches in Acts," in Leander E. Keck and J. Louis Martyn, eds., *Studies in Luke-Acts* (Nashville and NY: Abingdon P, 1966), pp. 208–216.

Stylistic analysis of the speeches of Peter and Paul in *Acts* shows them to be by the same hand—thus providing additional evidence for the contention that they are literary creations by the author of Acts, rather than by the speakers.

957. Sloan, Robert B. "'Signs and Wonders': A Rhetorical Clue to the Pentecost Discourse," in Naymond H. Keathley, ed., *With Steadfast Purpose: Essays on Acts in Honor of Henry Jackson Flanders, Jr.* (Baylor University, 1990), pp. 145–162.

The importance of Luke's use of *Joel* 2:28–32 in a narrative framework to communicate his kerygma. The "rhetorical dynamic" of the sermon connects the miracles of Jesus with his resurrection. Stylistic characteristics of the sermon.

958.   Sloan, Robert. "'Signs and Wonders': A Rhetorical Clue to
        the Pentecost Discourse." *EvQ* 68 (1991), 225–240.

        "Luke's theological method reflects a complex of authorities in-
        volving received christological traditions, historical events, Scrip-
        ture, and literary techniques." Rhetorical criticism helps us under-
        stand how Luke develops Peter's Pentecost sermon.

959.   Soards, Marion L. *The Speeches in Acts. Their Content, Con-
        text, and Concerns.* Louisville (Westminster/John Knox P),
        1994.

        "The speeches in *Acts* are more than a literary device, or a his-
        toriographic convention, or a theological vehicle—though they are
        all of these...." Luke uses them to unify his narrative "and, more
        important, he unified the image of an otherwise ... diverse early
        Christianity." The dynamic of analogy unifies his presentation.
        There is a "remarkable ... consistency in the forms and contexts of
        the speeches." How they are similar and dissimilar to other con-
        temporary writing.

960.   Soards, Marion L. "The Speeches in Acts in Relation to
        Other Pertinent Ancient Literature." *ETL* 70 (1994), 65–90.

        The speeches in Acts are often parallel in form and rhetoric to
        speeches in Greco-Roman historiography, though in context they
        more resemble portions of the Septuagint. In their purpose, how-
        ever, the speeches "are most like the work of the fragmentary
        writings of Hellenistic Jewish historians." The one distinctive fea-
        ture of the speeches is repetition.

961.   Spencer, F. Scott. *The Portrait of Philip in Acts. A Study of
        Roles and Relations.* Sheffield (JSOT P), 1992.

        Sociological, narrative-critical, and historical-critical analyses of
        the portrait of Philip in *Acts*, especially in relation to individuals
        and groups he evangelizes and to important fellow ministers in
        the early church—i.e., Peter and Paul. Philip emerges as a "truly
        significant and positive figure within Luke's narrative," as seen by
        focusing on three critical roles which he plays in the narrative: pi-
        oneering missionary, dynamic prophet, and cooperative servant.

962.   Sterling, Gregory E. "'Athletes of Virtue': An Analysis of the
        Summaries in Acts (2:41–47; 4:32–35; 5:12–16)." *JBL* 113
        (1994), 679–696.

        What ideological constructs or literary models may have influ-
        enced the shape of the summaries; how these summaries function

within the book, and evidence for arguing that the summaries "are authorial compositions based primarily on traditions embedded in the surrounding narratives which the author has generalized by means of a specific literary model, the description of religious-philosophical groups." This model is Greek in origin. The summaries are apologetic in function.

963. Tannehill, Robert C. "The Composition of Acts 3–5: Narrative Development and Echo Effect." *SBLSP* (1984), 217–240.

The elaborate patterns of repetition in *Acts* 3–5 have a number of complex functions, including helping readers remember things throughout a long narrative; emphasis; persuasion; more active involvement for the reader; highlighting change; preservation of unity; and lending resonance to the portrait of history provided therein.

964. van Unnik, W.C. "Luke's Second Book and the Rules of Hellenistic Historiography," in J. Kremer, ed., *Les Actes des Apôtres* (Leuven: Leuven UP, 1979), pp. 37–60.

Luke seems to have known and applied the various rules of Hellenistic historiography, as embodied in Dionysius and Lucian, in writing *Acts*. These include choice of a noble subject, a profitable one, appropriate beginnings and endings, selection of incident, unity, vividness, and use of speeches.

965. Wansborough, Dom Henry. "The Book of the Acts and History." *The Downside Review* #391 (1995), 96–103.

While speculation about Luke's sources and historical accuracy in *Acts* have been popular, his style may also yield fruitful results. It is smooth and sophisticated, and his genius for characterization is also evident, as is his penchant for repeating scenes.

966. Watson, Duane F. "Paul's Speech to the Ephesian Elders (Acts 20.17–38): Epideictic Rhetoric of Farewell," in #629, pp. 184–208.

Rhetorical analysis of Paul's speech in *Acts* 20 shows it to consist of historical preface (vv 17–18a), *Exordium* (18b–24), *Probatio* (25–31), *Peroratio* (32–35), and narrative summary (36–38). Review of the problems in analyzing this speech.

967.   Webber, Randall C. "'Why Were the Heathen So Arrogant?'
        The Socio-Rhetorical Strategy of Acts 3–4." *BTB* 22 (1992),
        19–25.

        The Christian and Sadducean combatants of *Acts* 3–4 conduct
        their confrontation according to widely accepted rhetorical rules of
        Greco-Roman rhetoric. When a Christian speaker uses "an exces-
        sively aggressive strategy," he is forced to back down.

*   Wiarda, Timothy. "Simon, Jesus of Nazareth, Son of Jonah,
        Son of John: Realistic Detail in the Gospels and Acts."
        See #678.

968.   Winter, Bruce W. and Andrew D. Clarke, eds. *The Book of
        Acts in Its Ancient Literary Setting (The Book of Acts in Its
        First Century Setting*, Vol. I). Grand Rapids (William B.
        Eerdmans) and Carlisle (The Paternoster P), 1993.

        Thirteen essays by fourteen different critics discussing *Acts* as
        influenced by ancient historical monographs, intellectual biogra-
        phies, HB themes and history, *Luke*, the Pauline corpus, ancient
        Greco-Roman rhetorical speech theory and practices, non-literary
        forensic speeches. Other subjects include how *Acts* has in turn in-
        fluenced later ecclesiastical histories, how it has been analyzed us-
        ing literary critical tools during the past two decades, and prob-
        lems raised by the Western text of *Acts*.

969.   Witherup, Ronald D., S.S. "Functional Redundancy in the
        Acts of the Apostles: A Case Study." *JSNT* 48 (1992), 67–
        86.

        The repetitions of Paul's conversion in *Acts* 9, 22, and 26 "are
        part of a narrative strategy which can be termed 'functional re-
        dundancy.'" Sternberg's five forms of repetition and variation ap-
        plied to *Acts* shows that seemingly insignificant differences "are
        actually essential to their meaning."

970.   Wolfe, Robert F. "Rhetorical Elements in the Speeches of
        Acts 7 and 17." *JTT* 6 (1993), 274–283.

        Summary of Robert Longacre's typology of persuasive dis-
        course, and its application to Paul's and Stephen's speeches in
        these two chapters. Macro segments (narrative-discourse-narra-
        tive) and micro segments in these speeches and scenes. "The con-
        stituent parts of the narratives serve to display and highlight the
        narrative and oratorical rhetoric." The first- and second-person

language "gives the narratives and speeches personalness and directness...."

See also #621, 806, 1126.

THE PAULINE LETTERS

971.   Botha, Pieter J.J. "The Verbal Art of the Pauline Letters: Rhetoric, Performance and Presence," in #624, pp. 409–428.

"... orality is an essential aspect of premodern communication," and even the "(rather limited) literacy of the time must be understood within [this] ... context...." Many uses of Greco-Roman rhetoric mislead because they ignore the orality of first-century culture. Issues which should be addressed include multi-authorship, the communal experience of letters, and "the oral performative aspect of letter reading."

972.   Brown, Lucinda A. "Asceticism and Ideology: The Language of Power in the Pastoral Epistles." *Semeia* 57 (1992), 77–94.

"The language of the Pastoral Epistles and its underlying ideological assumptions ... examined ... through an analysis of the experimental, relational, and expressive values of the text's lexical and grammatical systems, larger scale structures, and interactional conventions ... the use of ascetic language ... as a means of establishing social roles within the community and defining the parameters of the legitimate exercise of authority."

973.   Castelli, Elizabeth A. *Imitating Paul: A Discourse of Power.* Louisville (Westminster/John Knox P), 1991.

Ideological dimensions of Paul's letters; relationships between the letters and the early Christianity, using Paul's "appropriation of mimesis" as example, and based on Foucault; history of mimesis in Greco-Roman antiquity, especially in its religious dimension: dramatic ritual reenactment, and assimilation of the divine, as well as its aesthetic and political dimensions; close readings of passages which invoke imitation: *I Thessalonians* 1 and 2, *Philippians* 3, *I*

Corinthians 4 and 11. Paul's rhetoric of mimesis is a thoroughly first-century one. How his notion of this act functions in his letters as a discourse of power.

974.   Classen, C. Joachim. "St. Paul's Epistles and Ancient Greek and Roman Rhetoric," in #624, pp. 265–291.

Reflections on the history of rhetorical criticism of the Bible before 1974, especially the neglected influence of Philip Melanchthon. As his example shows, "there is no reason why one should restrict oneself to the rhetoric of the ancients in interpreting texts from antiquity...." Application of rhetorical theory to *Galatians*.

975.   Crafton, Jeffrey A. "The Dancing of an Attitude: Burkean Rhetorical Criticism and the Biblical Interpreter," in #624, pp. 429–442.

Rhetorical criticism "can and should be used to integrate the various techniques needed to interpret a text ... as an orientation which guides the interpretive endeavor." The Burkean approach is "especially capable" of answering this call because he shifts our attention toward what a text does. Pentad analysis of *2 Corinthians* explains the peculiarities of that book by identifying its symbolic action.

976.   Doty, William G. "The Epistles," in #20, pp. 445–457.

Greco-Roman Hellenistic letters are the "primary proto type" of the NT letters. "There is no one 'Christian letter form,' [however], any more than there is any one 'Christian language.'" Rhetorical features of the Pauline letter; its influence and formal characteristics: e.g., response to particular situations, allegorizing of scriptures, ethical admonition.

* Fowl, Stephen E. "Who's Characterizing Whom and the Difference This Makes: Locating and Centering Paul."

  See #944.

977. Jaquette, James L. *Discerning What Counts. The Function of the 'Adiaphora Topos' in Paul's Letters.* Atlanta (Scholars P), 1995.

   The "literary and social function of Paul's references to and discussions of [adiaphora]...." Their function in the Greco-Roman moralists, especially the Roman stoics. The possibility of entering into the thinking of first-century figures. Paul's adaptations of pagan moralistic traditions, and their "functional diversity." *Adiaphora* in *Philippians* 1 and 4, *Galatians* 2 and 3, *Romans* 14, *I Corinthians* 8–10, and *I Thessalonians* 5.

978. Malherbe, Abraham J. "MH ΓENoito in the Diatribe and Paul." *HTR* 73 (1980), 231–240.

   The ways in which the "by no means" strategy is used in the pagan diatribe and in Paul. Contrary to Bultmann, Paul's use of the formula has a counterpart only in Epictetus. They both use it as a transitional device, though in other ways their use of it differs.

* Moore, Stephen D. *Poststructuralism and the New Testament. Derrida and Foucault at the Foot of the Cross.*

  See #623.

979. Murphy-O'Connor, Jerome, O.P. *Paul the Letter-Writer. His World, His Options, His Skills.* Collegeville (The Liturgical P), 1995.

   The Pauline letters in their first-century context. Conditions of compositions at that time; formal features of the letters, especially their adaptations of current epistolary and rhetorical conventions; formation of the Pauline canon.

980. Newman, Carey C. "Christophany as a Sign of 'The End': A Semiotic Approach to Paul's Epistles." *Mosaic* 25, #3 (1992), 1–13.

   "Paul's conversion draws upon three tributaries—theophanies, prophetic calls, and apocalyptic throne visions." How the Christophany functions as a "pure signifier" in the Pauline corpus, using the theories of Lacan, Peter Brooks and Marianna Torqovnick.

Paul's letters evoke various narrative worlds, and the Christophany functions as an important sign—within those worlds.

981. Porter, Stanley E. "The Theoretical Justification for Application of Rhetorical Categories to Pauline Epistolary Literature," in #624, pp. 100–122.

If we wish to apply ancient Greco-Roman rhetoric to Paul's letters, we must be precise in our use of terms. We must, e.g., distinguish "rhetoric" in its universal sense of interpretation using both ancient and modern analytical models from "rhetoric" in its formal sense to describe particular, culture-specific used by practitioners of rhetoric. We find that doing the latter on Paul's letters "is not firmly grounded in the theoretical literature (or apparently the practice) of the time." The ancient rhetorical handbooks discuss on the style of epistolary material.

982. Reed, Jeffrey T. "Using Ancient Rhetorical Categories to Interpret Paul's Letters: A Question of Genre," in #624, pp. 292–324.

We need to exercise "methodological prudence" in applying ancient rhetorical categories to Paul's letters, since "*Functional* similarities between Paul's argumentative style and the rhetorical handbooks do not prove a *formal* relationship between them." While reading Paul from the perspective of ancient rhetoric can prove beneficial, "Paul probably did not incorporate a *system* of ancient rhetoric into the epistolary genre."

983. Silva, Moises. "The Pauline Style as Lexical Choice: *ΓΙΝΩΣΚΕΙΝ* and Related Verbs," in Donald A. Hagner and Murry J. Harris, eds., *Pauline Studies: Essays Presented to Professor F.F. Bruce on His 70th Birthday* (Exeter: Paternoster P and Grand Rapids: Eerdmans, 1980), pp. 184–207.

The need for a more systematic approach to the study of Pauline style. Proposed method for investigating lexical patterns in Paul in order to determine their relevance for exegesis. Ruling a direct object, passive constructions, ruling a clause, absolute uses, and fuller verbal expressions. The reliability of these lists for investigating authorship, synonymy, and stylistic comparison.

984. Stamps, Dennis L. "Rethinking the Rhetorical Situation: The Entextualization of the Situation in New Testament Epistles," in #624, pp. 193–210.

"... [the textual presentation] of the rhetorical situation becomes the basis or a premise for the argument of the letter as a whole and for the individual rhetorical units in the letter. But this textual presentation of the rhetorical situation not only acts as a premise, but is rhetorically persuasive in and of itself. Through the textual presentation of the literary-rhetorical situation, the audience and the speaker are conditioned to adhere to the new reality which the text posits. For the sake of the argument, the ideal reader and the implied speaker accept the textual situation as the situation in which the letter operates. In more literary terms, the textuality of the rhetorical situation means that the speaker and audience as literary constructions themselves only meet in the 'world-of-the-text.' One aspect of the world-of-the-text which the text constructs is the rhetorical situation."

985. Stanley, Christopher D. *Paul and the Language of Scripture. Citation Techniques in the Pauline Epistles and Contemporary Literature.* Cambridge (Cambridge UP), 1992.

A "careful sifting of the evidence" shows a near-identity between Paul and Greco-Roman writers with regard to acceptable parameters for citing literary texts. The same holds true for Paul and the methods of citation used in early Judaism. Through various techniques, quotations are often adapted by writers, yet these changes rarely affect the meaning of the original text. In literary conventions of the day, the intrusion of interpretational elements was not only unavoidable, but desirable.

* Thiselton, Anthony C. *New Horizons in Hermeneutics.*

See #7.

986. Weima, Jeffrey A.D. *Neglected Endings. The Significance of the Pauline Letter Closings.* Sheffield (Sheffield Academic P), 1994.

The need for, and value of, a comprehensive discussion of the Pauline letter closings lies in their similarity in function to what ancient rhetorical handbooks expected, as well as in their own innate importance as summaries of Pauline arguments and themes. The "high degree of formal and structural consistency" of the closings, and their significance for understanding the letters.

See also #72, 638, 639, 949, 989, 1074, 1126.

ROMANS

987. Boers, Hendrikus. *The Justification of the Gentiles. Paul's Letters to the Galatians and Romans.* Peabody (Hendrickson), 1994.

Semiotic, text-linguistic analysis of the two letters in terms of the macro-structure of each letter separately and then together; the semantic deep structure of Paul's thought and his "micro-universe." Analysis reveals the fallacy of assuming an opposition between faith and works in Paul, and the consistency of his thought.

988. Botha, J. "Social Values in the Rhetoric of Pauline Paraenetic Literature." *Neotestamentica* 28 #1 (1994), 109–126.

Paul's various argumentative strategies and the social values operative in them. Some of these values Paul took over from the broader culture. The syllogisms and enthymemata of Paul's paranesis in *Romans* 13. Rhetorical criticism ought to go beyond this to "inquire into the interests and power at stake in specific instances of social interaction."

989. Botha, Jan. *Subject to Whose Authority? Multiple Readings of Romans 13.* Atlanta (Scholars P), 1994.

Romans 13:1–7 read from a linguistic, a literary, a rhetorical, and a social-scientific perspective, respectively. Each method explained; a historical overview of its impact on NT study; and the reading itself. "... doing justice to the rhetoricity of the text implies that the phenomenon of intratextual social interaction ... must be studied." Various preconditions and implications of these methods when applied to an NT text.

990. Callow, John C. "Constituent Order in Copula Clauses: A Partial Study," in #618, pp. 68–89.

While we can define the copula clause and find many examples, unresolved questions include: factors that control placement of the subject phrase; vagueness of our definitions of emphasis and focus; connections between purpose, negation, and verb-initial clauses; and what causes an author to choose a verbless clause.

991. Campbell, Douglas A. "Determining the Gospel through Rhetorical Analysis in Paul's Letter to the Roman Chris-

tians," in L. Ann Jervis and Peter Richardson, eds., *Gospel in Paul: Studies on Corinthians, Galatians and Romans for Richard N. Longenecker* (Sheffield: Sheffield Academic P, 1994), pp. 315–336.

Rhetoric—i.e., argumentative discourse, "along with its implicit opponents, is the critical insight into the contingent dimension of Romans." It allows us "to recover Paul's underlying coherent convictions," and thus to reverse the failure of many scholars to distinguish correctly between Paul's contingent and his deepest convictions. Rhetoric, that is, enables us to differentiate between "Paul's positive declarations of his gospel both from his defences against ... his opponents and from his attacks on the ... gospel of those same opponents."

992. Campbell, Douglas A. *The Rhetoric of Righteousness in Romans 3.21–26.* Sheffield (JSOT P), 1992.

Its importance in Paul's broader argument, and dispute over its meaning, makes *Romans* 3:21–6 the pivotal and disputed passage in the letter. Analysis of recent attempts at interpretation shows that the critical preliminary decisions to make are syntactical, especially concerning awkward transitions. Rhetorical analysis of the passage clarifies syntax and function of clauses: it exhibits antithesis, paranomasia, parenthesis, epanaphora, and verses 25c–26c are an isocolic reduplication. Rhetorical analysis of its three significant atonement words clarifies those terms, and of his righteousness terminology. Conclusion offers an overall "suggested reading" of the passage.

993. Cosby, Michael R. "Paul's Persuasive Language in Romans 5," in #629, pp. 209–226.

Paul's use of parts of speech, *transitio*, word play, various rhetorical figures, metaphor, antithesis—all of which "increase substantially the impact of his words on his audience."

994. Donfried, Karl P., ed. *The Romans Debate: Revised and Expanded Edition.* Peabody, MA (Hendrickson), 1991.

Adds fourteen new essays, of which five are literary-critical: M.L. Stirewalt, Jr., "The Form and Function of the Greek Letter-Essay"; James D.G. Dunn, "The Formal and Theological Coherence of Romans" (*Commentary* 1988 Waco); William S. Campbell, "*Romans* III as a Key to the Structure and Thought of the Letter" (*Nov T* 23, pp. 22–40); Robert Jewett, "Following the Argument of

Romans" (expanded from *WW* 6, 382–389); D.E. Aune, *"Romans* as a Logos Protreptikos."

995.   Dunn, James D.G. "Paul Is Epistle to the Romans: An Analysis of Structure and Argument." *ANRW* 25.4 (1987), 2842–2890.

The importance of structural tensions, and of taking into account both "personal" and "essay" features of the letter. Rather than arguing for a specific form for *Romans*, e.g., epideictic or deliberative, we can "speak comfortably" only of "formal features which were part of the idiom of the age."

996.   Gieniusz, Andrzej. "Rom 7,1–6: Lack of Imagination? Function of the Passage in the Argumentation of Rom 6,1–7,6." *Biblica* 74 (1993), 389–400.

Literary analysis of the context of *Romans* 6–7 shows that the marriage image, usually thought incongruous, is in fact well-adapted to the point of the passage. It functions rhetorically as an *exemplum* and a summary of previous arguments. Even its incongruity with verse 1 has a thematic purpose.

997.   Guerra, Anthony J. *Romans and the Apologetic Tradition. The Purpose, Genre and Audience of Paul Is Letter.* Cambridge (Cambridge UP), 1995.

Romans belongs to the protreptic genre—a class of ancient writing "which urges the adoption of a particular way of life (or a deeper commitment to it) setting out its advantages, replying to objections, and demonstrating its superiority." Understanding *Romans* this way reveals its underlying unity, and locates it within the particular situation of the Roman church. A dual audience— Jewish and Christian—best accounts for the form and the context of the book.

998.   Hellholm, David. "Amplificatio in the Macro-Structure of Romans," in #624, pp. 123–151.

"Here, in Romans, we clearly encounter a highly conscious and stylistically reflective compositional effort that is operative on the macro—as well as on the micro—structural levels of the text. What we find in this letter is nothing less than a distinct *syntagmata-co-niuncta* structure in which both the more *langue*-determined *dispositio* and the more *parole*-conditioned *amplificatio* have been utilized to their utmost limits. What we ultimately encounter in Paul's accomplishment with regard to the compositional macro-

and micro-structures of *Romans* is in fact a dialectical interdependence between *langue* and *parole*, whereby in view of the *utilitas causae* the *parole* as *ordo artificialis* is as important as the *langue* as *ordo naturalis.*"

999.   Hellholm, David. "Enthymemic Argumentation in Paul: The Case of Romans 6," in Troels Engberg-Pedersen, ed., *Paul in His Hellenistic Context* (Minneapolis: Fortress P, 1995), pp. 119–179.

In this chapter Paul "makes direct use of the *probatio* of ancient rhetoric including inartificial, artificial (deductive and inductive) as well as practical proofs." First and second dialogue phases and their various parts; details of the inartificial and artificial proofs. Paul follows Aristotle's rules of argumentation fully.

1000.   Jervis, L. Ann. *The Purpose of Romans: A Comparative Letter Structure Investigation.* Sheffield (JSOT P), 1991.

Discourse analysis of the formal features of *Romans* can reveal the function of this letter, including matters of authorial intention. We first must recognize the importance of variation in these formal features. Analysis of Pauline opening formulas, thanksgivings, apostolic parousias, and conclusions, and their function in *Romans*. Paul was "chiefly exercising his apostolic mandate in the letter." Thus its purpose is missionary, not to prepare for a Pauline visit.

1001.   Jewett, Robert. "The Rhetorical Function of Numerical Sequences in Romans," in #629, pp. 227–245.

"... the large number of series associated with completeness convey the comprehensive argument concerning the triumph of divine righteousness through the gospel." Threes, fours, and sevens relate to description of the old and the new; or a decorative effect; fives and tens reinforce other major goals, e.g., interaction of Jewish and Gentile Christians.

1002.   Meyer, Charles D., Jr. "Chiastic Inversion in the Argument of Romans 3–8." *Nov T* 35 (1993), 30–47.

Recognition of Paul's elaborate chiasmus in *Romans* 3–8 helps us see the overall structure of his argument in the book. It accounts for, among other things, the disjunctions between chapters 4 and 5, and 7 and 8, the problematic position of 5:12–19, and the relationship between 3:1–8 and chapters 9–11.

1003. Miller, Neva F. "The Imperativals of Romans 12," in #618, pp. 162–182.

"... the verbal forms of Romans 12 constitute a system, and ... there is definite thought movement from the lesser to the greater and to the greatest achievement of love." Each form of the imperatival has its own function in encoding behavior.

1004. Porter, Stanley E. "The Argument of Romans 5: Can a Rhetorical Question Make a Difference?" *JBL* 111 (1992), 655–677.

Failure to note "significant and concentrated use" of diatribal elements in *Romans* 5 has led to inadequate interpretations of Paul's argument about what it means to be reconciled to God through the death of Jesus, and therefore of its place in the book of *Romans* as a whole.

1005. Schoeni, Marc. "The Hyperbolic Sublime as a Master Trope in Romans," in #624, pp. 171–192.

Any cultural synthesis at work in Paul, between the Jewish and Hellenistic worlds he inhabited, is "sublime" in that "it does not annihilate the heterogeneity of its parts." The Jewishness of Paul in the juxtaposition of "sublime" and "counter sublime" in the midrashic interpretive religious discourse in general, and in the NT.

1006. Spaulding, Lynn Spencer. "The Significance of the Differing Audiences in Galatians and Romans," in Dr. Barry L. Callen, ed., *Listening to the Word of God: A Tribute to Dr. Boyce W. Blackwedder* (Anderson, IN: Warner P, 1990), pp. 103–119.

Reader response theory demonstrates that many of the theological differences can be accounted for by Paul's needing to address quite different audiences—that audiences determine a great deal of the meaning of texts. An example is Paul's deliberately negative use of *Leviticus* 18: 5 in *Galatians* and deliberately positive use of *Leviticus* 18:5 in *Romans*. The implied readers determine the differences between the two treatments of the same text.

*   Stanley, Christopher D. *Paul and the Language of Scripture. Citation Techniques in the Pauline Epistles and Contemporary Literature.*

See #985.

1007.   Stowers, Stanley K. "Romans 7.7–25 as a Speech-in-Character (προσωποποιΐα)," in Troels Engberg-Pedersen, ed., *Paul in His Hellenistic Context* (Minneapolis: Fortress P, 1995), pp. 180–202.

Definition of "speech-in-character" as an ancient literary and rhetorical technique. How Paul employs it in *Romans 7:7–25*; characterization in chapter 7, and its place within the larger context of the letter's rhetoric. Origen first recognized the presence of this device in *Romans 7*. "... the characterization echoes broader cultural types from Greek, Latin and Jewish literature...."

1008.   Stowers, Stanley K. "Text as Interpretation: Paul and Ancient Readings of Paul," in Jacob Neusner and Ernest S. Frerichs, eds., *New Perspectives on Ancient Judaism: Volume Three: Judaic and Christian Interpretation of Texts: Contents and Contexts* (Lanham: UP America, 1987), pp. 17–27.

"... it is misleading to think of the church transmitting a text in which Paul's meaning was fully and objectively present and that in a secondary step the church appropriated and applied that meaning in light of their own circumstances. That some of Paul's meaning was understood is clear. What is called 'interpretation,' however, occurred at every level. To have a meaningful text at all is a constructive activity, and practical social context determines the generic patterns for making a text meaningful.... [T]ext editing is not just a matter of punctuating sentences. It has larger generic implications. The way a text is edited corresponds to the editor's larger generic conception of the work, whether that conception be explicit or an unrecognized set of assumptions. Without diminishing the helpfulness of critical editions, I suggest that scholars ought to forget that to have a text at all is an act of interpretation." Application to *Romans 2*.

1009.   Vorster, Johannes N. "Strategies of Persuasion in Romans 1.16–17," in #624, pp. 152–170.

We should integrate various audience-oriented disciplines into any discussion of rhetoric. When we thus expand the boundaries of rhetoric, we find other strategies to be complementary. Re-

stricting rhetoric to questions of structure "ignores the social relationships from which and toward which the argument develops." In this light, "Paul's objective is not the introduction of
God's righteousness, but rather the positive assessment and con-
firmation of the good news."

1010.   Weima, Jeffrey A.D. "Preaching the Gospel in Rome: A
         Study of the Epistolary Framework of Romans," in L.
         Ann Jervis and Peter Richardson, eds., *Gospel in Paul:
         Studies on Corinthians, Galatians and Romans for Richard N.
         Longenecker* (Sheffield: Sheffield Academic P, 1994), pp.
         337–366.

         Examining the letter structure of *Romans* "is an essential first
         step in ... understanding ... the intention of Paul in that letter.
         More specifically, ... the theme of 'gospel' as it occurs in the epis-
         tolary framework of Romans (1.1–15; 15.14–16.27)." This frame-
         work "establish[es] the authority of Paul's apostleship and his
         gospel over the Roman Christians in a way that wins their accep-
         tance of his gospel as it has been preached in the body of the let-
         ter."

1011.   Wire, Antoinette Clark. "'Since God is One': Rhetoric as
         Theology and History in Paul's Romans," in #622, pp.
         210–227.

         "In reading ancient texts we fumble about to compensate for
         the knowledge readers were then expected to have, and we never
         fully understand the rhetoric as history or theology. But the text
         sharply and finely focused on persuading a specific audience ...
         has the greatest possibility, because of its integration, to bring
         that world to life.... [W]ords that seek to shape history and theol-
         ogy may be the best evidence of that history and theology. Ro-
         mans I take to be this kind of text."

See also #63, 977, 1074.

1 CORINTHIANS

*   Beardslee, William A. "What Is It About? Reference in
         New Testament Literary Criticism."

         See #631.

1012. Brown, Alexandra R. "Seized by the Cross: The Death of Jesus in Paul's Transformative Discourse." *SBLSP* (1993), 740–757.

In Paul's rhetorical strategy, "the language of the cross functions as performative agent of perpetual transformation in an apocalyptic context.... [F]or Paul the revelatory word of the cross ... is the sole and necessary catalyst for the transformation of mind he intends."

*   Callow, John C. "Constituent Order in Copula Clauses: A Partial Study."

See #990.

1013. Callow, Kathleen. "The Disappearing Δέ in 1 Corinthians," in #618, pp. 183–193.

The multiple functions of Δέ in *1 Corinthians*. "The evidence of 1 Corinthians ... is that [it] is a particle of calm, reasonable progression, a step at a time. The absence of Δέ is occasioned by the dominance of any factor operating not linearly, but emotionally and holistically."

1014. Callow, Kathleen, "Patterns of Thematic Development in Corinthians 5:1–13," in #618, pp. 194–206.

How discourse analysis reveals the thematic pattern of these verses through the text's wide variety of discourse signals. The thematic patterns here all relate to matters of motivation.

1015. Campbell, Barth. "Flesh and Spirit in 1 Cor 5:5: An Exercise in Rhetorical Criticism of the NT." *JETS* 36 (1993), 331–342.

"Paul's argumentation in 5:1–13 is a deliberative rhetorical unit whose proposition advocates an action ... whose purposes are proximate ... and ultimate.... The proof consists of two arguments, in both of which Paul desires that the Corinthians rid themselves of wickedness in order to be pure." How Paul's rhetorical patterns helps us define the meaning of *sarx* and *pneuma*.

*   Cotterell, Peter, and Max Turner. *Linguistics and Biblical Interpretation.*

See #620.

1016.   Deming, Will. "A Diatribe Pattern in 1 Corinthians 7:21–22:
        A New Perspective on Paul's Directions to Slaves." *Nov
        T* 37 (1995), 130–137.

> Paul employs the diatribe of ancient rhetoric in *1 Corinthians* 7,
> while altering it in two ways: the insertion of 21b, and the use of
> the imperatival clause in 21a. 21b probably attempts to control
> the rhetorical pitch of 21a more than it does to heighten it. 21
> should be interpreted, then, as meaning that Christian slaves may
> justifiably regard their slavery with indifference, but "should not
> ... forgo an opportunity to gain their freedom."

1017.   Duncan, Thomas S. "The Style and Language of Saint Paul
        in His First Letter to the Corinthians." *B Sac* 83 (1926),
        129–143.

> Paul "used the devices of rhetoric ... freely, sometimes as a
> natural expression of the form of his own thought and sometimes
> consciously...." *1 Corinthians* is his most rhetorical letter, the
> "excess of rhetorical ornamentation" to be explained by the hard
> battle he is waging. Most likely, his rhetorical training came via
> the Asianic schools and probably not from comprehensive
> schooling in ancient oratory.

1018.   Khiok-Khng, Yeo. *Rhetorical Interaction in 1 Corinthians 8
        and 10. A Formal Analysis with Preliminary Suggestions for
        a Chinese, Cross-Cultural Hermeneutic.* Leiden (E.J. Brill),
        1995.

> Rhetorical analysis shows us "that Paul is responding to differ-
> ent issues out of two exigencies in 1 Corinthians 8 and 10. In 1
> Corinthians 10:1–22 he employs midrashic rhetoric to exhort the
> Corinthians to flee from idolatry. In 1 Corinthians 8:1–13 and
> 10:23–11:1 he uses the rhetorics of knowledge and love to create a
> community dialogue in order for the 'strong' and the 'weak' to
> interact over the issue of eating idol food." A cross-cultural read-
> ing of these texts needs to consider as well the nature of the an-
> cient and modern audiences.

1019.   Khiok-Khng, Yeo. "The Rhetorical Hermeneutic of 1 Corin-
        thians 8 and Chinese Ancestor Worship." *BI* 2 (1994),
        294–311.

> A rhetorical analysis of *1 Corinthians* 8 helps us overcome the
> traditional focus on the content of Paul's theology alone, suggest-
> ing that "all traditions can participate in the interpretive process

whereby the uniqueness of each is differentiated, affirmed, and esteemed...."

*   Levison, John R. "Did the Spirit Inspire Rhetoric? An Exploration of George Kennedy's Definition of Early Christian Rhetoric."

     See #789.

1020.   Mitchell, Margaret M. *Paul and the Rhetoric of Reconciliation: An Exegetical Investigation of the Language and Composition of 1 Corinthians.* Tübingen (J.C.B. Mohr), 1991.

     1 Corinthians employs deliberative rhetoric to achieve both thematic and rhetorical unity as a means of urging behavioral unity (concord) among its original intended audience. Since it fits the class of deliberative rhetoric so well by employing Greco-Roman *topoi* generally used for urging divided groups to unify, it cannot be assigned to the categories of forensic or epideictic rhetoric as some previous critics have done.

1021.   Mitchell, Margaret M. "Rhetorical Shorthand in Pauline Argumentation: The Functions of 'the Gospel' in the Corinthian Correspondence," in L. Ann Jervis and Peter Richardson, eds., *Gospel in Paul: Studies on Corinthians, Galatians and Romans for Richard N. Longenecker* (Sheffield: Sheffield Academic P, 1994), pp. 63–88.

     Paul's "different ways of assessing the gospel in the Corinthian correspondence in the light of Graeco-Roman techniques of rhetorical shorthand." Paul grounds his arguments on an underlying gospel narrative through brevity of expression, synecdoche, and metaphor. "Because these shorthand formulations are geared for each specific argumentative context and purpose, they are essential clues for exegesis...."

1022.   Pogoloff, Stephen M. *Logos and Sophia: The Rhetorical Situation of 1 Corinthians.* Atlanta (Scholars P), 1992.

     Background of ancient rhetoric and its modern rediscovery, especially form and content, situational rhetoric. The background of the situation of the church in first-century Corinth, and how Paul addresses his concerns over their ethical behavior and their typical Hellenistic concern over status.

1023.   Reiling, J. "Wisdom and the Spirit: An Exegesis of 1 Corinthians 2, 6–16," in T. Boarda, et al., eds., *Text and*

Testimony: Essays on New Testament and Apocryphal Literature in Honour of A.F.J. Klijn (Kampen: J.H. Kok, 1988), pp. 200–211.

Paul pursued three objectives in *I Corinthians*: a theological one concerning how knowledge of salvation is obtained; a rhetoric-paranetic one which leads him first to a condemnation of wisdom and then to praising it in order to force the Corinthians to confront their own internal jealousy; and a personal one in which Paul wishes to make his own position clearer but has difficulty doing so. "In terms of ancient rhetoric Paul's way of using the language of the Corinthians can be understood as *ironia*.... [That] these three objectives do not always agree well together ... explains the strains and tensions [in] ... the text."

1024.   Sigountos, James G. "The Genre of 1 Corinthians 13." *NTS* 40 (1994), 246–260.

I *Corinthians* 13 fits into the rhetorical form of encomium, one of the most stable forms in Greek literature. This helps explain its similarities to commonly mentioned parallels. The techniques of epideictic rhetoric help explain the chapter's outline. Rhetorical theory underlines that *I Corinthians* 13 is not only a "beautiful statement about a cardinal virtue," but also a "stinging indictment of the ... Corinthian church."

1025.   Smit, Joop. "Argument and Genre of 1 Corinthians 12–14," in #624, pp. 211–230.

Chapters 12 and 14 both exhibit characteristics of the deliberative genre, with the criterion of utility playing the major role. *I Corinthians* 13, then, functions as a demonstrative excursus, using not argumentation but persuasion, since it is suitable for impressing ideas and values upon an audience. Importance of stylistic considerations, especially series of parallelisms.

1026.   Smit, J.F.M. "Two Puzzles: I Corinthians 12.31 and 13.3: A Rhetorical Solution." *NTS* 39 (1993), 246–264.

"1 Corinthians 12:31–13:13 belongs to the *genus demonstrativum* ...; style, content and persuasive strategy of this passage correspond entirely to the rules in the classical handbooks of rhetoric appertaining to this genre [see Minor I, #2124]. This helps us understand the "two minor puzzles" posed by 12:31 and 13:3. Paul uses exaggeration and irony to make his point.

* Stanley, Christopher D. *Paul and the Language of Scripture. Citation Techniques in the Pauline Epistles and Contemporary Literature.*

   See #985.

1027. Watson, Duane F. "Paul's Rhetorical Strategy in 1 Corinthians 15," in #624, pp. 231–249.

   "... Paul uses deliberative rhetoric in this chapter to advise the audience to adhere to the traditional understanding of the bodily resurrection, incorporating a sophisticated use of *confirmatio* and *refutatio*...."

1028. Witherington, Ben III. *Conflict and Community in Corinth. A Socio-Rhetorical Commentary on 1 and 2 Corinthians.* Grand Rapids (Eerdmans) and Carlisle (The Paternoster P), 1995.

   An examination of the social context and rhetorical form of 1 and 2 *Corinthians* and their relationship to classical literature and Roman history. Background and structure of each letter, and detailed analysis of each argument.

See also #973, 977, 1054.

2 CORINTHIANS

1029. Andrews, Scott B. "Too Weak Not to Lead: The Form and Function of 2 Corinthians 11.23b–33." *NTS* 41 (1995) 263–276.

   "Paul's catalogue of hardships in 11.23b–33 conforms to an ancient form of *peristasis* catalogues.... In the larger context of 2 Corinthians 10–13, Paul uses the *peristasis* catalogue in order to continue the comparison with his opponents which begins at 10.12 and ends at 12.18.... The catalogue of hardship ... functions to place him in the role of populist leader or demagogue."

1030. Danker, Fredrick W. "Paul's Debt to the De Corona of Demosthenes: A Study of Rhetorical Techniques in Second Corinthians," in #629, pp. 262–280.

"... chs. 10–13 are an appropriate rhetorical climax to Paul's application of the reciprocity paradigm that appears in chapters 1–9.... In another sense, 2 Corinthians may be read as a parody of the Greco-Roman epideictic pattern...."

1031.   Garrett, Susan R. "The God of This World and the Afflic-tion of Paul: 2 Corinthians 4:1–12," in David L. Balch, et al., eds., *Greeks, Romans, and Christians: Essays in Honor of Abraham J. Malherbe* (Minneapolis: Fortress P, 1990), pp. 99–117.

"The influence of Hellenistic popular philosophy on Paul's portrayal of his endurance ... extends considerably beyond a su-perficial borrowing of vocabulary: Paul's literary use of the por-trait of the afflicted sage shows a deep familiarity with, and sym-pathy for, its functions in the works of popular philosophers. In 2 Corinthians, Paul deftly employs the motif to persuade his read-ers that they ought to be proud of him" because of the suffering he has withstood. Paul's portrayal also has a "Jewish apocalyptic aspect."

1032.   Holland, Glenn. "Speaking Like a Fool: Irony in 2 Corinthi-ans 10–13," in #624, pp. 250–264.

Irony and parody in these chapters as Paul's clever rhetorical means of emphasizing the theme of the "paradox of strength hidden in apparent weakness," as "parallel to the *kenosis* of Christ himself."

1033.   Hughes, Frank Witt. "The Rhetoric of Reconciliation: 2 Corinthians 1.1–2.13 and 7.5–8.24," in #629, pp. 246–261.

"Since there is a clear thematic unity which is matched by a demonstrable unity of rhetorical structure, it is likely that 1.1–2.13 and 7.5–8.24 are an integral letter." It is a deliberative letter, though making some use of epideictic consolation.

1034.   Joubert, S.J. "Behind the Mask of Rhetoric: 2 Corinthians 8 and the Intratextual Relation Between Paul and the Corinthians." *Neotestamentica* 26 (1992), 101–112.

The roles of the encoded author and readers within the intra-textual discourse related to the sequence of subjects discussed by Paul, and his verbal repertoire "all contribute to an intimate dis-course situation in 2 Cor 8." These and other rhetorical skills shown by Paul as means of moving his readers to a specific view of the collection.

1035. Loubser, J.A. "A New Look at Paradox and Irony in 2 Corinthians 10–13." *Neotestamentica* 26 (1992), 507–521.

The nature of Pauline irony. *2 Corinthians* 10–13 as ironic discourse with three intersecting levels: dissimulative, existential, and paradoxical. By means of irony, Paul heightens pathos, enabling us to see the passage as a *peroratio*. Thus these chapters are not a separate letter.

1036. Macky, Peter W. "St. Paul's Collage of Metaphors in II Corinthians 5: 1–10: Ornamental or Exploratory?" *PEGL* 11 (1991), 162–173.

We should take Paul's "highly symbolic form" seriously, seeing it as "more literary than expository, ... more as Poetic Vision (like Ezekiel 1) than as Dogmatics." By doing this we will "see more deeply into Paul's thought." The literary beauty and complexity of Paul's "text" metaphor. (Response to this and two other essays on Paul's metaphors in this issue by Glenn S. Holland, pp. 185–190.)

* Mitchell, Margaret M. "Rhetorical Shorthand in Pauline Argumentation: The Functions of 'the Gospel' in the Corinthian Correspondence."

See #1021.

1037. de Silva, David A. "Measuring Penultimate Against Ultimate Reality: An Investigation of the Integrity and Argumentation of 2 Corinthians." *JSNT* 52 (1993), 41–70.

Rhetorical critical analysis of *2 Corinthians* 1–9 demonstrates its thematic and argumentative integrity. Therefore, chapters 8 and 9 are definitely part of the same literary whole as chapters 1–7.

1038. de Silva, David A. "Recasting the Moment of Decision: 2 Corinthians 6:14–7:1 in Its Literary Context." *AUSS* 31 (1993), 3–16.

6:14–7:1 (together with 6:11–13 and 7:2–3) "constitute the climax of an appeal" by Paul for re-establishment of the relationship of the apostle to the congregation. Thus, the arguments for considering it an integral part of the letter are stronger than those which see it as a non-Pauline interruption.

*   Stanley, Christopher D. *Paul and the Language of Scripture. Citation Techniques in the Pauline Epistles and Contemporary Literature.*

       See #985.

See also #71, 975.

GALATIANS

*   Boers, Hendrikus. *The Justification of the Gentiles. Paul's Letters to the Galatians and Romans.*

       See #987.

1039.   Castelli, Elizabeth A. "Allegories of Hagar: Reading Galatians 4.21–31 with Postmodern Feminist Eyes," in #622, pp. 228–250.

       A "multiple reading—a simultaneous reading of allegory, Paul's use of allegory, Hagar, and theoretical interventions into the practices and politics of interpretation." The antihegemonic nature of allegorical readings. "If Fischer and Abedi's understanding of Hagar as herself the figure for voices of multiplicity ... is accepted, then allegories of Hagar offer, perhaps, a keenly critical example of the radical potential of political interpretation as allegory."

*   Classen, C. Joachim. "St. Paul's Epistles and Ancient Greek and Roman Rhetoric."

       See #974.

1040.   Cranford, Lorin L. "A Rhetorical Reading of Galatians." *SWJT* 37 (1994), 4–10.

       We should not view Paul as using either *Jewish* or *Hellenistic* sources, but rather as creatively blending both in a holistic approach to his task. The significance of the letter structure of *Galatians* for its interpretation.

1041.   Fairweather, Janet. "The Epistle to the Galatians and Classical Rhetoric." *TB* 45 (1994), 1–38, 213–243.

St. John Chrysostom applied rhetorical criticism to *Galatians* in a way that modern readers should notice. Paul, it seems, was conscious of rhetorical concepts, thought it is debatable whether he formally studied them in his youth. A close reading of *Galatians* plus a general consideration of Paul's handling of the five parts of rhetoric show that, despite some use of techniques from the orators, his conceptual framework was different and the bases of his argumentation "distinct and innovative."

1042. Hall, Robert G. "Historical Inference and Rhetorical Effect: Another Look at Galatians 1 and 2," in #629, pp. 308–320.

"Since ancient rhetoricians urged writers of narrations to re-interpret history in the interest of persuasion, and since Paul structures his narration according to the rhetorical principles accepted in his age, Galatians is not an ideal historical source."

1043. Hansen, G. Walter. "A Paradigm of the Apocalypse: The Gospel in the Light of Epistolary Analysis," in L. Ann Jervis and Peter Richardson, eds., *Gospel in Paul: Studies on Corinthians, Galatians and Romans for Richard N. Longenecker* (Sheffield: Sheffield Academic P, 1994), pp. 194–209.

"When we use the most prominent points of the rebuke-request structure [in Greek papyrus letters] of ... Galatians as vantage points from which to view the rest of the letter, we are given a fresh perspective of the purpose [of] ... each part of the letter.... Most significant of all is the way Paul constructs the rebuke section of the letter (1.6–4.11) to prepare the way for his initial request for the Galatian believers to imitate his example (4.12)."

1044. Hester, James D. "Placing the Blame: The Presence of Epideictic in Galatians 1 and 2," in #629, pp. 281–307.

Paul's use and modification of various parts of epideictic, especially the exordium and the chreia, "to bring the Galatians into a new argumentative situation, where they are not outsiders to the debate concerning the nature and practice of faith...."

1045. Hughes, Frank W. "The Gospel and Its Rhetoric in Galatians," in L. Ann Jervis and Peter Richardson, eds., *Gospel in Paul* (Sheffield: JSOT P, 1994), pp. 210–221.

The flexibility of the term "gospel" for Paul, in *Galatians* and elsewhere. Its appearance in the narratio as a kind of shorthand.

1046.   Lategan, Bernard. "Textual Space as Rhetorical Device," in #624, pp. 397–408.

How Paul uses textual space in persuasion, "in the light of recent developments in rhetorical and hermeneutical theory and practice.... The use of textual space and the indication of preferred positions [in Galatians] are ... much more than clever tricks in Paul's rhetorical repertoire. They offer the reader a new self understanding, leading to new attitudes and actions."

1047.   Loubser, J.A. "The Contrast Slavery/Freedom as a Persuasive Device in Galatians." *Neotestamentica* 28 #1 (1994), 163–176.

Aspects of the slavery/freedom contrast which serve as persuasive devices in Galatians include the wide distribution of the theme, the speech act of 4:21–31, the conflict in value systems, and rhetorical devices, e.g., drastic language, pathos, and antithesis. The contrast has several strong referential functions, including appeals to his audience's attempt to improve their social position and the law-free gospel.

1048.   Muddiman, John. "An Anatomy of Galatians," in #17, pp. 257–270.

An anatomy is the "doctrine of the structure of organized bodies," and an epistle qualifies as such. "In Galatians, the conventional rhetorical structure [reveals] several other layers of discourse" beyond the obvious one of counter-attack on opponents. The anatomical approach "asks ... of any passage, at what level, or within what system does this operate." It has the advantage of alerting us to dimensions of Paul's discourse otherwise unnoticed, as well as of explaining seeming anomalies.

1049.   *Neotestamentica* 26 (1992), #2, pp. 257–484.

Twenty articles by as many scholars applying various forms of rhetorical criticism to specific passages in NT letters. Fifteen of these analyze passages in *Galatians*. Other articles on *II Corinthians* 10–13 by J.A. Loubser (see #1035), G. Aichele and J.A. Smit on resurrection gospel stories (#649).

1050.   Parunak, H. Van Dyke. "Dimensions of Discourse Structure: A Multidimensional Analysis of the Components and Transitions of Paul's Epistle to the Galatians," in #618, pp. 207–239.

The transitional nature of 2:15–21, the introductory chiastic summary of 1:11–12, and the role of grammatical person as key to the structure of 2:15–21 and 3:1–6:10 are all better understood through discourse analysis.

1051. Pelser, G.M.M., et al. *Discourse Analysis of Galatians* [Addendum to *Neotestamentica* 26 #2, 1992].

Semantic discourse analysis of *Galatians*, consisting of diagrams of the macrostructure, and of each of twenty-two identified pericopes (pericope texts in Greek, with some summaries in English).

1052. Perriman, Andrew C. "The Rhetorical Strategy of Galatians 4:21–5:1." *EvQ* 65 (1993), 27–42.

Paul's rhetorical strategy in his "allegorical" treatment of Abraham in Galatians 4–5 has been misinterpreted. It is not in fact an allegory after the manner of Philo and the rabbis, but a deliberate attempt to startle and provoke his readers into a new understanding.

1053. Russell, Walter B. "Rhetorical Analysis of the Book of Galatians." *B Sac* 150, #s 599, pp. 341–358, and #600 (1993), pp. 416–439.

Survey of previous rhetorical analyses of *Galatians* shows the rudimentary stage of its use on biblical texts. Defense of its use on Paul, despite potential for abuse. Outline of the preferred approach, based on Kennedy. The epistle's blending of rhetorical techniques and epistolary form. The difficulty of the fifth step: deciding on the rhetorical arrangement of the material.

* Spaulding, Lynn Spencer. "The Significance of the Differing Audiences in Galatians and Romans."

See #1006.

* Stanley, Christopher D. *Paul and the Language of Scripture. Citation Techniques in the Pauline Epistles and Contemporary Literature.*

See #985.

1054. Vos, Johann S. "Paul's Argumentation in Galatians 1–2." *HTR* 87 (1994), 1–16.

The multiple functions of the narrative *confirmatio* of *Galatians* 1:13–2:14. It is apologetic in "that Paul was defending the truth of his gospel," but not apologetic in the sense that he was not "arguing mainly from a defensive position...." This may be clarified by comparing *Galatians* 1–2 with *I Corinthians* 15:1–11. Thus we should prefer Melanchthon's category of "didactic genre" to any derived from the rhetorical handbooks.

See also #71, 974, 977.

EPHESIANS

1055.   Breeze, Mary. "Hortatory Discourse in Ephesians." *JTT* 5 (1992), 313–347.

Analysis of the information structure of *Ephesians* reveals that the core of the letter is the "exhortation information" of the second half (chapters 4–6). The author was not so much worried about actual impurities of conduct at Ephesus as he was about potential dangers and temptations in the corrupt environment in which they lived.

1056.   Lincoln, Andrew T. "'Stand, Therefore ...': Ephesians 6:10–20 as *Peroratio*." *BI* 3 (1995), 99–114.

Ephesians 6:10–20 "contains the major elements expected of a peroratio by the ancient rhetoricians and also has features in common with ancient accounts of speeches of generals before battle." Recognizing the peroratio illuminates its links with the rest of the letter, the dispute about armor, and the depiction of Paul's imprisonment.

See also #1079.

PHILIPPIANS

1057.   Basevi, Claudio, and Juan Chapa. "Philippians 2.6–11: The Rhetorical Function of a Pauline 'Hymn,'" in #624, pp. 338–356.

"... Philippians 2.5–11 should be viewed as an encomium of Christ which demands a poetical form and has the foundation for an exhortation to the afflicted community of Christians in Philippi. Knowing what Christ was and what he did, they would be encouraged to stay faithful to the gospel as well as united to Christ, to Paul, and amongst themselves."

1058. Black, David Alan. "The Discourse Structure of Philippians: A Study in Textlinguistics." *Nov T* 37 (1995), 16–49.

"... Philippians is an integral composition whose primary rhetorical function is deliberative." "'Unity for the sake of the gospel' provides the overarching framework and motif" within which other themes are introduced. Comprehensive outline of the letter's macrostructure.

1059. Gundry, Robert H. "Style and Substance in 'The Myth of God Incarnate' According to Philippians 2:6–11," in #17, pp. 271–293.

The importance of chiasms and other related parallelism in *Philippians* 2 lies partly in their favoring "the synonynity of the form of God with equality to God." They also favor the view that the passage "represents Paul's own exalted prose ... rather than an early Christian hymn...."

1060. Jaquette, J.L. "A Not-So-Noble Death: Figured Speech, Friendship and Suicide in Philippians 1:21–26." *Neotestamentica* 28 #1 (1994), 177–192.

Philippians is a hortatory or psychogogic letter of friendship which treats suicide in terms of moral exemplification—thus its allusions serve Paul's rhetorical strategy. The speech of the letter is figured or oblique, and "framed specifically for purposes of persuasiveness in delicate matters...." Thus Arthur Droge's thesis that Paul's discussion of life and death alludes to Greco-Roman discussions of suicide is correct, but for reasons he did not articulate.

1061. Koperski, Veronica. "Textlinguistics and the Integrity of Philippians: A Critique of Wolfgang Schenk's Arguments for a Compilation Hypothesis." *ETL* 68 (1992), 331–367.

Textlinguistic analysis of *Philippians* demonstrates the presence of a careful structure with connecting elements. In fact, Wolfgang Schenk's own methods in his 1984 *Die Philipperbriefe des Paulus* reinforces this position, despite his attempts there to prove the opposite.

1062.   Kraftchick, Steven J. "A Necessary Detour: Paul's Meta-
        phorical Understanding of the Philippian Hymn." *HBT*
        15 (1993), 1–37.

> "... considering metaphor as a mode of cognition enables us to
> maintain the 'is/is not' nature of the hymn in relationship to the
> believers Paul addressed. Because the difference between the
> myth and its hearers is maintained by considering it metaphori-
> cally, the hymn can be appropriated for ethical exhortation with-
> out fear of collapsing the mythical nature of the hymn into a form
> of reporting...."

1063.   Luter, A. Boyd, and Michelle V. Lee. "Philippians as Chi-
        asmus: Key to the Structure, Unity and Theme Ques-
        tions." *NTS* 41 (1995), 89–101.

> Seeing the structure of *Philippians* as a chiasmus, with its pivot
> point at 2:17–3:1, enables us to understand the structure and
> theme of the book and to prove its unity. The structure of *Philip-
> pians* seems to fulfill eight of Rosenberg's nine criteria of a true
> chiasmus.

1064.   Marshall, John W. "Paul's Ethical Appeal in Philippians,"
        in #624, pp. 357–374.

> Understanding *Philippians* as a persuasive document means
> understanding its ethos. Aristotle analyzed ethos into three quali-
> ties: good sense, good will, and virtuous excellence, all of which
> Paul demonstrates in himself in *Philippians*, and all of which he
> maintains throughout his discourse.

1065.   Porter, Stanley, and D.A. Carson, eds. *Discourse Analysis
        and Other Topics in Biblical Greek.* Sheffield (Sheffield
        Academic P), 1995.

> Six essays in Part I, of which four are on Philippians and two
> on the NT as a whole. On the former: George H. Guthrie, "Cohe-
> sion Shifts and Stitches"; Stephen H. Levinsohn, "Constituent
> Order and the Article"; Jeffrey T. Reed, "Identifying Theme";
> Moisés Silva, "Discourse Analysis." On the latter: Stanley E.
> Porter, a survey of recent work, and a "response to several at-
> tempts" to analyze biblical discourse.

1066. Snyman, A.H. "Persuasion in Philippians 4.1–20," in #624, pp. 325–337.

Classical rhetorical theory should not be applied rigidly to N.T. texts, but rather should be "used as a frame of reference for empirical study," especially since ancient rhetoric itself was "extremely fluid" in rules and application. Applied to *Philippians*, we find all three major modes of persuasion present in the peroration: ethos, logos, and pathos, and all three used successfully.

See also #632, 973, 977.

COLOSSIANS

1067. Baugh, Steven M. "The Poetic Form of Colossians 1:15–20." *WTJ* 47 (1985), 227–244.

The overall pattern of *Colossians* 1:15–20 is a "simple chiasm much like poetry and prose from the OT and from other Semitic works." Its model is thus not Hellenistic but Hebraic. It does not have perfectly balanced, symmetrical strophes, as Semitic hymns need not have.

1068. Christopher, Gregory T. "A Discourse Analysis of Colossians 2:16–3:17." *GTJ* 11 (1990), 205–220.

Colossians 2:16–3:17 forms a unit of hortatory discourse whose structural framework is a chiasmus and whose argument is in climactic order.

* Seeley, David. "Poststructuralist Criticism and Biblical History."

See #646.

See also #646, 716, 1079.

1 THESSALONIANS

1069.   Chapa, Juan. "Consolatory Patterns? 1 Thessalonians 4,
         13.18; 5,11," in #1070, pp. 220–228.

         The "extent to which we are justified in seeing Greek or Hel-
         lenistic literature of consolation behind this section of *1 Thessalo-
         nians*." The consolation genre in the Greco-Roman world and its
         importance and fame as rhetoric and epistolography.

1070.   Collins, Raymond F., ed. *The Thessalonian Correspondence.*
         Leuven (Leuven UP), 1990.

         Thirty-seven essays, divided into four sections: Background,
         "The Writing of a First Letter" (rhetoric, structure, influence on),
         Thought, "The Writing of a Second Letter" (literary and theologi-
         cal issues).

1071.   Hughes, Frank Witt. "The Rhetoric of 1 Thessalonians," in
         #1070, pp. 94–116.

         Comparing *1 Thessalonians* "to several traditions within Greco-
         Roman rhetoric aids in the identification of the letter's rhetorical
         situation, [which in turn] ... can become a useful matrix for
         exploring some of the historical questions asked by N.T.
         scholars." Detailed rhetorical outline of the book.

1072.   Kloppenborg, John S. "ΦΙΛΑΔΕΛΦΙΑ, ΘΕΟΔΙΔΑΚΤΟΣ and
         the Dioscuri: Rhetorical Engagement in 1 Thessalonians
         4.9–12." *NTS* 39 (1993), 265–289.

         "To see in 1 Thessalonians 4.9–12 a covert allusion to the popu-
         lar traditions connected with the Dioscuri implies that Paul en-
         gaged in a lively, learned and subtle dialogue with the culture of
         his audience and was willing to draw upon its best traditions and
         turn them to his own use."

1073.   Lambrecht, Jan, S.J. "Thanksgivings in 1 Thessalonians 1–
         3," in #1070, pp. 183–205.

         A suggested structure of *I Thessalonians* 1–3, based on its
         thanksgivings, and taking off from the work of Paul Schubert
         (1939). The structure of the thanksgivings themselves. They are
         characterized by a basic bipolarity, and a three-dimensional time-
         structure.

1074. Schlueter, Carol J. *Filling Up the Measure. Polemical Hyperbole in 1 Thessalonians 2.14–16.* Sheffield (Sheffield Academic P), 1994.

These verses have been a problem passage since the 19th century because of their conflict with *Romans* 9–11. Their likely authenticity, and the need to try to focus on the passage in its own right. Paul's exaggerations and their rhetorical function in the context of Greco-Roman rhetoric and the "sweeping generalized hyperbole of the Dead Sea sect." Comparison with polemical hyperbole in other Pauline letters, and their levels of intensity, depending on the group being attacked.

1075. Smith, Abraham. *Comfort One Another. Reconstructing the Rhetoric and Audience of 1 Thessalonians.* Louisville (Westminster/John Knox P), 1995.

Thessalonians as a letter of consolation in the Greco-Roman tradition. How the letter of consolation functioned to "restore individuals to a level of personal freedom and transcendence over constantly changing circumstances." How Paul exploited Hellenistic rhetoric and the topoi and form of the consolatory letter in *I Thessalonians.*

1076. Wuellner, Wilhelm. "The Argumentative Structure of I Thessalonians as Paradoxical Encomium," in #1070, pp. 117–136.

"... the interpretation of 1 Thessalonians as letter is best served by prioritizing our concern for the rhetorical rather than the epistolary genre, let alone the historical and theological preoccupations." Further, it is the rhetoric of, not the rhetoric in, *1 Thessalonians*, that matters. The best framework for identifying the wholeness and coherence of its argument is the popular subgenre of epideictic known as *paradoxon enkomion.*

See also #63, 973, 977.

2 THESSALONIANS

1077. Callow, John. *A Semantic Structure Analysis of Second Thessalonians,* ed. Michael F. Kopesec. Dallas (Summer Institute of Linguistics), 1982.

Theory and uses of semantic structure analysis. Explanation of the semantic structure analysis of 2 *Thessalonians* in terms of the communication situation, constituent organization, thematic outline, and division into semantic units.

1078.   Menken, M.J.J. "The Structure of 2 Thessalonians," in #1070, pp. 373–382.

2 *Thessalonians* is carefully constructed in three parts, each displaying a concentric structure. The whole may be a golden section. Various verbal and numerical and rhetorical repetitions and devices show the interrelationship among the three parts.

1079.   Schmidt, Daryl D. "The Syntactical Style of 2 Thessalonians: How Pauline Is It?," in #1070, pp. 383–393.

Stylistic analysis of 2 *Thessalonians* shows such close relationship to that of *Ephesians* and *Colossians*, and such distinct differences from the rest of the genuine Pauline corpus, that we must conclude Paul did not write it.

1 TIMOTHY

1080.   Reed, J.T. "Cohesive Ties in 1 Timothy: In Defense of the Epistle's Unity." *Neotestamentica* 26 (1992), 131–147.

Application of the theory of cohesive ties to *I Timothy* supports the move toward viewing the pastoral epistles as containing coherent arguments, not collections of miscellaneous materials. Interaction of central tokens with claims reveal the "primary participant structure" of the text as Paul and Timothy; the corresponding event structure of the letter.

1081.   Reed, Jeffrey T. "Discourse Features in New Testament Letters. With Special Reference to the Structure of 1 Timothy." *JTT* 6 (1993), 228–252.

Discourse features of the epistolary genre as they are used in *I Timothy*, especially the important distinction in the genre between obligatory and optional elements. These elements can be analyzed for their "contribution to textual cohesiveness." How this works in 1 *Timothy* to produce cohesive structure when the letter is read through Timothy's eyes.

1082.   Stiefel, Jennifer H. "Women Deacons in 1 Timothy: A Linguistic and Literary Look at 'Women Likewise ...' (Timothy 3.11)." *NTS* 41 (1995), 442–457.

Careful scrutiny of the syntax of 3:11 and the literary structure of the passage on deacons "discerns new evidence for the identification of these women as partners in ministry with the explicitly named men of the passage."

2 TIMOTHY

See #632.

TITUS

See #1126.

PHILEMON   ·

1083.   Allen, David L. "The Discourse Structure of Philemon: A Study of Textlinguistics," in David Alan Black, ed., *Scribes and Scripture: New Testament Essays in Honor of J. Harold Greenlee* (Winona Lake: Eisenbrauns, 1992), pp. 77–96.

Definition of textlinguistics (discourse analysis), and of the specific version used by Robert Longacre. Philemon as hortatory discourse: sentence and paragraph segmentation, structure of the salutation, of vv. 4–7, 8–16, 17–20, and 21–22; "macrostructure, constituent structure, and texture of Philemon."

1084.   Banker, John. *Semantic Structure Analysis of Philemon.* Dallas (Summer Institute of Linguistics), 1990.

Explanation of semantic structure analysis. Application of the method to *Philemon* in terms of the communication situation, constituent organization of the epistle by division and section, and identification of semantic units. Themes of each of the epistle, division, and section constituents.

1085. Martin, Clarice J. "The Rhetorical Function of Commercial Language in Paul's Letter to Philemon (Verse 18)," in #629, pp. 321–337.

"The rhetorical function of the commercial language in v. 18 of *Philemon*, then ... [is more than stylistic or euphemistic; it] has enabled Paul skillfully and masterfully to formulate a convincing and practicable case for conforming (realigning) Philemon's will to his own."

1086. Wilson, Andrew. "The Pragmatics of Politeness and Pauline Epistolography: A Case Study of the Letter to Philemon." *JSNT* 48 (1992), 107–119.

Using Geoffrey Leech's interpersonal rhetoric—specifically politeness theory of modern linguistic pragmatics, we gain "a valuable approach to the Pauline writings by directing attention to the ways in which ... in Philemon considerations of politeness have significantly affected the way in which Paul makes his request." Other Pauline letters may also be illuminated by this method.

OTHER LETTERS

See #63.

HEBREWS

1087. Black, David Alan. "A Note on the Structure of Hebrews 12, 1–2." *Biblica* 68 (1987), 543–551.

Syntactic analysis of this passage reveals a chiastic structure which emphasizes the theme of "running the race with endurance." The text of 12:2 appears to be homological or even hymnic. Both chiasm and hymn show how well schooled the author was in the art of composition.

1088.   Brawley, Robert L. "Discoursive Structure and the Unseen in Hebrews 2:8 and 11:1: A Neglected Aspect of the Context." *CBQ* 55 (1993), 81–98.

"... the context for understanding Hebrews 11:1 needs to be expanded beyond the current opinions about the architectonic structure, the progressive clarification of ambiguity, and the conceptual background, so that it includes the correlation between 2:8 and 11:1.... [T]he theme of what is not seen in Heb 2:8 is a preliminary qualification reducing the ambiguity of the meaning of faith in 11:1...."

*   Cotterell, Peter, and Max Turner. *Linguistics and Biblical Interpretation.*

See #620.

1089.   Ebert, Daniel J., IV. "The Chiastic Structure of the Prologue to Hebrews." *TJ* n.s. 13 (1992), 163–179.

While the intricate structure and theological complexity of the opening sentence of Hebrews has long been recognized, previous commentators have failed to see its overall symmetrical design. Thus it is almost certainly not a hymn fragment from another source. And the chiastic structure is designed "to prepare the reader for the main themes of the treatise: the Son as prophet, priest, and king."

1090.   Guthrie, George H. *The Structure of Hebrews: A Text-Linguistic Analysis.* Leiden (E.J. Brill), 1994.

Review of proposals on the structure of *Hebrews* from the ancient world up through today shows five basic approaches: "structural agnosticism," conceptual/thematic, rhetorical, literary, and linguistic. Difficulties in deciding structure stem from its original delivery orally, where logical exposition alternated with challenging exhortation, and from failure to take transitional devices seriously. These difficulties can be surmounted through textlinguistics analysis.

1091.   Jobes, Karen H. "The Function of Paronomasia in Hebrews 10:5–7." *TJ* n.s. 13 (1992), 181–191.

The author's misquotation of Psalm 40 in *Hebrews* 10 is deliberate—an example of the Greco-Roman rhetorical technique of paronomasia which was intended to call the reader's attention to continuity and yet discontinuity between David and Christ.

1092.   Olbricht, Thomas H. "Hebrews as Amplification," in #624, pp. 375–387.

The *Hebrews* author employed the Greco-Roman rhetorical device of amplification, but did so not from experience as Hellenistic orators did, but via comparison, drawing heavily on biblical material, on the evidence of the transcendental.

1093.   Rice, George E. "The Chiastic Structure of the Central Section of the Epistle to the Hebrews." *AUSS* 19 (1981), 243–246.

A chiasm in *Hebrews* 6:19–20 previously unidentified. Its importance is that it contains in miniature four different theological themes developed fully in 7:1–10:39.

1094.   Swetnam, James. "On the Literary Genre of the 'Epistle,' to the Hebrews." *Nov T* 11 (1969), 261–269.

Hartwig Thyen's *Der Stil der Jüdisch-Hellenistischen Homilie* (1955) must be the starting point, though his is not the definitive solution. We should also investigate possible Palestinian homiletic tradition.

See also #632.

JAMES

1095.   Cargal, Timothy B. *Restoring the Diaspora. Discursive Structure and Purpose in the Epistle of James.* Atlanta (Scholars P), 1993.

Explanation and illustration of two paradigms for reading James: the historical and the linguistic (structural semiotic). Choice of latter for analysis, following the theory of A.J. Greimas: discursive structure of units, oppositions of actions in each section, and progressive development of themes in each section. Such analysis shows far more organization and structure in the letter than is usually recognized.

1096.   Crotty, Robert B. "The Literary Structure of the Letter of James." *ABR* 40 (1992), 45–57.

We can clear up the confusion if we recognize the pivotal importance of 1:16–18, and its parallel to 5:19–20. The structure is chiastic, with centers at 2:12–13, 5:1–6. Its theme emerges as that of "good speech," and eventually good action, though these "invoke a violent struggle within the individual."

1097. Elliott, John H. "The Epistle of James in Rhetorical and Social Scientific Perspective: Holiness-Wholeness and Patterns of Replication." *BTB* 23 (1993), 71–81.

Despite the prevailing view that *James* consists of "disjointed hortatory topoi and lacks literary and thematic integrity," rhetorical and social-scientific analysis "reveals a complex and coherent argument in which purity and pollution concerns figure prominently."

1098. Terry, Ralph Bruce. "Some Aspects of the Discourse Structure of the Book of James." *JTT* 5 (1992), 106–125.

Robert Longacre's methodology of text analysis is of value "in discovering structural relationships in a discourse that has previously defied attempts to understand them." The complex macrostructure of *James*, particularly the chiastic and lexical relationships; the presence of several types of peak material, and the function of 3:13–4:10 as a kind of hortatory climax.

1099. Watson, Duane F. "James 2 in Light of Greco-Roman Schemes of Argumentation." *NTS* 39 (1993), 94–121.

James 2 "is constructed according to a standard elaboration pattern for argumentation discussed by the Greco-Roman rhetoricians." *James* 2 is "particularly diatribal." "The difficulties posed by Jas 2:18–20 can be explained with elements of the diatribe and figures common to the confirmatio, especially the dilemma. The chapter shows the early church "molding its received traditions into persuasive aural and written forms of its time."

1100. Watson, Duane F. "The Rhetoric of James 3:1–12 and a Classical Pattern of Argumentation." *Nov T* 35 (1993), 48–64.

James 3:1–12 "is the author's own unified composition, constructed according to a standard elaboration pattern for argumentation discussed by Greco-Roman rhetorical works." Thus this chapter shows not "the bumping and clashing of ideas" argued by Dibelius, but a "shifting from one portion of the argumentation to another, using its various literary forms."

1 PETER

1101.   Kendall, David W. "The Literary and Theological Function
        of 1 Peter 1:3–12," in Charles H. Talbert, ed., *Perspectives
        on First Peter* (Macon: Mercer UP, 1986), pp. 103–120.

        The literary and theological relationship between 1 Peter 1:3–12
        and 1:13–5:11, and how this relationship illuminates the literary
        structure and major theme of the letter. "... each section of 1 Peter
        finds an introduction in 1:3–23, ... [thus providing] additional
        evidence in support of the recent scholarly consensus on the
        unity of the epistle." This relationship shows that the primary
        theme of 1 Peter is to "clarify and reinforce the distinctive charac-
        ter of Christian life-style."

1102.   Martin, Troy W. *Metaphor and Composition in 1 Peter*. At-
        lanta (Scholars P), 1992.

        Survey of history of compositional analyses of I Peter, and their
        usefulness for resolving literary issues; Greco-Roman letter con-
        ventions and their relevance to I Peter; significance of paranesis
        genre for explaining composition of I Peter; metaphor and transi-
        tion as tools for resolving residual problems of literary structure
        of I Peter.

1103.   Slaughter, James R. "The Importance of Literary Argument
        for Understanding 1 Peter." *B Sac* 152 (1995), 72–91.

        Why 1 Peter must be studied as a literary work. How the au-
        thor wove together five primary motifs—the believer's behavior,
        treatment, deference, motivation by Christ's example, and antici-
        pation of future glory—into one underlying message concerning
        the necessity for believers to "reflect a spirit of deference in all re-
        lationships as they follow Christ's example and anticipate future
        glory."

1104.   Thompson, James W. "The Rhetoric of 1 Peter." *RQ* 36
        (1994), 237–250.

        The persuasive force of 1 Peter derives from its unity and co-
        herence. The book is a rhetorical unit, distinguished at beginning
        and end by an *inclusio*. Aristotelian rhetorical analysis shows it to
        be a piece of deliberative rhetoric, with a consistent appeal to au-
        thority.

1105. Thurén, Lauri. *The Rhetorical Strategy of 1 Peter, With Special Regard to Ambiguous Expressions*. Åbo (Åbo Academy P), 1990.

How rhetorical criticism reveals the deliberate ambiguity of much of *I Peter*. It is a "piece of ancient mass communication," a letter with characteristics of epideictic discourse. How its argumentative material is arranged.

2 PETER

1106. Titrud, Kermit. "The Function of καί in the Greek New Testament and an Application to 2 Peter," in #618, pp. 240–270.

The subtleties of the meanings of this word have long been ignored. Of fifty-eight occurrences in *2 Peter*, twelve function adverbially. In about half the remaining occurrences where it functions as a coordinating conjunction, it is used to introduce opposition.

1 JOHN

1107. Hansford, Keir L. "The Underlying Poetic Structure of 1 John." *JTT* 5 (1992), 126–174.

1 John is a "highly structured text, probably a homily or sermon, with poetic parallelism and chiastic structures ... [deliberately employed] to make his message more pleasurable and memorable...."

1108. Longacre, Robert E. "Towards an Exegesis of 1 John Based on the Discourse Analysis of the Greek Text," in #618, pp. 271–286.

Division of the book into structural paragraphs as indicated by features of its surface structure. Distribution of performative verbs reveals the disproportionately long introduction (as compared to its body and closure). It is a hortatory discourse whose peaks peculiarly develop the book's message. The macrostructure of the book.

1109.   Mojola, A. Ototsi. "Theories of Metaphor in Translation: With Some Reference to John 1.1 and I John 1.1." *BTr* 44 (1993), 341–347.

The merits and drawbacks of two theories of metaphor—substitution/comparison and interaction—and their application to logos in these two passages, especially problems of translation.

1110.   Neufeld, Dietmar. *Reconceiving Texts as Speech Acts. An Analysis of I John.* Leiden (E.J. Brill), 1994.

Examination of key passages involving either doctrine or ethics "from the perspective of a modified version of J.L. Austin's speech act theory." The author of *I John* "employs a number of self-involving speech acts ... that leave neither the author and [sic] readers uninvolved and unchanged. The author uses these speech acts to create a literary world where the cash value of the christological statements is seen in corresponding ethical conduct and proper confession."

1111.   Sibinga, J. Smit. "A Study in I John," in *Studies in John, Presented to Professor Dr. T.N. Sevenster on the Occasion of His Seventieth Birthday* (Leiden: E.J. Brill, 1970), pp. 194–208.

Analysis of the syllable pattern in *1 John* reveals the letter's intricate structure. Sometimes this formal structure illuminates the logic of a passage. Structure in *1 John* often relies on patterns of numbers of syllables, as well as frequent inclusio/chiasmus.

1112.   Talbert, Charles H. *Reading John: A Literary and Theological Commentary on the Fourth Gospel and the Johannine Epistles.* NY (Crossroad), 1992.

Focuses not on verse by verse, but large thought units through close reading of the final form of the text. Relationship of the texts to their Christian, Jewish, and Greco-Roman milieu.

*   Timmins, Nicholas G. "Variations in Style in the Johannine Literature."

See #899.

1113. Watson, Duane F. "Amplification Techniques in 1 John: The Interaction of Rhetorical Style and Invention." *JSNT* 51 (1993), 99–123.

Repetitiveness of this letter explained by author's use of amplification techniques common in Greco-Roman rhetoric "as a major part of his inventional strategy." These techniques are an integral part of the author's epideictic rhetoric designed to distinguish between the Johannine tradition and its errant forms.

1114. Watson, Duane F. "An Epideictic Strategy for Increasing Adherence to Community Values: I John 1:1–2:27." *PEGL* 11 (1991), 144–152.

1:1–2:27 is a carefully structured portion utilizing epideictic rhetoric to refute opponents' theology and to argue that readers adhere to traditional theology. Breakdown of the passage into rhetorical units. "The choice of an epideictic strategy rather than a deliberative one indicates that the … audience is still faithful to the Johannine tradition."

See also #926.

2 JOHN

* Talbert, Charles H. *Reading John: A Literary and Theological Commentary on the Fourth Gospel and the Johannine Epistles.*
See #1112.

3 JOHN

* Talbert, Charles H. *Reading John: A Literary and Theological Commentary on the Fourth Gospel and the Johannine Epistles.*
See #1112.

JUDE

1115. Charles, J. Daryl. *Literary Strategy in the Epistle of Jude.* Scranton (U of Scranton P), London and Toronto (Associated UP), 1993.

Literary-rhetorical analysis of *Jude*; the letter in its Palestinian milieu; use of the OT and of extrabiblical source material in Jude. The letter is a "rhetorical-theological polemic ... which employs a highly stylized literary approach." The author uses word-play, parallelism, symmetry, alliteration, and vivid imagery.

1116. Joubert, Stephan J. "Persuasion in the Letter of Jude." *JSNT* 58 (1995), 75–87.

Rhetorical analysis enables us to perceive that Jude's overall goal is to "redefine his readers' perceptions of reality...." He employs to this end various techniques of vituperatio, his examples ranging from the godless people to the OT to nature.

1117. Osburn, Carroll D. "Discourse Analysis and Jewish Apocalyptic in the Epistle of Jude," in #618, pp. 287–319.

Literary analysis reveals "no basis for viewing Jude's epistle as pseudo-epistolary.... The extensive use of Jewish apocalyptic ... seems to relate the authors and his readers to Jewish background." The intruders whom Jude attacks "have every appearance of historicity...."

1118. Wendland, E.R. "A Comparative Study of 'Rhetorical Criticism,' Ancient and Modern—with Special Reference to the Larger Structure and Function of the Epistle of Jude." *Neotestamentica* 28 (1994), 193–228.

Review of rhetorical criticism in general, and in particular of its application by Watson, Bauckham, Stowers and Neyrey to *Jude* (and to NT letters generally). A "mutually complementary, more macrotext-oriented procedure is possible, however; how such an analysis would work on Jude, and it would restore such "minor" letters to their rightful influence.

REVELATION

1119. Aune, David E. "The Apocalypse of John and the Problem of Genre." *Semeia* 36 (1986), 65–96.

Modifications needing to be made to the analyses of the genre of Revelation by Collins and Hellholm. "The profound embedment of the speech of God summarizing the central message of the Apocalypse (*Revelation* 21:5–8) is the core of a literary structure which is a surrogate for the cultic barriers which separate the profane from the sacred, the hidden from the revealed."

1120. Aune, David E. "Intertextuality and the Genre of the Apocalypse." *SBLSP* (1991), 142–160.

"... the sequence of literary forms in the Apocalypse conforms to no known ancient literary conventions." We do not know, then, whether ancient readers had any way of anticipating each new turn in the narrative. The interesting synthesis of apocalyptic and prophetic elements through their juxtaposition in Revelation—perhaps to give a new lease on life to prophetic traditions.

1121. Bauckham, Richard. *The Climax of Prophecy. Studies on the Book of Revelation.* Edinburgh (T. and T. Clark), 1993.

A series of essays that attempts to understand "both the form and the meaning of the Apocalypse in its literary and historical contexts." This is done through studying its "distinctive literary techniques, ... disciplined and deliberate allusion to specific Old Testament texts," indebtedness to the form and content of Jewish and Christian apocalypses, and to the first-century Roman world.

1122. Collins, Adela Yarbro. "Numerical Symbolism in Jewish and Early Christian Apocalyptic Literature." *ANRW* 21.2 (1984), 1221–1287.

Use of numbers in *Revelation* is rhetorical and symbolic, but rarely if ever for the purpose of predicting the future. Such use "is part of the fundamental human enterprise of creating order in experience and environment and discovering analogies in various realms of experience."

1123. Giblin, Charles Homer, S.J. "Recapitulation and the Literary Coherence of John's Apocalypse." *CBQ* 56 (1994), 81–95.

The plot line of John's vision and its "progressive articulation" through recapitulation. How motifs develop out of these repetitions. This should help us avoid the temptation to historicize the vision by interpreting aspects of that vision as "specific, encoded factual events in some framework of clock-and-calendar time ..." since John's own time frame is typological.

1124.   Goldsmith, Steven. *Unbuilding Jerusalem: Apocalypse and Romantic Representation.* Ithaca and London (Cornell UP), 1993.

Part I: How a formalist aesthetic "enters into the claim apocalyptic texts have made to a normative authority independent of historical situation." How conservative ideology and "an idea of ahistorical literary form became mutually constitutive in both biblical apocalypse and its exegesis." Revelation as the product of tension between prophecy and canon, where canon seeks to control and master prophecy.

1125.   Hellholm, David. "The Problem of Apocalyptic Genre and the Apocalypse of John." *Semeia* 36 (1986), 13–64.

Paradigmatic analysis of generic concepts needed, supplemented by text-linguistic analysis. Such an approach can take into account not only content, form, and function, but syntagmatic structures of *Revelation* as well. The parallels with the Shepherd of Hermas, suggesting invariant generic characteristics.

1126.   Kenny, Anthony. *A Stylometric Study of the New Testament.* Oxford (Clarendon P), 1986.

Study of the quantifiable features of the style of the NT, primarily to help determine authorship of various books. Results show that Luke wrote *Acts*, that John did not write *Revelation*. The Pauline epistles (even the genuine ones) show greater diversity in style than do any two gospels. Titus is least likely to be by Paul, but the others probably are.

1127.   Lerner, Robert E. "Ecstatic Dissent." *Speculum* 67 (1992), 33–57.

Three medieval interpreters of scripture, and how they defended their revolutionary interpretations through claiming ecstatic inspiration from the Holy Spirit. Of the three, Joachim of Fiore's reading of *Revelation* was most like modern literary criticism.

1128.   Linton, Gregory. "Reading the Apocalypse as an Apocalypse." *SBLSP* (1991), 161–186.

Revelation is "highly intertextual," a mixed genre which constantly breaks out of its frame. It is a "writerly text ... that allows the reader to participate in producing its meaning. Because of its intertextuality, it is also polyvalent, allowing readers to produce multiple interpretations." Thus it has no one genre, and no one nature or essence.

1129.   Mathewson, Dave. "Revelation in Recent Genre Criticism: Some Implications for Interpretation." *TJ* n.s. 13 (1992), 193–213.

Survey of recent discussions of the apocalyptic genre and "their potential value for interpreting the perplexing book of Revelation." While the writer uses a well-known genre of his day, there are also discontinuities between Revelation and pagan examples. It is apocalyptic, prophetic, and epistolary.

1130.   O'Leary, Stephen D. "A Dramatistic Theory of Apocalyptic Rhetoric." *QJS* 79 (1993), 385–426.

How apocalyptic rhetoric "creates its own demands and expectations." It is a "tragic discourse that announces radical discontinuity [and yet] paradoxically leads to a comic reaffirmation of continuity...." How modern apocalyptic writings have survived repeated disconfirmation by continually reconceiving the relationship of past and future.

1131.   Pippin, Tina. *Death and Desire: The Rhetoric of Gender in the Apocalypse of John*. Louisville (Westminster/John Knox P), 1992.

Political and literary reading of themes of death and desire, and of gender codes and oppositions, in *Revelation*. Deconstructive theory applied to the narrative tensions in the text.

1132.   Pippin, Tina. "Peering into the Abyss: A Postmodern Reading of the Biblical Bottomless Pit," in #622, pp. 251–267.

"The abyss is an entry point into a strange and fragmented reading of the Apocalypse, a reading that is postmodern because it is not rooted in any historical-critical starting point." Intertextual dimensions of the abyss as prison-house; chaos as otherness, and therefore female like the abyss. "In the abyss, 'all is interpretation and exegesis,' and there is no end to this process.... The

Apocalypse is not a history book of the late twentieth or the late first century."

1133.   Poythress, Vern Sheridan. "Genre and Hermeneutics in Rev. 20:1–6." *JETS* 36 (1993), 41–54.

Symbolic communication in *Revelation* 13:1–8 and 19:7–8 exist on four levels: linguistic, visionary, referential, and symbolical. Difficulties arise with more controversial passages, e.g., Revelation 11:1–13. The four levels in Revelation 20, as compared to 13 and 19. The mistake of literalists who collapse other levels into the referential. Recognizing the visionary form of 20:1–6 reopens questions concerning referents because of the freedom and fluidity with which it is used, the "flexibility and relative indirectness of the correspondence between vision and referent...."

1134.   du Rand, Jan A. "'Now the Salvation of Our God Has Come....' A Narrative Perspective on the Hymns in Revelation." *Neotestamentica* 27 (1993), 313–330.

"The hymns in the Apocalypse of John function as interpretative commentary on decisive events in the unfolding of the plot. From narratological perspective, it is clear that the reader ... representing the faithful, experiences a catharsis in associating with the hymns...." Rhetorical/strophic analysis of the hymns.

*   Reed, Walter L. *Dialogues of the Word: The Bible as Literature According to Bakhtin.*
          See #6.

1135.   Ruiz, Jean-Pierre. "Betwixt and Between on the Lord's Day: Liturgy and the Apocalypse." *SBLSP* (1992), 654–672.

"... the Apocalypse is a script for oral performance in a ritual setting." How this setting affects the book's organization, and how social and literary analyses may fruitfully interact in an analysis based on ritual theory. Revelation "represents a reconfiguration of congregational prophecy in early Christianity in the direction of textualization."

1136.   Ryken, Leland. "Revelation," in #20, pp. 458–469.

Because it "prefers the imaginative to the propositional," Revelation is "the most thoroughly literary book in the Bible." Five fallacious beliefs about this book; the "convergence of genres" in the book should not blind us to its essential generic identity: visionary prophecy. The importance of symbolism as a basic literary mode; other characteristics of its style and rhetoric.

1137.   Smith, Christopher R. "The Structure of the Book of Revelation in the Light of Apocalyptic Literary Conventions." *Nov T* 36 (1994), 373–393.

If in the welter of conflicting theories of the structure of *Revelation* we can agree that it should be sought in the "conventions of its literary genre, or hermeneutical inquiry after indicated authorial intent." We may assume it to be an apocalyptic work; comparison of various such works, e.g., Third Baruch and Second Enoch leads to a typical apocalyptic pattern in *Revelation* of "reviewing history past as a prelude to prediction of history future." This leads to a seven-part structure with a transition at 10:1–11.

1138.   Snyder, Barbara Wootten. "Triple-Form and Space/Time Transitions: Literary Structuring Devices in the Apocalypse." *SBLSP* (1991), 440–450.

The most important literary techniques used in structuring *Revelation* are its triple form: apocalypse, prophecy, and epistle; the prophetic call narrative; time-space transitions at key points where John is transported in the spirit; and the concentric structure of chapters 17–22.

1139.   Steiner, George. "The Scandal of Revelation." *Salmagundi* #98–99 (1993), 42–70.

How the two deaths of Socrates and Jesus have largely determined "the fabric of western sensibility." The question of "whether the revealed admits of a rational hermeneutic" in the accounts of Jesus' death. How the two deaths have been compared in Western culture, and the mystery of the original event in each case. The dead end of our civilization brought about by these two texts.

1140.   Steinmann, Andrew E. "The Tripartite Structure of the Sixth Seal, the Sixth Trumpet, and the Sixth Bowl of John's Apocalypse (Revelation 6:12–7:17; 9:13–11:14; 16:12–16)." *JETS* 35 (1992), 69–79.

Recognizing the tripartite unity of these passages in *Revelation* can remove disagreements about the meaning and structure of the book. The ancient "recapitulation" theory of its structure is shown to be the correct one.

1141.   Thompson, Leonard L. "Mooring the Revelation in the Mediterranean." *SBLSP* (1992), 635–653.

> "... interpreters of *Revelation* miss an important dimension of its meaning if they consider only what is written without also considering the author's point in writing what is written." He is not only constructing an imaginary literary world; he uses language to redraw the social map: "lowering boundaries between his audience and himself, while raising them between audience and other groups."

*   Tilborg, Sjef Van. "Metaphorical versus Visionary Language."

> See #333.

*   Weathers, Robert A. "Leland Ryken's Literary Approach to Biblical Interpretation: An Evangelical Model."

> See #59.

1142.   Webber, Randall C. "The Apocalypse as Utopia: Ancient and Modern Subjectivity." *SBLSP* (1993), 104–118.

> *Revelation* may be read as a utopia "not because it belongs naturally in that category but because modern academic readers may find the comparison informative. Utopia, like apocalyptic, is a modern generic construction ... and is useful for the comparison of ideal and worst-case political states ranging from ... Plato to ... Orwell."

See also #3, 11, 63, 71.

Author Index